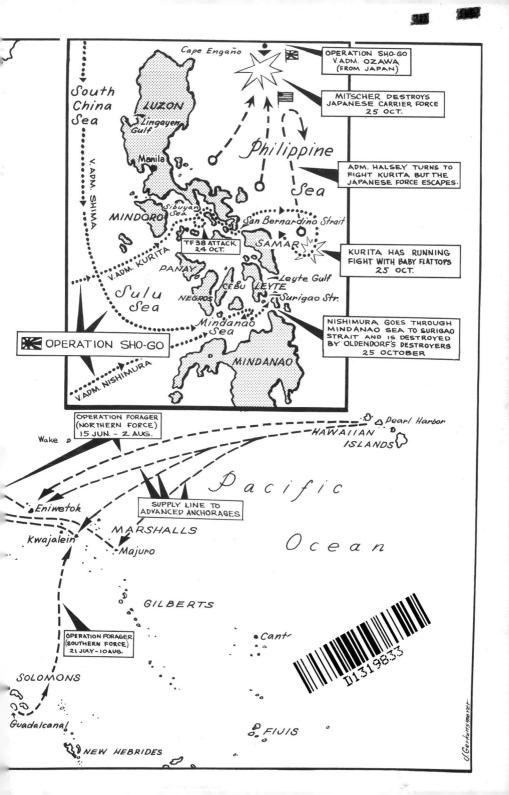

BATTLES OF
THE PHILIPPINE SEA

BATTLES OF
THE PHILIPPINE SEA

CHARLES A. LOCKWOOD *Vice Admiral, U.S. Navy, Ret.*

HANS CHRISTIAN ADAMSON *Colonel, U.S. Air Force, Ret.*

Thomas Y. Crowell Company   Established 1834, New York

Sources of miscellaneous quotations from participants in
the battles may be found in the bibliography.

To those who fought so gallantly
on and above land; on, over, and under the sea
in the great amphibious
and
aircraft carrier operations
in
the philippine sea
june–october 1944

CONTENTS

ILLUSTRATIONS

PHOTOS

xi

Guns on battleship IOWA *fire on Philippines*

GIs hit beach at Leyte

Soldiers building sandbag pier at Leyte beach

Coastguardsman giving water to wounded GI

Filipinos greeting American liberators on Leyte beach

Kamikaze shot down 25 October 1944

Admiral Jisaburo Ozawa

Battleships and cruisers of Admiral Oldendorf's fleet

MISSISSINEWA *in flames after submarine attack*

Rescue crew during Kamikaze attack, Mindoro

Kamikaze shot down astern carrier SANGAMON

MAPS

INTRODUCTION

A MAN BORN near the turn of this century has lived through changes greater than all others in history. In no part of man's affairs have revolutions been greater, nor brighter with promise for freedom if followed with wisdom, than at sea.

Admiral Charles Lockwood, the naval co-author of this book, has lived through and greatly influenced many of these changes. At the start of his distinguished career, when he entered the Naval Academy in 1908, navies were in the throes of the latest of the revolutions that have affected them in accelerating tempo for a century and a half.

In the 19th century, as materials and technology improved, navies changed from sail to steam, from smoothbore to rifled guns, from wood to iron, from emphasis on the basic elements of seamanship, navigation, and gunnery to broad fields of science that encompassed many other matters as well. The American Civil War dramatically highlighted the increased capabilities that these brought to seapower, particularly in armor, which had just begun in the Navy, long-range striking power against shore fortifications, and freedom from wind and tide.

That these were godsends indeed for a nation understanding them proved itself time after time in the Civil War. The successful Union campaigns in combined operations against forts had no parallel in history. It was fortunate for the United States and her future leadership of freedom that the Civil War did not come a generation earlier when navies had not attained these new capabilities to overcome shore fortifications.

In the forty-three years after Appomattox, before Charles Lockwood entered the Naval Academy, other remarkable technical developments had forged even more potent promise. For generations before the Civil War the ship of the (battle) line had sailed the seas as the mighty core of seapower—the ship that could take and give the most.

The battle of *Monitor* and *Merrimack* (*Virginia*) highlighted this famed warship's passing, but neither then nor in the immediate decades following did a single type evolve to take its place. Then in Charles Lockwood's youthful years there emerged seapower's new ship of the line, the battleship.

One of young Lockwood's first cruises was on a battleship. It is fitting therefore that this latest of many fine books he and his talented colleague Colonel Hans Christian Adamson, USAF (Ret.), have written should include the last graphic battle between these champions of the sea. Witness to the speed of change through which we live, the battleship's period of glory spanned little more than a generation. But it was fortunate indeed for America and freedom that these warships sailed and served in these years.

As the battleship consolidated into a type, developments that would mark the end of its pre-eminence gathered speed. Improved precision in manufacturing, tools, machines, communications (especially radio); more powerful batteries, generators, and other electrical equipment; refined petroleum and the internal combustion engine—these advances made possible two dramatic newcomers that brought seapower new dimensions of limitless possibilities: a practical submarine and the airplane.

The submarine came first. On the eve of World War I it had grown into a reasonably reliable and effective warship for the times, though still not much faster or much more comfortable than the crude manpower-propelled CSS *Hunley* that sank the USS *Housatonic* off Charleston in 1864. For a young man seeking opportunity and responsibilities, however, these mattered little. Hence, after his battleship service, as World War I broke, Ensign Lockwood turned to submarines in 1914.

Most of his duties for the next quarter of a century were with this great element of seapower (just as Colonel Adamson's lay in the air and elsewhere). The Navy Department sent him to England as naval attaché during the middle of the dark winter of bombing, 1940–1941, where I happily served with him. Then in the spring of 1942 he went to the Pacific, first commanding submarines in the Southwest Pacific; later, in February 1943, to command submarines, Pacific Fleet, under Admiral Nimitz. Here again, in my gunnery and training tasks, I often witnessed his wisdom, skill, and leadership.

Thus Admiral Lockwood had played a large and growing part in the events leading to victory in the Pacific by the time of the far-reaching battles in the Philippine Sea that this volume covers. The vastness of this story challenges all the wide experience of the adventurous, productive careers of Admiral Lockwood and of Colonel Adamson. Setting the stage admirably for the Philippine Sea battles, the authors introduce the reader to the Pacific War when the United States was changing from the offensive-defensive to the all-out offensive. Japan had laid careful plans for defense of a powerful perimeter. Yet her leaders failed to appreciate the massive, crushing force of modern seapower, as refined by the United States Navy.

Much of America's strength and salvation has lain at sea from the time of George Washington. One of the great strategists of the sea, Washington said often—and proved at Yorktown—that for the American Revolution seapower was "the pivot upon which everything turned."

Since the American Revolution, the importance of power on the sea has steadily increased. In World War II it reached a peak with the submarine, aircraft carrier, and battleship. The significant growth stands out most strikingly in the increased ability of sea-based strength to overwhelm land defenses. Steam, in freeing ships from wind and tide, had brought progressively greater mobility and flexibility. Armor had given ships much of the resistance of forts. Improved engines, providing increased speed and steaming radius, gave greater freedom of action and made warships harder to hit.

At the same time, stereo range finders, then radar, combined with electricity operating at speed of light, and the remarkable "mechanical brains" of fire control computers gave ships' guns precise accuracy even at high speed on the unsteady sea.

The submarine and aircraft were first heralded as replacing surface navies. Instead, by wise integration, they brought the United States Navy incredible new power. Incorporating aircraft as part of total fleet strength, the Navy developed the aircraft carrier with its embarked dive bombers, torpedo planes, and fighters into one of the most powerful wartime forces in history. The submarine likewise steadily increased in deadliness. Under Admiral Lockwood, they had penetrated Japan's home seas by the time the battles for Leyte were fought.

Meanwhile the United States Navy had made large strides to counter these new weapons of enemy submarines and airplanes. In the years between the world wars, and with increasing acceleration after Pearl Harbor, the Navy developed sophisticated and successful defenses against the airplane that became almost invulnerable. These included carrier fighter and attack planes, radar, fighter direction, voice radio, antiaircraft guns, influence fuze, and automatic directors that "lock on" the target and solve the fire-control problem instantly.

In the quarter century following World War I, the crude anti-aircraft methods progressed to one of the most complex and efficient systems man has ever evolved. Radar measured the range to an attacking plane accurately with the speed of light even when the plane was far out of sight. Fire-control computers, parents of today's electronic brains, solved the problem of hitting the swift, invisible target miles away in the sky. The influence fuze insured destruction. Hard hitting rapid firing guns made United States warships so safe from air attack that the Japanese had to switch to the Kamikaze tactics so graphically covered in this volume.

From Guadalcanal on, the power of the U.S. Navy had multiplied in offense and in defense, particularly in amphibious assault. As this volume so well relates all this giant force was now unleashed against Japan's inner barrier; what would be the outcome?

We will not see again a drama like this to which Admiral Lockwood and Colonel Adamson have turned their skilled pens. In reading this fascinating narrative of battles reaching over the vast sea we can know that in this case, history will not repeat; for here both the battleship and carrier jointly exhibited their potentials and the submarine played its own silent vital role. The battleship, as we know it, has had its days of glory.

The heavy ship, with its precise and sustained striking power that guns supply, will always be valuable, especially in amphibious operations and keeping the peace. But the carrier and the submarine with their increased flexibility, reach, and surprise capabilities, have replaced it as the pre-eminent factor at sea, the backbone of seapower.

The era described in this book has passed. The battleship with its mighty guns and rugged defense brought many new capabilities against the land. In passing, it handed on the torch to the airplane, submarine, and the guided missile-gun ship, each of which has injected its own new potentials.

Although Japan had to strike by sea, her large goals lay ashore —Manchuria, North China, Southeast Asia, the Philippines. So these giant battles to shatter the inner barrier that culminated in the far-spreading battles for Leyte have significance far beyond the sweeping play of events they unfolded. In them lies the age-long battles between tyranny and freedom, between man's brutalities and his dreams, between land and sea.

The battles for Leyte that bring this fine book to a climax in a sense highlighted the developments of our lifetime and of all the last century—developments which have demonstrated the advantage of having an increased portion of a nation's military power based afloat. That based ashore has unique advantages navies can not replace. Yet the unique advantages of navies ever become more potent—an omen of hope for our destiny and for all those who seek freedom.

E. M. Eller, Rear Admiral, USN, Ret.
Director of Naval History,
Washington, D. C.

BATTLES OF
THE PHILIPPINE SEA

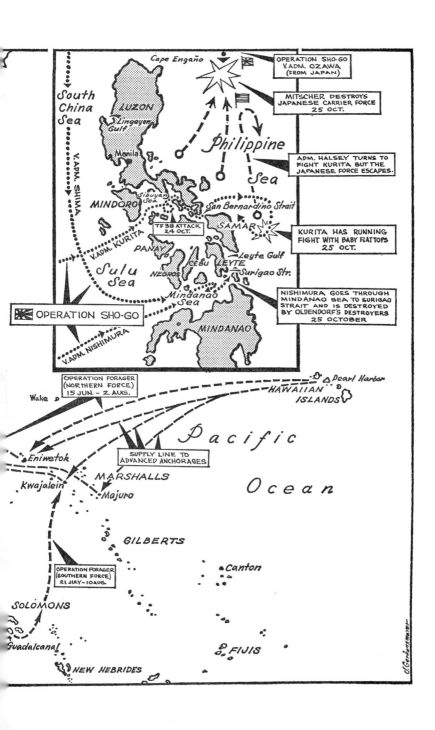

Chapter One

THE BLACK LINE
OF DEFENSE

AT TEN O'CLOCK ON THE MORNING of 30 September 1943 Emperor
Hirohito entered the Imperial Council Chamber of his moat-framed
palace in Tokyo. Seated before him were a dozen or so admirals and
generals in high staff positions and frock-coated civilians of cabinet
and slightly lesser rank. Among those present were Premier and War
Minister Hideki Tojo; Admiral Osami Nagaro, chief of the Navy
General Staff; and Vice Admiral Mineichi Koga, commander in chief
of the Imperial Combined Fleet. Heading the civilian contingent was
Yoshimichi Hara, president of the emperor's Privy Council.

The group had gathered for the most significant conference since
1941 when Japanese forces had swarmed locustlike over widespread
regions in the Pacific and East Asia to establish, with bullets, bombs,
and bayonets, what they called a co-prosperity sphere. The purpose
of the meeting was to obtain Imperial approval for a plan designed to
recapture the offensive, which had been seized by General MacArthur
and Admiral Nimitz.

The plan centered on a heavy black line that was drawn on a large-
scale chart on the wall. The chart depicted ocean areas from Hawaii
to the China Seas, from the Kuriles in the north to New Guinea and
the Coral Sea in the south. The heavy black line followed a winding
course from the Kuriles southward, dodging at varying distances to
the east of the groups of islands that rise out of the ocean from Japan
to New Guinea like irregularly spaced stepping stones.

First, in the order of their appearance north to south, were the
Nampo Shoto. These islands lie east and south of Honshu and bear
such charming names as The Father, The Mother, and The Son-in-
Law. Below them are the Bonins (Chichi Jima), the Volcano (Iwo
Jima), the Marianas (Saipan, Tinian, Rota, and Guam). Here the
line curved eastward to just beyond Truk in the Carolines—the Japanese Gibraltar of the Pacific. Next it turned west past the Palaus

(Babelthuap, Peleliu), ran southwest to cross New Guinea well to the east of Biak Island, then westerly to the Timor Sea and beyond.

The line was the product of painfully searching inquiries into the true status of Japan's dwindling power to wage war and the trend of operations by Admiral Chester W. Nimitz' amphibious assault fleets and General Douglas MacArthur's sea and air forces in the Bismarck Archipelago. There was every indication that the fortunes of war now favored America. Her carrier strength was obviously growing, as evidenced by carrier strikes in far apart areas from the Aleutians to Tarawa and Makin in the Gilberts and the equally sudden appearance of the Navy's floating airdromes off Marcus and Wake, all of which had been heavily hit that very month. As if that were not enough, submarines operating out of Hawaii and Australia smacked torpedoes at an alarming rate into Japanese cargo vessels laden with fuel oil, food, and industrial necessities of which Japan was in increasingly short supply. Something had to be done. Japan's fleet strength had failed to recover from the Midway disaster in 1942, which cost her four carriers, one cruiser, and one destroyer—not to mention the complete eradication of four air groups and the loss of more than one hundred of the Imperial Navy's best carrier pilots.

To Japan, the major threat was the U.S. carrier fleet and its protective screens of fighting ships with their heavy guns. Only in the air could Japan hope to cope with her enemies. Hence she needed carriers as well as planes and pilots. To fill those requirements she had, above all, to gain time. But how? The answer was a change in position from aggressive planning to a delaying action defense program. That black line on the chart was actually a barricade; Nippon's equivalent of Verdun's famous "they shall not pass."

Behind that line ran the island bridge over which Japanese warbirds could shuttle back and forth between the homeland and outlying bases. Many of the stepping stones were large enough for airfields or landing strips and sufficiently close together for easy daylight hops. From the Marianas the airways extended eastward to the outside perimeter islands, the Gilberts and Marshalls; they also covered Truk and the rest of the Carolines. All Central Pacific islands east of Truk —which the Japanese had never expected to give up—were now listed expendable. So were the Bismarcks and Admiralties to the south, and New Guinea as far west as Biak Island and Vogelkop Peninsula. But that did not mean that these areas were to be surrendered. Quite the contrary. Their garrisons would sacrifice themselves

*Chart of the Area Commands in the Pacific Theatre with
the "absolute national defense line" adopted by Japan on
30 September 1943. North, Central, and South Pacific
were under Admiral Nimitz; Southwest Pacific, under
General MacArthur. A year later this line had been driven
as far west as Leyte, on the opposite rim of the Philippine
Sea.*

to stall and delay the American westward drive. These perimeter resistance areas were all-important in Japan's program to gain time for
a showdown in 1945. It must not fail. But if the American forces
should seize the perimeter areas before then, the Imperial Navy was
to swing into immediate action at full strength, and do the best it
could to repulse and eradicate the attackers.

The session in the palace lasted more than seven hours during which generals, admirals, cabinet members, and subordinates explained the military-economic-political policy designed to give Japan time to strengthen her aerial combat capacity. All plans to that end, civil and military, were integrated in the "General Outline of the War Direction Policy." The black line on the chart was officially designated "the absolute national defense line."

Following protocol, the emperor made no comments, asked no questions. According to the rules, he could either take it or leave it. To do the former, he had only to remain silent. The gathering was, however, not just a one-way session. Privy Council President Hara acted as a devil's advocate by asking penetrating and critical questions. Aviation production was his special target. He wanted to know if the 40,000 planes called for by the end of 1944 could actually be built, a seemingly impossible quota when production in August and September, both peak months, had reached only 1,360 and 1,470 planes respectively. Challenging the premise that the new operational plan was a surefire way to victory, he asked Admiral Nagano point-blank if he believed that to be the case. The admiral hedged by saying that he could not promise or predict victory.

This was too much for General Tojo to take. Flushed and angry, he butted in and said that the plan had his wholehearted endorsement; that its objective could be reached; and that he had unqualified confidence in ultimate Japanese victory.

President Hara, who seemed to know when to quit a fight, hastily moved for adjournment. The emperor never spoke a word, and thus the project had been given Imperial acceptance.

Thousands of miles away were the staff operations rooms of General MacArthur in Brisbane, Australia, and of Admiral Nimitz at Pearl Harbor. These commanders eyed Pacific oceanic charts similar to the one displayed in the Imperial Council Chamber, but they regarded them from different viewpoints and with differing objectives. To be sure, neither chart showed Japan's switch in combat attitude indicated by that secret black "they shall not pass" line. Nor did they show markings that denoted future operations and combat objectives of the admiral who was commander in chief of the North, Central, and South Pacific Ocean Areas or those of the general who was supreme commander of Allied Forces in the Southwest Pacific Area. That did not mean that the two leaders were without plans. Their plans, however, were wholly different from each other.

If General MacArthur had his way, there would be but one road to

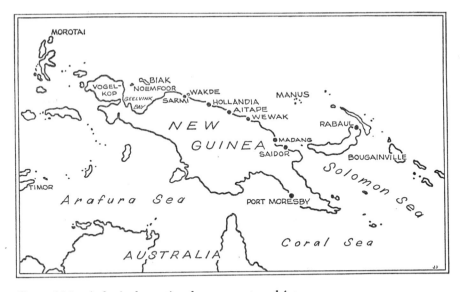

*General MacArthur's dramatic advance, westward from
Saidor along the northern coast of New Guinea, bogged
down when he struck tiny Biak, vital stronghold on Japan's
defense perimeter. Manus and Hollandia became important
amphibious staging points for Admiral Kinkaid's Seventh
Fleet ("MacArthur's Navy").*

Tokyo: his own exclusive MacArthur Boulevard. He proposed to
leapfrog strong amphibious forces westward along the northern coast
of New Guinea, and then, supported by Admiral Nimitz' powerful
Central Pacific Fleet, to assault and occupy Mindanao. After that he
would steam up through the Philippine Sea, making landings at strategic points, liberating the Filipinos as he went; then on to Tokyo by
way of Formosa and Okinawa.

Admiral Nimitz strongly opposed the idea that the Navy should be
reduced to a supporting role under General MacArthur. In line with
long-established Navy precepts, he held that the straightest and best
route to the Philippines led through the Central Pacific. First he
would take the Gilberts, the Marshalls, and Truk. Then he would
seize the Marianas and neutralize Iwo Jima. Thus he would cut and
straddle the Japanese lifeline and establish a foothold on the rim of
the Philippine Sea, control of which was essential for operations
against Japan itself. That body of water lies between Pajaris Island,

at the top of the Marianas, and Luzon Strait below Formosa. To the south, it reaches from the Palaus to Mindanao. The sea covers an area of about 1,140,000 square (nautical) miles, runs about 1,300 miles east to west, and some 800 miles north to south. (Incidentally, all mileages used in this volume are nautical. They measure 6,080 feet as against a statute mile's 5,280 feet.)

After crossing the Philippine Sea, Admiral Nimitz reasoned, landings could be made either on Luzon in the Philippines or on Formosa. He would not, however, take time out to liberate all the Filipinos but would sail on Tokyo and make assault landings on strategic points en route. Convinced of the necessity of disposing of the Imperial Navy before he approached the home islands, the admiral hoped—but felt far from certain—that assaults on such supersensitive spots as the Marianas would compel Admiral Koga to bring the Combined Fleet out of retirement. At this period many experts believed that only an American naval attack on Tokyo itself would lure the entire fleet into battle.

In far off Washington sat the umpires who would pass on the routes proposed by the two Pacific commanders. They were the joint chiefs of staff (JCS), comprising Admiral William D. Leahy, chief of staff to the President in the latter's role as commander in chief of the Armed Forces; Admiral Ernest J. King, commander in chief of the U.S. Fleet and chief of Naval Operations; General George C. Marshall, C of S of the Army; and General Henry (Hap) Arnold, chief of the Army Air Force. In the fall of 1943 the JCS combined the plans of the admiral and the general in a general directive for 1943–44 but subject to change. In late September 1943 it was a toss-up which direction the war in the Pacific would take.

Early in October General Arnold, who had leaned with General Marshall toward General MacArthur's plan, switched to the support of Admiral Nimitz' project. He had decided that the Marianas—some 1,200 miles from Tokyo—would make ideal bases for his upcoming ultralong-range B-29 bombers. The directive was rewritten to include quick buildups of B-29 bases in the Marianas. Realizing that this meant the Navy might take a separate route to Tokyo, General MacArthur tried to have the B-29s incorporated into his concept. But General Arnold wanted the superbombers under his own command and won his point. The final JCS directive, however, was not to be issued until the following March.

Some analysts have written that a deep cleft existed between Gen-

eral MacArthur and Admiral Nimitz. This is not correct. Their opposing views were based on honest differences of opinion; neither
personal animosity nor ambitious rivalry entered into their relation-
ship, which, on the whole, was one of willing and efficient cooperation. When the general needed carriers, as well as Big Boys (battleships and cruisers) and Small Boys (destroyers and destroyer escorts), he borrowed them from the admiral. And when the admiral
needed air support provided by long-range land-based bombers, the
general always obliged. Such mutual support was to keep wheels,
wings, and keels in both commands moving toward flattening Japanese installations.

General MacArthur and Admiral Nimitz had much in common.
Both had highly trained command minds that cut through underbush
to reach the core of projects and problems; both had that extraordi-
nary quality of leadership that inspires loyalty; both were endowed
with the champion's will to win; both respected rules and traditions
but had the guts to throw them over and make off-the-cuff decisions
in emergencies; both were tall, well-knit men, lean as greyhounds and
straight as ramrods.

But here similarity ceases. The admiral's eyes were serene and
blue, his bushy hair was blond salted with gray, his soft speech still
carried a trace of his native Texan drawl. The general's eyes were
dark and fiery, his thinning hair was straight and jet black, his speech
was quick and modulated. The admiral seldom rode the emotional
pendulum; joy or sorrow would set the general off on lusty zooms or
steep dives. During moments of tense waiting, when great combat is-
sues hung in the balance, the admiral would drawl appropriate Lin-
colnesque jokes while he calmly practiced on his pistol range or
tossed ringers with horseshoes just outside his office. At such moments the general would, as a rule, sit stonily in his chair, chewing on
the stem of a corncob pipe, which usually needed relighting.

The slowdown in American–Allied combat tempo, which Japanese
strategists had anticipated, did not materialize. Almost every day
brought alarming reports to Tokyo. In the South Pacific, General
MacArthur kept hammering the Bismarck Archipelago with the stout
assistance of Air Command Solomons (Airsol), composed of Army,
Navy, and Marine squadrons, beefed up by Royal New Zealand Air
Force cadres and General George C. Kenney's Army Air Force, reinforced by the Royal Australian Air Force. To the valiant men who
flew search planes, fighters, bombers and torpedo-planes in these out-

fits belongs a large slice of credit for Allied victories in those hotly contested islands. Powerful blows were struck by Admiral William F. Halsey's South Pacific Fleet and MacArthur's own amphibious forces to forge a ring of steel around Rabaul. These strongly fortified positions on New Britain, as well as on Bougainville near by to the southeast, were important cards in Japan's hands. Despite almost continuous bombing and strafing, both strongholds continued to send land-based combat planes aloft. To large numbers of these Japanese fliers, death was wingman. But those who died were replaced by other fliers drawn by Admiral Koga from Truk and from carrier contingents and the air bases in the Carolines, Gilberts, Marshalls, and Palaus.

October 1943 began with General MacArthur capturing Finsch-hafen on New Guinea, a harbinger of westward moves to come. The project to neutralize Rabaul and crush Bougainville continued.

Meanwhile at Pearl Harbor, Admiral Nimitz assembled forces to break the outer perimeter of General Tojo's "absolute national defense line" by grabbing the Gilberts. His combat capacity had been increased during the year by a thin but fairly regular dribble of heavy carriers (CV) of the *Essex* class, light carriers (CVL) of the *Independence* class, and escort carriers (CVE) including some of the unique make-do *Sangamon* class, namely oiler hulls converted into jeep flattops. The core of the Central Pacific Fleet, commanded by Vice Admiral Raymond A. Spruance, had a seagoing battering ram made up of 6 CVs, 5 CVLs, 8 CVEs, 7 old battleships (OBB), and 5 new ones (BB). Added to this were 9 heavy (CA) and 5 light (CL) cruisers, 59 destroyers (DD), 29 transports, supply ships, and various landing craft. Rear Admiral Charles A. Pownall commanded the fast carrier task force; the amphibious force was headed by Rear Admiral Richmond K. Turner; the landing forces were commanded by Major General Holland M. Smith, USMC. This fleet was now being readied to pound the Gilberts into submission.

Guided by the resistance mustered by the enemy in the South Pacific, Admiral Nimitz, aided by General MacArthur, expanded or built air facilities in the Ellice Islands. Flying from these bases, Army, Navy, and Marine search and photo reconnaissance missions observed and photographed the Gilberts and lower Marshalls to evaluate results of bombing and strafing missions by other pilots. They also scanned the seas for signs of the Japanese Second Fleet, which that fall had twice steamed from its base on Truk to the rim of the eastward perimeter in search of American warships that were not there. The island-based air groups were commanded by Rear Admiral John H. Hoover.

While the bombings were going on the 2nd Marines trained on New Zealand beaches for their landings in the Gilberts. Admiral Nimitz' new carriers, with their complements of green pilots, made strikes on such "soft" targets as Wake Island, where they received their baptism of fire and acquired a taste for combat. The Japanese could testify to their adequacy.

Truk, where Admiral Koga had his headquarters aboard the super-battleship *Musashi,* was a center of major activity as well as base for part of Vice Admiral Takeo Kurita's Second Fleet. Vice Admiral Jisaburo Ozawa's Third Fleet of carriers and their screens was based at Lingga Roads near Singapore.

Admiral Koga had the calculator brain of the born staff officer. Endowed with courage, sagacity, and tenacity, he worked diligently and well in the face of tremendous odds. Japan's intentions had been to fortify Truk's inner and outer perimeters in the Carolines, Marshalls, and Gilberts, as well as to increase their garrisons and air units. But either Admiral Koga did not have the means to increase garrisons and defenses or else Japan dawdled too long to initiate such efforts. As for island air installations, the numbers of planes decreased rather than increased as time went on. By and large, the ground defenses of the perimeter islands were low on men but strong in antiaircraft guns and artillery. These weapons were well manned; there was plenty of ammo on hand. Also, the terrain of the islands was such that a few defenders could stand up against more numerous assault troops.

In November a tidal wave of air strikes and surface actions swept the seas from the Kuriles to Rabaul. On 1 November 1943 General MacArthur launched the invasion of Bougainville. The following day ships of Admiral Halsey's South Pacific Fleet, commanded by Rear Admiral Stanton Merrill, entered upon and won the Battle of Empress Augusta Bay. Rushing to the rescue of Bougainville, Rear Admiral Sentaro Omori sailed his cruiser-destroyer force out of Rabaul, but he badly bungled the job and was relieved of his command by Admiral Koga. Sensing disaster ahead, Admiral Koga sped Admiral Kurita with a fast cruiser-destroyer force from Truk to head off the invasion. At the same time, he expedited 173 assorted warplanes to the scene from the Gilberts and nearby points although planes in the islands were being destroyed by U.S. fliers at a rate that almost matched the pace of aircraft production in the homeland.

Admiral Kurita, a hard-bitten career sailor, through his own ability had risen to his position as commander, progressively, of destroyers, cruisers, and battleships. He was a battlewagon driver who believed in the power of big guns and lots of them in preference to the carrier concept. Alas, he fared no better in the Bismarcks than did his predecessor, Admiral Omori. In fact, Kurita's cruisers did not fire a single salvo. Airsol patrols sighted his force being refueled in Rabaul harbor. There a flattop, on loan to Admiral Halsey from Admiral Nimitz and commanded by Rear Admiral Frederick C. Sherman, caught Kurita with his hooks in the mud. Despite frantic efforts to barge out of the harbor, six of Kurita's cruisers and two destroyers were so damaged that they could barely stagger back to Truk.

Admiral Koga, now thoroughly alarmed, waited for the next American onslaught. It came upon him during the early hours of 19 November when Koga's headquarters were informed by Commander Goro Matsuura, on Tarawa, that one of his search planes, in its dawn sweep, had sighted a huge fleet approaching the Gilberts.

Matsuura did not know it, but his search pilot had been the first Japanese to see the greatest carrier-assault force that, up to then, ever sailed any sea. Soon the Gilberts shook under bombardments from fighting ships and carriers. Next came assault waves of Marines and a regimental combat team of the 27th Infantry. An RCT is an infantry regiment to which a battalion of field artillery and smaller units of other arms have been added. Makin Atoll was the first objective taken—and the easiest. Then came Tarawa Atoll. In the eyes of the enemy High Command, the defense was a failure because it lacked the delaying features Japanese leaders had hoped for. Less than a week of fighting and it was all over but the mopping up. But the Japanese died almost to a man and American casualties ran into the thousands. One carrier, CVE *Liscome Bay,* was torpedoed by a lone Japanese submarine that came out of nowhere and disappeared whence it came.

As Commander Submarines Pacific (ComSubPac), Vice Admiral Charles A. Lockwood placed subs near Mille in the eastern Marshalls and off Tarawa before the assaults. Their job was to rescue aviators downed in enemy waters. After the strikes, one of the subs, the *Nautilus,* transported seventy-eight Marines to Apamama Island under cover of night. She was nearly sunk—Marines and all—when a "friendly" destroyer and a cruiser attacked her with shellfire. Three additional subs patrolled waters between the Gilberts and Ponape in the Carolines to discover and prevent any sneak sortie by Koga from Truk. One of these subs, the *Sculpin,* while attacking a convoy, was so damaged by depth charges dropped by an enemy destroyer that her skipper was forced to surface with the intention of fighting it out with his guns. Two enemy shells killed the skipper, Lieutenant Commander F. A. Connaway, along with other officers and men on the bridge or in the conning tower below. Lieutenant G. E. Brown, the diving officer, assuming command, decided to abandon ship and scuttle the *Sculpin.* Remaining aboard, by his own wish, was Captain John P. Cromwell, who decided that he was too familiar with future war plans to risk capture.

The loss of the Gilberts left Koga with only eight air bases for the protection of Truk's outer perimeter. They were on Eniwetok, Jaluit, Kwajalein, Maloelap, Mille, Nauru, Wake, and Wotje. Koga and his officers believed that Truk itself, a cluster of islands around a lagoon some 70 miles in diameter, was well protected against attack. Koga's patrols flew widespread search patterns, and radar swept the horizon. At first sighting, the enemy would be attacked by long-range planes, which would be reinforced by short-range aircraft if the approach continued. Meanwhile Kurita's Second Fleet would stand to sea under a full head of steam, all hands at battle stations. This fleet had no carriers; all flattops were either carefully hoarded by Ozawa or being used to train carrier pilots in home waters. In the whole year since the Battle of Santa Cruz in October 1942, not a single Rising Sun carrier had been seen in the Pacific combat zone. A similar reluctance to appear in public had seized Japanese battleships about a month later when they bid Guadalcanal adieu. After the Gilberts debacle, Koga tried to repair his crumbling outer fences and prepared to meet Admiral Nimitz if and when his far-ranging fast carrier fleet should attempt to crash the barrier. But there was to be no respite for the Japanese.

On 26 November Vice Admiral Thomas C. Kinkaid, who as commander of the North Pacific Fleet had distinguished himself in the joint Navy–Army operations to drive the enemy out of the Aleutians, was given command of General MacArthur's amphibious force. He landed the 12th Cavalry RTC at Arawe, New Britain, on 15 December. On that occasion amtracs (amphibious landing vehicles) sprayed rockets for the first time in the Pacific war. They scored so heavily that rocket launchers were installed on LCIs (landing tanks, infantry) as well. Eleven days later Admiral Kinkaid landed the 1st Marine Division on Cape Gloucester, New Britain. On 2 January he set the 126th Infantry RTC ashore on New Guinea's Huon Peninsula at Saidor, which was to become a jumping board for General MacArthur's leapfrogging along New Guinea's coast en route to Tokyo. Thus the year ended without Japan gaining the time she so desperately needed to recapture the initiative.

In the south, MacArthur, Halsey, Kinkaid, and company drew the noose tighter around Rabaul. After 18 February no Japanese planes remained in the Bismarcks. Then came the capture of Manus in the Admiralties northwest of the Bismarcks. Manus was not only large enough for the staging and care of troops but its Seeadler Harbor was also the best and largest in the area. Among the many islands in the Admiralties several were big and flat enough for air installations that ranged from airfields to strips. In the far north the sound of bursting bombs became an almost weekly occurrence in the Kuriles, under fire from long-range Army and Navy bombers.

In Pearl Harbor Admiral Nimitz was in close touch with Admirals Spruance, Turner, Mitscher, and Hoover, as well as General Holland M. Smith, better known as "Howling Mad" Smith by virtue of his low boiling point. (Smith, incidentally, got along very well with Admiral Turner, whose temper had earned him the *nom de guerre* Terrible Turner.) What occupied the attentions of these officers, plus those of ComSubPac and ServForPac (Services Forces Pacific Fleet), commanded by Vice Admiral William F. Calhoun, was the impending occupation of the Marshalls. Admiral Nimitz, in particular, had his eyes fixed on the great possibilities for anchorages in the huge lagoons of Kwajalein, Eniwetok, and Majuro atolls. Possession of them would enable him to move his fleet 2,000 miles closer to Japan and only 1,000 miles from the Marianas.

In determining the Marshalls invasion schedule, Admiral Nimitz made one of those deft bypassing plays that threw the enemy off balance. He decided to disregard Wotje, Maleolap, Mille, and Jaluit despite their airstrips and garrisons. Instead, he would descend upon Kwajalein, the main atoll in the heart of the group where the Japanese would least expect an initial attack. As for garrisons on bypassed islands, he would keep their heads down and planes grounded by massive air strikes and surface bombardments. Excellent periscope panoramic photos of beachheads and shore conditions had been obtained by three photographic submarine missions. The subs also acted as lifeguards at Eniwetok, Kusaie, and Ponape; other subs guarded exits from Truk as well as those from fleet bases in Japan.

The two men who were to play top roles in this expedition were Spruance and Mitscher. Admiral Spruance was tall, square-shouldered, narrow-hipped. His face habitually wore the grave expression of the bust of a Roman senator. A naval tactician of great skill, his spectacular victory at Midway in 1942 so impressed Admiral Nimitz that he made Raymond Spruance his deputy as well as C of S. In the fall of 1943 he became commander of the vastly enlarged and reorganized Central Pacific Fleet, soon to become the Fifth Fleet. He was a quiet, deliberate man, capable of making vital decisions and sticking to them.

Marc A. Mitscher was a sea bird of a different color. He had turned to naval aviation as early as 1915 and was among those who helped build our first carrier, the *Saratoga,* on which he served for three years. His first CV command was the *Hornet,* from which he launched the Doolittle Tokyo raiders in 1942. Jockey-sized, he weighed in at about 135 pounds. Taciturn, almost grumpy, he nonetheless enjoyed a reputation as a good man to serve under. Aboard ship he wore a lobsterman's cap on his bald head and ensconced himself on a long-legged steel armchair at the after end of his flag bridge; to keep the wind out of his face, he always faced the stern.

Together, Admirals Spruance and Mitscher made a wonderful and virtually unbeatable team. While the former was boss of the fleet of which Mitcher's Task Force 58 was a part, the latter had certain tactical powers in his own right. The fleet commander flew his flag in one of the fast new Big Boys of TF 58's gun-support screen; the fast carrier task force's boss hoisted his flag aboard one of his towering flattops. Admiral Spruance came to favor the CA *Indianapolis,* whereas Admiral Mitscher came to prefer CV *Lexington.*

By 19 January 1944, when the fast carrier task force was on the Marshalls' horizon, Admiral Hoover's land-based planes had brought at least temporary paralysis to defenders on islands to be bypassed. While steaming off Kwajalein, Admiral Mitscher sent deckload after deckload of carrier planes on strike missions while screen support guns belched their deadly salvos. After three days and nights of this torrent of explosives, the 4th Marines and 7th Infantry moved toward the beaches. Again, it was no easy Sunday stroll. Resistance did not end until 4 February. Opposition on Roi Namur was especially fierce. Still, of the 53,000 assault troops, only 43,000 hit the beach. Since no more were needed, this left a reserve of 10,000 men with nowhere to go but Eniwetok, a large atoll some 360 miles to the northwest. The duration of resistance at Kwajalein had been shorter than expected. There had been no Japanese reception committee at all at Majuro Atoll, where TF 58 had already found anchorage, primitive but secure. Only one of Mitscher's four task groups steamed to Eniwetok for the invasion. But the other three did not remain at anchor for long.

On 16 February 1944 Admirals Spruance and Mitscher—to use the phrase of Admiral Nimitz—"returned at Truk the visit made by the Japanese Fleet at Pearl Harbor on 7 December, 1941, and made a partial settlement of the debt." For reasons unknown, Japanese radar and snoopers failed to sight a single boat in the concentration of nine submarines sent by ComSubPac to surround Truk a few days before the fleet's arrival. Also, the elaborate reception prepared by Koga was never executed. First news of the unbidden visitors came when Admiral Mitscher's planes raced toward their objectives, preceded by the roar and rip of shells hurled by Admiral Spruance's fire-support ships. This treatment had become known as a Spruance Haircut at Kwajalein, where heavy and devastating bombardment from the large-bore rifles of battleships at close inshore range blasted and razed everything in sight—proof that although battleships might no longer be the queens of the line, they carried a heftier punch than any other invasion weapon.

Though not generally realized, the real bone- and stone-crushing jobs, prior to landings, were done not by carrier bombardiers but by gunners aboard the grand old battleships. But, unlike Admiral Kurita at Rabaul, the Second Fleet was not to be caught with its anchors down. On 10 February, when the Marshalls were doomed, Admiral Koga, aware of his insecure position, sent Admiral Kurita and most of his fleet to the Palaus on the edge of the Philippine Sea. Left at Truk were only two light cruisers, three destroyers, one ammunition ship, and some naval odds and ends. Of the planes that rose to beat back Admiral Mitscher's deckloads of fighters, 127 were blasted to pieces or splashed into the sea. That ended airborne resistance; but on the ground, AAs and other artillery were still going strong. For two days Truk endured strike on strike. To foil would-be escapes by ships in the harbor, Admiral Spruance circled the atoll with a supporting force of two battleships, two cruisers, and four destroyers. Air and sea actions accounted for 300 planes shot down, wrecked, or damaged. The cruisers, destroyers, and ammo ship that had remained were sunk, as were a miscellany of oilers, gunboats, cargo vessels, and a seaplane tender. Shore facilities such as gasoline and ammo dumps, runways, hangars, barracks, revetments, and gun positions were wrecked. On the American side, twenty-five aircraft were lost and CV *Intrepid* was badly hit when one of the few "meatball" (slang for Japanese emblem on planes) Jills, Bettys, or Kates (torpedo-bombers) that attacked during the night landed a torpedo into her rudder and steering compartment. She made it home under her own power, however, by rigging a sail on the flight deck and steering with her engines.

An important discovery was made about Truk in that operation. Admiral Nimitz learned that the Gibraltar of the Pacific did not measure up to its reputation; it was not worth the time and trouble to take it. Like Rabaul, Admiral Spruance reported, it could be by-passed, left to shrivel up and fade away. Admiral Nimitz suggested that Truk be removed from the invasion list. The suggestion was accepted.

Admiral Koga and his superiors in Japan became painfully aware that the "absolute national defense line" was less capably protected than they had believed. For all practical purposes, the bulge into the Carolines from the Marianas down to the Palaus had been wiped out. With Truk in jeopardy, the lifeline itself was exposed. Important stepping stones in the Marianas and Palaus were vulnerable, and so was the Philippine Sea. Admiral Koga transferred his fleet headquarters to the Palau Islands. Truk was not abandoned but reduced to a delaying point in the Carolines perimeter, which would be supplied by air or submarines, the real cargo boats of the Japanese Navy.

In desperation, Admiral Koga flew to Japan for conferences at Imperial Staff levels. He proposed air reinforcements be distributed along the lifeline and guaranteed that the strategic center—Saipan, Tinian, Guam, Peleliu, and Babelthuap—would be pierced only over the dead bodies of all defenders, including his own. The plan formulated in 1943 to reorganize the Imperial Fleet along the American lines of carrier task groups protected by heavy gunpower was now slated to be put into execution. Next, Koga proposed to supplement their striking strength by increasing land-based Army and Navy air complements along the absolute defense lifeline, so that they could cooperate with carrier planes in attacking American fleets. Like the High Command, Koga was inflexibly sold on the idea that Japan would be able to select the time and place for naval action by the simple means of letting an enemy assault fleet start landing operations, a rather vulnerable period; then the Japanese fleet, coiled to strike, would launch planes as would the island air bases. Thus the invaders would be caught in a massive crossfire; the effectiveness of the attack would be increased by sending carrier pilots on shuttle-runs. After hitting the American fleet, pinned down between Japanese ships and the shore, the Japanese planes would streak toward friendly airfields, fill their tanks, and take on fresh ammunition to attack again on the return run. This arrangement had another aspect. Aware that carrier pilots were given deplorably inadequate training, the considerable risks incurred by inept pilots taking off and landing on carrier decks between strikes would be cut in half. Obviously Japan expected American assaults in the Philippine Sea perimeter to be aimed at the Mariana–Palaus line.

Garrisons on the lifeline islands would be beefed up by the transfer of troops from Manchuria, where the 31st Army with some 30,000 men was formed and commanded by Lieutenant General Hideyshi Obata. This transfer was admittedly risky, because American subs out of Pearl Harbor, Brisbane, and Fremantle were perforating maru bottoms with deadly aim and great frequency. From Pearl Harbor day to the time of the adoption of the new operational plan in September 1943, Allied submarines had sunk or damaged 436 cargomen with a loss of 2,143,000 tons of shipping. Since then, monthly sinkings by American subs alone had reached 200,000 tons. Despite the risks involved, the Japanese troops were transported from Manchuria to the Philippine Sea perimeter in convoys. Unfortunately for her, Japan had neither the time nor the means to establish a naval escort command to protect valuable convoys.

To defend the homeland from sudden attack, Operation TO was set up by the Imperial General Staff. It would boost the air groups at Yokusuta, Japan's principal land-based air station, to the largest possible proportions with torpedo, search, fighter, and bomber planes. Their mission would be to attack and exterminate approaching enemies.

But, contrary to program, Japan's air quotas were not being filled. Instead of producing some 3,500 planes a month to reach 40,000 at the end of the year, the turnout in February was only about 1,800. To replace the 2,500 pilots lost in the South Pacific alone was virtually impossible. Nonetheless, it was agreed to scatter 1,644 planes, which did not exist, down the lifeline. In a slow trickle, new planes were flown down the latitudes over the stepping stones, many with inadequately trained pilots. Vice Admiral Kakuji Kakuta, a naval flier of long standing, had command of this operation. He subjected his inexperienced fliers to frequent patrols up and down the lifeline, even though pilots, like planes, were hard to replace. Whereas Uncle Sam trained carrier pilots for about two years, their Japanese counterparts—the best and brightest youths of the country—had only a few months in which to become carrier-ready.

The Imperial Navy had only two heavy (CV) carriers left of her once formidable flattop fleet; a third CV would soon be added. Only six light (CVLs) carriers, of which two had been tankers and one a naval supply ship, were on hand. In dock for conversion were two old battleships whose after turrets were being removed to make way for stubby little flight decks. The air groups of the CVs had been chewed to pieces in the Rabaul debacle; those of the CVLs were still to be completed.

A weary Admiral Koga returned to the Palaus from Japan, but for him no rest was in store. A few days after hoisting his flag on the *Musashi,* carriers of Admiral Mitscher's TF 58 raided the Marianas.

In the bypassed Gilberts, Marshalls, and Carolines, including Truk, General Kenney's long-range Army bombers and Admiral Hoover's land-based Navy, Marine, and Army fliers devastated virtually every visible rock pile, coral clump, and sand heap. Only the Palau Islands had remained untouched. In the South Pacific, General MacArthur prepared for a 400-mile amphibious jump to Aitape and Hollandia, where his landings would have the support of two carrier task groups from TF 58. In ridding the entire South Sea region of Japanese forces, General MacArthur had made sure that his flanks and rear were not exposed to enemy attack during his westward moves on New Guinea.

Admiral Nimitz, in exterminating enemy positions from the Kuriles to the Carolines—by invasions, air strikes, and protracted bombings —was transforming the Central Pacific into a safe and convenient corridor to the islands that formed General Tojo's defense line.

The United States actions were basically preparatory moves for twin drives that were to crack the Japanese lifeline and provide entry to the Philippine Sea. Numerous difficulties were still ahead and months would be required to set up plans and bring them to fruition. Even so, this complicated program was executed with such unexpected speed that it threw Japan into a precarious situation from which she was never permitted to recover.

Chapter Two

DRIVES TOWARD
THE PHILIPPINE SEA

CincPac Communique No. 281, Feb. 23, 1944:

A strong Pacific Fleet Task Force, including several hundred carrier-based planes, struck Saipan and Tinian Islands in the Marianas Group on Feb. 22. Further details are not now available.

These few calm words from Admiral Nimitz did not reveal the true import of the attack. No one, least of all the Japanese, guessed that this was the first faint dawning of the day when the Empire's last-stand island defense line and barrier to the Philippine Sea would be cracked wide open.

The task force referred to was composed of two task groups totaling some half-dozen carriers accompanied by their respective fire-support screens. Rear Admiral Marc A. Mitscher was in command, the first time in his long naval career when his ambition to be the sole boss, the strategic as well as the tactical head of a task force, was realized. After the assault on Truk on 16 February, Task Force 58 had split up. Admiral Spruance headed for Kwajalein. Of the three task groups that remained, one made for Majuro with orders to give the Japanese installations on bypassed Jaluit Atoll a first-rate drubbing en route.

The other two task groups were commanded by Rear Admirals A. E. Montgomery and F. C. Sherman. Admiral Mitscher, as force commander, flew his flag in the CV *Yorktown*. When orders came for the two task groups to take a northern heading instead of going east to Majuro, all hands in all ships began to wonder what was up. Speculation increased when the Force approached a refueling area, where several fleet oilers, an escort carrier, and their screening destroyers

19

awaited them. Something unexpected was in the wind. After the Marshalls invasion and the assault on Truk there was widespread feeling aboard that Majuro, although primitive and not much of a resort, at least promised liberty to go ashore. There might even be time for two cans of beer and a swim.

Soon the work and excitement of taking oil aboard for the fuel tanks, aviation gas, ammunition, stores, provisions, mail, and water drew everyone's attention. There is a strong sporting element in the tricky and skill-demanding task of refueling at sea. This was done within a predesignated area that was usually 75 miles long and 25 miles wide. Steaming at close quarters, from 20 to 70 feet apart, at identical speeds, an oiler would pass large and heavy hoses to carriers, battleships, and cruisers as they moved, one by one, into position. (The Small Boys would be refueled by the Big Boys as needed.) Through those umbilical tubes, the black bunker oil flowed in 1,000-gallon streams until the Oil King, who watched the fuel gauges, gave the stop signal. During these operations, which usually took several hours, men with heavy, long-handled, broad-bladed axes stood by each hose to sever it with a single blow if alarms should be sounded. Aloft, combat air patrols (CAP) scanned sky and water.

The CVE that accompanied the oilers was specially equipped to fill plane and air personnel losses on carriers by catapulting manned planes to them from her stubby decks. This was a brand new type of carrier operational efficiency. It saved flattops, in protracted operations, from having losses sap their combat strength or from having to spend valuable time returning to base to fill their air group quotas.

Soon after the refueling was completed and the Force was on course, Admiral Mitscher let it be known that Saipan, Tinian, Rota, and Guam were the targets, and that the operation was named Cherry Tree in honor of George Washington.

"I cannot tell a lie," said Mitscher in a message to his force. "D-day is Washington's birthday. Let's chop down a few Nip cherry trees."

On the afternoon of 21 February—D-day minus one—a nosy Betty slipped through the CAP cordon of fighters and saw the force. Making for home, the Japanese plane was caught in the sights of a Hellcat pilot, whose guns froze after a short initial burst. The incident was reported to Admiral Mitscher, who now knew that his coming was no longer a secret. After examining the situation he decided to move into launching range against whatever obstacles the Japanese defenders might put in his way. Since his targets were to westward and because the tradewinds always blow out of an easterly corner in those latitudes, the taciturn, leathery little force commander decided that he would not delay his chances of getting within striking distance at daylight by making time-consuming 180-degree turns to launch and recover night fighters while heading into the wind.

On this occasion he planned to let the gunnery skills aboard his carriers and screening vessels handle the situation if a torpedo attack —as was expected—should develop. Admiral Mitscher had great faith in the ability of the new VT proximity fuzes for antiaircraft guns, to knock planes out of the sky. These fuzes differed from the orthodox type, which exploded a projectile a given length of time after it was fired. Instead, an electronic brain in the VT fuze detonated the shell when it was within adequate range of a plane. This fuze was so new and so secret that strict orders forbade its use over areas where a dud might fall into Japanese hands. Because of their amazing talent for imitation, it was feared that such a gift from above would enable the Japanese to develop similar fuzes.

In short order the screening vessels slipped into combat patterns that looked like huge wheels, one for each task group, of which the carriers were the hubs. Around these hubs the Big Boys formed a tight inner circle and the Small Boys an equally tight outer ring. The rapid and heavy firepower of these men-of-war provided the floating airdromes with strong defense perimeters. Despite these advantages, one cannot help wondering if similar action would have been taken if someone else had been in command. While not unqualifiedly reckless, the decision was akin to placing a heavy bet on a long-shot racehorse, a bet few commanders would dare to make. With good reason, carrier commanders feared night torpedo-plane attacks, and not many would have had the temerity to expose themselves deliberately to that danger as Admiral Mitscher did that night.

With his task force in combat readiness and the two wheels several miles apart, the admiral steamed toward the sunset and into the gathering darkness, each vessel keeping station in the circular formations. For this, good navigation and clever seamanship were essential. Speed was not reduced, although the long wakes spread by fast screws were as visible on the sea as electric signs on Times Square.

At 2100, when night covered the sea and the blacked-out ships, Admiral Mitscher was informed by Captain Arleigh A. Burke—of South Pacific destroyer fame and now his chief of staff—that *York-*

town's CIC (combat information center) had radar reports indicating that planes were approaching from the south at levels so low that they seemed to skim the water. The expected torpedo attack was on its way.

All personnel already stood at battle stations from topside gunners to fire-control parties below decks. Over the TBS (ship-to-ship radio phone) crackled an alert, followed by orders to execute sharp starboard turns to a northerly heading at flank speed—about 30 knots —and for the carriers to prepare for such evasive action as would be required. Presently the radar dots indicated a formation of twenty planes. Next came instructions to fire at will.

The cards were dealt; now it was up to the two task groups to play them. Admiral Mitscher left the flag-plot and took his accustomed seat on his long-legged chair facing aft on the flag bridge, which was in the *Yorktown*'s massive island and just below the captain's bridge. He lit a cigarette in cupped hands, took a deep drag, and quietly waited for hell to pop in all directions. The night, dark as the inside of a rubber cow (Navy blimp), was suddenly slashed to pieces by a multitude of gun flashes followed by the winking glares of exploding projectiles. The racket they set up was ear-splitting. Undeterred by this awesome zone of death, the torpedo-heaving Jills, Judys, and Kates kept pressing in. The first attack wave was aimed at Admiral Montgomery's group, which included the *Yorktown*. In the darkness the enemy planes were utterly undetectable. They became visible only when flamed by a hit or exposed briefly by the *flash-flash-flash* of bursting shells. According to eyewitnesses, the first attack, pressed very stubbornly, cost the Japanese eight torpedo-planes, without a hit being scored by them. Flying off to re-form, they next drove on Admiral Sherman's task group. When this wave had spent itself, not a ship had been scratched, but two more torpedo-planes had been shot down. Despite their 50 percent losses, the attackers did not turn back. Like a pack of wolves, they bore down on the carriers in individual torpedo-level rushes, from which five participants never returned.

With the pearly predawn, the five survivors of twenty Judys, Jills, and Kates disappeared. Their places, however, were soon taken by an assortment of fighters, bombers, dive-bombers, and torpedo-bombers. Admiral Kakuta, who ran the air show from his headquarters on Tinian, was giving his opponents the works. But the thrust was blunted by the massive CAP sent aloft at first light. The weather was dirty; strong gusts of wind, moist with rain, swept sea and sky. The latter was so heavily overcast that not even one of those patches of blue called Dutchmen's Breeches brightened the low ceiling's gray gloom. When the new set of attackers droned in under the low, scudding clouds, they ran smack into a brood of Hellcats who tore into them with a will. The Japanese formations were soon blasted apart. Zekes, instead of riding shotgun for bombers and divers, were cornered into dogfights that usually ended at an enemy pilot's first chance to dash into the clouds for sanctuary. The unprotected bombers and divers did not stand on formality but flew off. One Judy dive-bomber, mortally hurt, spiraled slowly seaward as chunks of fuselage, wings, and tail were sawed off by streams of bullets from a Hellcat's guns. Another dived down, trailing flame and smoke, to splash into the sea.

In the distance and far below the milling contestants, carriers and screens cut various evasive capers while tense gun crews waited for their inning. In the aerial scramble, two Bettys slipped past the guardian Hellcats, crashed through the screens, and streaked, wave-hopping, for the CV *Belleau Wood*. But before they came within torpedo-launching range, the big flattop's gunners made hash of them.

Thus ended the dawn attack. As soon as it was over, carrier elevators spewed deckloads of fighters, dive-bombers, and torpedo-bombers, loaded and ready, upon the flight decks. Flying conditions were bad, but that is not unusual off Saipan where the weather is as notoriously unstable as it is over the Bay of Biscay. If, reasoned Admiral Mitscher, conditions were good enough for the Japanese to find the Americans, they were good enough for the Americans to find the Japanese. In rapid succession planes roared off, climbed, assembled, and turned toward their targets manned by a flock of hatchetmen eager to whack down Japanese cherry trees.

Admiral Mitscher was not as complacent about the weather as he appeared to be. He had hoped for bright sunshine and high visibility for two important reasons: Although the first and foremost duty of a carrier task force is to strike and destroy its objectives, this operation was also a huge search mission for gathering the fullest possible information about each of the four target islands, particularly Saipan, the chief and first invasion objective.

The JCS directives dealing with the direction the war in the Pacific would take had not been issued, but Admiral Nimitz felt fairly certain that they would appear soon and that they would include his recommendation for the invasion of the Marianas. Believing that preparation is the largest single factor in victory, Nimitz wanted his planners to know all that could be learned about the Marianas—not the entire 450-mile-long group of volcanic rocks, but the four principal islands at the bottom of the chain. That need was especially true with respect to Saipan and Tinian, which had virtually been closed to outsiders since Japan acquired them after World War I. Nearly all available maps, charts, and general information dated back to the days before Japan took over from Germany. These outdated sources were inadequate for planning and timing invasions. Where and in what strength were army, navy, and air installations and garrisons? Where were blockhouses, pillboxes, heavy coast defense guns, and other fortifications situated? What was the situation with respect to Saipan's most desirable landing beaches on the western side of the island? These were but a few of the questions that had to be answered.

As Admiral Mitscher's pilots winged toward the Marianas, Lieutenant Commander Edgar E. Stebbins, a veteran Avenger pilot, whiled away time in his carrier's ready room with four Hellcat fliers. Stebbins had a very important secret mission for which his torpedo-bomber had been converted into a well-camouflaged photographic plane: cameras and photographers were housed in the bay where bombs or tin fish usually hung on the release racks. Their task was to take, at predetermined altitudes, photographs of the islands, including obliques of mountains, foothills, and beaches, all to be used in building the scale topographical models used by commanders and their staffs. To screen the Avenger from enemy attack, four Hellcats would serve as escorts. Much hung on the success of this secret mission, not only with respect to photography but also in keeping Japanese observers from guessing its real purpose. Such a guess would point to invasion probabilities and pinpoint the island group on which beach-heads would be established for amphibious landings. But on that morning there seemed very little chance that Commander Stebbins would make even one exposure.

The pilots in the first wave of attack, however, reported a slight but perceptible breakup of the overcast. They actually found holes through which they could drop some two miles through the cloud cover and look for ground targets. Here and there they met air opposition, which was not very effectual; but the numerous antiaircraft batteries and other artillery positions were so well served that it made the fliers feel good to know that in the sea west of the Nipponese islands five ComSubPac subs were posted to rescue airmen who ditched. Alas, the crews of five disabled planes crashed on land before they could reach the sea and the subs. There were no rescues that day off Saipan. On the other hand, the subs sank over 20,000 tons of shipping; an equal tonnage was sunk by air attacks, which also covered runways, seaplane aprons, and other air facilities, as well as fuel dumps, barracks, and other buildings. In the course of these operations the aviators took notice of the ground below them, but visibility was so restricted that there was next to nothing to observe.

As the sun passed its zenith it also came out of hiding, and eventually the weather was good enough for aerial photographs. Making a beeline for the southern end of Saipan, Stebbins in his Avenger went to work over Aslito field while his Hellcats made sweeps over ground batteries to make gunners run for cover. Next he took low-level obliques of both sides of the mountain ranges and foothills that cover the 12½-mile length of the island and also the foothills that spread over its 5-mile width. Similar photographs were taken of potential landing beaches, the reef that skirted them, the shallow lagoon between reef and beach, and the hills and mountains that rise behind the beaches like the balconies and galleries in a theater. That strip of sandy beach seemed mighty narrow, and the pilot felt sorry for the foot-slogging Marines and GIs who might have to hit it. Pictures were also taken of two landing strips on the island and of Mt. Tapotchau, a dead volcano whose 1,554-foot dome dominates Saipan.

Next came Tinian, 10 miles long and half as wide. It lies 3 miles south of Saipan and has fewer mountains and a more cultivated look. Yet landing beaches seemed scarce along its winding coastline; however, the Avenger located and photographed three airfields. Commander Stebbins paid a brief visit to Rota, the runt of the lot, whose chief prewar industries had been the making of "Scotch" whisky and "French" wines. He had finished photographing its airstrip when an AA shell exploded too close for comfort, and he performed a strategic retreat. Guam, about which much was known because it was an American possession until the Japanese seized it in 1941, was not on the list. The largest of the Marianas, 206 square miles, it has little to offer north of its center—only a vast and high plateau of almost barren limestone and no beachhead opportunities along the cliff-lined shores. The southern half, although volcanic, hilly, and thick with jungle, offered good landing prospects on its west coast above and below Orote Point, next to which lies one of the best sheltered harbors on the Philippine Sea.

By the time Commander Stebbins landed, all other planes had returned and Operation Cherry Tree was a thing of the past. Admiral Mitscher was well satisfied with the results. And with good reason. He had proved that American carriers could sail—in spite of enemy opposition—to the edge of General Tojo's barrier and send planes over it with the greatest of ease. Even more important, he had demonstrated that a carrier task force has enough gunpower to repel a night torpedo attack without having to put aviators aloft. That evening, as the task force headed for Majuro—and beaches, bathing, and beer—the bulletin boards of all vessels in the task force displayed a message from Admiral Mitscher:

> After the Nips' loss of face at Truk, we expected a fight; we had a fight; we won a fight. I am proud to state that I firmly believe that this force can knock Hell out of the Japs anywhere, any time. I . . . give you a stupendous Well Done!

In the report he submitted later to Admiral Spruance, the seldom loquacious task force commander declared, in reference to the night torpedo attack, that the defense was "historic for courage and determination of purpose."

While CincPac's report claimed only a total of 116 enemy craft destroyed—29 in the air over the targets and 87 on the ground—the Japanese, after the war, admitted to the loss of 168 planes. Of these, 101 were on the ground, including a large unit of brand new Bettys that had flown in from Iwo Jima that very morning without a fighter escort to protect them. These scores, impressive as they are, were in this instance rather incidental. For the long-range war effort, the photographs taken by Lieutenant Commander Stebbins were the real fruits of a well-accomplished mission.

At about the time Admiral Nimitz sent Task Force 58 to the Marianas, the JCS Strategic Survey Committee, a very august body, removed some of the uncertainties, which had prevailed in Washington, Pearl Harbor, and Brisbane high echelons, with respect to the shape the war in the Pacific would take. In a mid-February memorandum it spoke strongly in favor of a JCS "Specific Directive for the Defeat of Japan," which had won approval from the combined chiefs of staff in December 1943. But this directive, which endorsed two drives independent of each other and left the liberation of the Philippines uncertain, still awaited approval. Meanwhile, General MacArthur had continued to exert pressure in Washington to make his drive the only one and to include the liberation of the Philippines. In effect, the Strategic Survey Committee said that the time had come to get the show on the road. A few weeks later, after conferences in the capital with Admiral Nimitz and his chief of staff for operations, Rear Admiral Forrest P. Sherman, the JCS action directive was issued on 12 March 1944. Briefly summarized, it stated that occupation of Formosa and the China east coast would be the ultimate 1944 objectives. To reach them, there would be a two-pronged approach, with the following timetables:

> General MacArthur: Occupation, on 22 April, of the north coast of New Guinea with landings at Hollandia to be supported by Admiral Nimitz' fast carrier task force and other vessels; landings on Mindanao (Philippines) to begin 15 November, also to be supported by carriers and other elements of the Central Pacific Fleet.
> Admiral Nimitz: Occupation of Saipan, Tinian, and Guam to begin 15 June; occupation of the Palaus to begin 15 September. Then on to Mindanao with General MacArthur. The admiral's recommendations to bypass Truk in the Carolines and Rota in the Marianas were adopted.
> From Mindanao both forces, still under separate commands, would move northward through the Philippine Sea, but final decision as to making landings on Luzon (Philippines) or nonstop runs to Formosa, was held in abeyance.

General MacArthur took the two-pronged drive in his stride. After all, Admiral Nimitz was, as the Rangers used to say in Texas, a good man to ride the river with. But not liberating the Philippines! That was another story. The general would oppose their being bypassed with every power at his command.

Thanks to advance planning by himself and his staff, Admiral Nimitz was able, sixteen days after the JCS directive was issued, to forward complete directives to his three force commanders—Admirals Spruance, Lockwood, and Calhoun. They were the men through whose organizations detailed operational plans would emerge. To integrate the many parts of an amphibious undertaking on the scale of Operation Forager, as it was named, was like assembling a giant jigsaw puzzle whose thousands of pieces, of various shapes and sizes, had to be fitted together with utmost precision. In

England, to be sure, General Dwight D. Eisenhower faced a similar hurdle. While much larger numbers of men and vessels were involved, the distance across the English Channel was short and did not offer such complex logistic problems. In the Pacific there were no precedents to go by. No fleet of corresponding size and carrying so many invasion troops—127,571—had ever launched attacks from such remote staging and supply bases as Hawaii, 3,500 miles from the Marianas, 2,300 miles from the Solomons. While stopovers for refueling, reprovisioning, and such were planned in the Marshalls, the voyage from those islands to the Marianas was still from 1,000 to 1,400 miles. These are respectable distances even to a modern fleet. Every situation had to be anticipated, every need foreseen. The problems of logistics—a catch-all term for the mathematics of transportation and supply, together with the movements of troops—were incredibly complex, and the word itself was soon loathed by those whose thinking it occupied day and night.

Admiral Spruance, as commander of the Central Pacific Fleet—to be called the Fifth Fleet from here on—had the responsibility of seeing to it that a bewildering assortment of men-of-war, as well as noncombatant naval vessels, were completely provisioned for long voyages and that sailing, combat, and other operational orders were written, double checked and dovetailed.

Actually the Fifth Fleet, in which Admiral Spruance would fly his flag in the CA *Indianapolis,* comprised two major and completely separate forces: The fast carrier task force (TF 58), led by Admiral Marc Mitscher in the CV *Lexington,* and the joint expeditionary force (TF 51), commanded by Admiral Kelly Turner aboard the commandship *Rocky Mount.*

Task Force 58 was a hard-hitting, highly mobile unit of 7 heavy and 8 light carriers, capable of filling the skies with 954 planes made up of 488 fighters (including 42 night-fighters), 210 dive-bombers, 191 torpedo-bombers, and 65 floatplanes. Because carriers are notoriously helpless under attack, the four task groups of TF 58 were protected by screens formed by 7 new fast battleships, 3 heavy and 6 light cruisers, 4 antiaircraft cruisers, and 58 destroyers, making a total of 93 ships in Admiral Mitscher's force.

Though TF 58 had manifold problems, the task of assembling and supplying its sea and air combat elements was less difficult than the job that faced Admiral Turner. Fortunately he had had experience in assembling and handling amphibious assault forces, beginning with the first such force to be organized in the early days of the Pacific war. To help him reach his goals, the admiral had many sturdy assistants. Top among these were Marine General H. M. Smith, who would assume over-all command of troops after they had disembarked from Admiral Turner's transports and gone ashore in landing craft; and Admiral W. L. Calhoun, whose staff could sniff out transports and other merchant bottoms that did not seem to exist and find supplies that apparently were unavailable.

For Operation Forager, General Smith broke the ice that had kept first-rate Marine pilots out of the carrier end of the conflict. The flying Marines, who claimed 1,500 of the 2,500 Japanese planes shot down in the South Pacific, felt they were entitled to more action than just keeping the hair of Japanese on bypassed islands closely cropped. General Smith shared that viewpoint.

Up to now, the flattops, large and small, had been exclusive naval aviation country, but thanks to General Smith's powers of persuasion, Admirals Nimitz, Spruance, and Turner agreed to place two Marine observation squadrons and their tiny grasshopper planes aboard the latter's TF 51 escort carriers. From these they would take off for Saipan to base there and provide spotter service for ground commanders. The truth was that the Marines in other landings had found carrier pilots too slow in answering calls for spotting services. These delays were caused not by any lack of cooperation on the Navy's part but by the long chain of command through which the calls had to filter before they reached the point of execution. The new arrangement was to prove so satisfactory that after Saipan Admiral Nimitz placed four escort carriers at General Smith's disposal. Marine fighter pilots joined flattop Hellcats that very fall, when more carrier fighters were needed to deal with the steadily increasing attacks by squadrons of Kamikaze pilots.

Another innovation for Operation Forager was the installation of rocket launchers under the wings of some of CV *Lexington*'s Avengers. At first regarded with suspicion, the Tiny Tim rockets eventually were accepted by carrier fliers. Like long, torpedo-shaped tracers, these high-explosive, self-propelled missiles left smoke trails that revealed where they were going and how they hit.

Always open to new ideas, Admiral Turner also experimented with a new method in scouting and clearing beachhead approaches of mines or other obstacles in the paths of assault troops. This new type of reconnaissance was performed by steady-nerved, strong young men who could swim like fish and dive like dolphins. Organized into underwater demolition teams, their duties were divided into three phases. The first of these was to make soundings, look for mines, potholes, and other obstacles in the lagoons between the landing beaches and the offshore coral reef that flanked them. To make soundings in very shallow water they used a rather ingenious system, measuring depths by means of dark rings painted around their bodies at one-foot intervals. Where waters were deep, 24-foot lengths of fishline—also marked in feet—were employed. The UDTs explored reefs for passages big enough for boats, as well as the coral barrier itself for places where amphibious tractors could cross; failing to find them, they located spots where charges of tetratol—a special underwater explosive—would provide crossings for amtracs, tanks, and other amphibious self-propelled vehicles. These operations were usually performed while the many weapons of gun-support groups delivered routine softening-up bombardments designed to silence enemy batteries and dispose of their crews.

The second phase of the UDT operation was to prepare charts—invaluable to invasion commanders—which showed boat passages, depths, mines, distances, and obstructions, and outlined safety lanes for landing craft to follow as well as points along the reef where self-propelled tanks and such could waddle across thanks to either nature or to tetratol.

The third phase was to destroy mines and bottom and reef obstacles with explosives. Incidentally, they would find no mines in the lagoon off Saipan. A UDT unit of about a hundred men, under Commander Draper Kauffman, would perform their difficult and dangerous tasks at Saipan. Four would be killed and five would be wounded by enemy small-arms fire.

But before UDTs could probe the lagoon and fliers release airborne rockets in preparation for the landing of troops, Admiral Turner had to corral enough ships to get his troops there with their supplies. In Hawaii he had to combat-load one Infantry and two Marine divisions. In the Solomons other Marine and Infantry contingents had to be similarly embarked, all of which meant a mountain of tonnage. To handle it, the admiral needed a minimum of 77 transports, 34 cargo ships, and 98 related auxiliaries, such as oilers, hospital ships, mine sweepers, and ocean-going tugs.

Many of the troop transports had been passenger ships, some even luxury liners that bore names famous the world over; but by the time

Admiral Calhoun had converted them, they were luxurious no longer. All space-consuming furniture and bulkheads had been removed and replaced by tier upon tier of bunks made of iron piping. Into these spaces troops were crowded so tightly that they made sardines seem loosely packed. The interiors were as hot as ovens by day, steamy as Turkish baths by night. There was hardly walking space topside, not even to exercise the Marine-trained combat dogs, because deck cargoes covered almost every inch of space. It was not a pleasant way to travel, and it was made even less so by having to stand in long and slowly moving lines at meal hours.

The new attack transports embarked few troops because their task was to lift stores, equipment, and ammunition for the assault troops. Last came the humble AK cargo boats, which carried SeaBees for new construction and repair of bomb-blasted airfields, garrison and base personnel, and material for garrison facilities.

To set the troops ashore, Admiral Turner had to have 152 large and small landing ships and craft for tanks, 8 landing ships, docks (LSD), to ferry smaller landing craft in their huge interiors, and 25 landing craft, infantry (LCI), some of which would serve as gun or rocket boats. Ships under Admiral Turner's command totaled 551—a big jump from the 88 he commanded at Guadalcanal almost two years earlier. The total given here includes 14 escort carriers with 301 planes, plus screening and gun-support groups that contained 7 battleships, 7 heavy and 5 light destroyers, all assigned to Admiral Turner's force to provide protection en route, as well as air and gun support before, during, and after landings. There were also 94 destroyers, 28 destroyer escorts, and 2 spanking new command ships equipped with elaborate communications facilities. One of these was *Rocky Mount,* the admiral's own flagship; the other was *Appalachian,* flagship of Rear Admiral Richard L. Conolly, commander of that part of the joint expeditionary force which, coming up from the South Pacific, would rendezvous with the main force in the Marshalls.

Both of these fleets had large contingents of Coast Guard personnel who filled important gaps between the numbers of experienced sailors available in the Navy and landlubbers just out of boot camps who hardly knew the difference between ship's time and an anchor watch. The contributions of the Coast Guard were felt and appreciated by all naval ranks in the Pacific. They commanded and operated transports, helped materially in putting troops ashore in landing craft, and saw to it that wounded men were given medical care at the earliest possible moment. Often they worked under intense enemy fire and their casualties were heavy. The Coast Guardsmen distinguished themselves by their courage, know-how, and sacrifices.

Plans for Operation Forager also called for land-based planes, commanded by Vice Admiral John Hoover, commander Forward Area, Central Pacific, and Major General Willis Hale, AAF—for both of whom the battle of the Marianas began long before Operation Forager was born—to stage long-range bombing-strafing and inconspicuous photo reconnaissance missions over the target islands in fairly steady streams. Because Saipan was beyond the range where land-based aircraft could provide the substantial and sustained air support they had given in previous invasions, reliance for such support was placed on the "Tailhook Navy," a term derived from the tailhooks on carrier planes that catch flight deck arresting gear, which brake their otherwise too-rapid landing rolls on crowded carrier flight decks.

Submarines also were needed. They would conduct combat patrols on shipping lanes between Japan and the Marianas; long-range observation assignments and a unique panoramic photo reconnaissance of the Marianas would be staged by a submerged sub. Last but not least were air-sub rescue missions off hostile shores during air strikes, combined with the sinking of escaping enemy ships. To perform these various duties in connection with Operation Forager, forty-eight submarines would eventually be assigned.

To conduct an extensive and exacting photo-snooping tour around Saipan and Tinian, Lieutenant Commander James D. Grant, skipper of the *Greenling,* who had made a specialty of pre-invasion reconnoiterings of landing beaches in the South Pacific, was selected. His assignment was to take panoramic photos that covered every foot of shoreline of the two islands. To do this he was given three cameras, two Navy photo technicians, stacks of film, and all the time he needed, provided the job was completed the day before yesterday. Being an experienced submariner, Jim Grant knew when to be patient. To get the wanted panoramic footage meant making many long stops with periscope exposed for all to see; it also meant making many short runs from one position to the next. At some places *Greenling* worked within the 50-fathom line; at other points she hovered below the surface just beyond the 100-fathom line. It all depended on the numbers of Japanese observation positions, beach patrols, airplanes, destroyers, patrol boats, and mines that were about. Once, off Tinian, Grant was taking pictures inside the 100-fathom line while his technicians developed them, when an ominous grating sound was heard passing down the entire starboard side of the hull. No ships were anchored near by, so it had to be the cable of an anchored mine. Needless to say, Grant continued his work from outside 100 fathoms in that locality.

"We were somewhat apprehensive in the beginning about running close inshore with the big periscope exposed continuously," said Commander Grant in recalling his mission in a letter to Admiral Lockwood.

> With endless stops for photographing and obtaining fixes, to run the scope down would have saved only seconds; also, thousands of up, down, up, down, periscope hoists could have put the scope out of kilter. It was a hazard we had to take; another was that we had to use the other scope at intervals for sweeping, thus creating an additional wake and radar target.
>
> While we were operating on the north and west coasts of Saipan we gathered, from depth-charge and bomb explosions, that the Japanese were hunting subs—but they were not hunting us. Whether the presence of other subs was strategy or happenstance, it was our fortune, because *Greenling* was emitting radar interference all over the islands, as were the other subs. I learned later that they were Slade Cutter in *Seahorse* and Herbie Jukes in *Kingfish*. Anyway, the Japs would send out their planes and destroyers day and night. I believe they were baffled by the activities of our subs and must have thought that we had an armada of them in the Philippine Sea. Whenever things got too hot off one island, *Greenling* simply shifted islands and used her radar sparingly.

Grant expressed the belief that *Greenling* was never actually spotted by human eyes or even radar during the forty long days when Saipan and Tinian sat before his cameras as *Greenling* moved for three minutes from fix to fix at a speed of 3 knots. The greatest danger he faced on those occasions was that of broaching, that is, when a submarine, moving close to the surface, exposes her upper works by accidental surfacing. Said Commander Grant on that score:

> I had no fears of broaching. My two diving teams could dive or surface the boat without showing a ripple. In operating the sub, they could operate almost as well backward as for-

ward. A handy ability in restricted waters wherein a regular turn could not be made.

When the panoramas were flown back to Pearl and delivered to the secret intelligence section of CincPac, the experts expressed themselves as highly pleased.

The job had taken a long time and *Greenling* got no bag of enemy shipping, but what she accomplished was eminently valuable to the war effort.

A fairly accurate estimate of the entire Forager operation reveals that about 300,000 Navy, Marine, and Army personnel—aloft, ashore, and on beachheads—participated in one way or another in the assaults upon Saipan, Tinian, and Guam. Including subs, the action called for 682 vessels and 2,125 carrier or land-based aircraft. Of the latter, 269 Army, 258 Navy, and 352 Marine planes were committed for various missions. It is said that pictures tell more than words. On the other hand, there are occasions when figures tell more than pictures, and this is one of them. Even those who have never had to sweat over logistics puzzles should by now have a fair idea of what it meant to have that many stomachs, cargo holds, ammunition magazines, fuel tanks, to fill and refill for weeks on end—and the nearest supply base 1,000 miles away by sea.

To launch and maintain Operation Forager more was needed than shoes, ships, and sealing wax, men, materiel, and guns. Bases had to be provided in the Marshalls. This is where the anchorages in the lagoons of the atoll paradise that included Majuro, Kwajalein, and Eniwetok—each some 300 miles apart—come into focus; and where Commodore W. R. "Nick" Carter, boss of Service Squadron 10, transformed three natural anchorages from idle lagoons into virtually complete naval bases in no time. Here fighting craft of every kind— and airplanes, too—depended upon ServRon 10 for maintenance, repair, ammunition, and fuel; for stores, provisions, and medical supplies. Here mail was handled, clothing issued, and recreation facilities provided. Here were refrigerator ships with cargoes of fresh, frozen meats, vegetables, and fruits on which the carrier and submarine crews had priority claims. But even in havens like these lagoons there were constant ill winds. The land-walls that framed them were too low to break the force of the wind, although they did give protection against the long ocean swells. In the lagoons, which were large enough to accommodate hundreds of ships, small vessels, including submarines and destroyers, often found the going rough. Usually moored to the apron strings of their mother ships, there were times when they tossed rather wildly. Harbor boats, unloading from or loading into larger ships, faced annoying interference from wind conditions.

The first small base detachment of ServRon 10 reached the Marshalls soon after the islands were taken in February 1944. By the time Operation Forager was launched, Commodore Carter had support from 2 submarine tenders, 4 destroyer tenders, 6 repair ships, and 3 repair shop barges for light and heavy work. Also there were 6 floating dry docks that could handle jobs from battleships to destroyer escorts, 4 ammunition ships, and 13 ammunition barges, which seems a lot of ammo until one realizes that an average shipload contained about 75 items and weighed about 6,500 tons. ServRon 10, in addition, had 15 storage barges for freight, spare parts, marine stores, torpedoes, and other supplies; also 23 oil and gasoline storage barges that held millions of gallons of fuel oil, diesel oil, and aviation gas. There were 15 old Liberty ship tankers for storage and local transport service, 6 large concrete supply barges, 11 water barges, and a distillery ship that transformed sea water into fresh water. Present, too, were 5 cold-storage vessels and many other vessels needed to make the Navy function.

Too much cannot be said in praise of the men who labored patiently and well at these anchorages, often around the clock, to make the Navy run. Carter's men handled practically everything, even the so-called barracks, or hotel barges, that housed about seventy-five men. They were steep-sided, drab-looking affairs, with rows of tiny portholes, and resembled barns on keels. But they bore such illustrious names as Ritz-Carlton, The Palace, Waldorf-Astoria, and Mayflower; in addition to energy and enterprise, ServRon 10 had a sense of humor.

Despite all precautions, slipups occur in the best of outfits, and Operation Forager was no exception. A case in point, which gave ServRon 10 many sleepless hours, popped up at Saipan. The bombardment ammunition of one of the gun-support groups ran low; Admiral Spruance ordered Commodore Carter to send him two ammunition ships, loaded to capacity, at once. To transfer live and heavy ammunition—a 16-inch shell weighs 1,900 pounds; a 14-inch, 1,275 pounds; an 8-inch, 260 pounds—at sea under combat conditions takes nerve, skill, and luck. An ammo carrier is a very vulnerable ship. One hit in the right place—and almost any place is the right one—and the ship would explode and do more damage to other vessels in seconds than the whole Imperial Navy could accomplish in a year. Nick Carter sent them off expecting the worst. But, as he observed in a letter, "Admiral Spruance took such good care of the transfer that, after Saipan, we never hesitated to send ammunition ships forward whenever and wherever they were requested."

Throughout March, land-based Navy, Marine, and Army planes led the way to the occupation of many bypassed islands in the Marshalls and Carolines and continued to make life unpleasantly uncertain for enemy garrisons on the remainder. These groups of islands cover some 500 miles east-west and about 250 miles north-south, and too many still housed enemy installations that hung on with grim tenacity despite steady rounds of bombings and strafings. It seemed utterly impossible that Tokyo could reinforce these island garrisons —by air or submarines—so that ground resistance could continue to throw heavy gunfire into the air or planes could sprout, again and again, along damaged runways. But the Japanese managed to do it. Ponape, for instance, after repeated attacks by land-based planes and a moderate version of a Spruance Haircut by carrier planes, was able to send fifteen Zekes aloft as late as 27 March. The Americans were astonished by the sight of so many fighters, but not so overcome that they failed to score nine certain kills and three probables. The main purpose of these continuing assaults was to keep enemy aircraft out of the sky so that snoopers could not report on the massing of seapower in the Marshalls or, when the time came, observe the departure or course of the Marianas-bound fleet. This was a matter of utmost importance, because the success of initial air assaults depended largely on the advantages of tactical surprise.

Toward the end of March three task groups of TF 58 and their screens slipped out of Majuro and swung south and west under the Carolines to avoid being seen by enemy snoopers. They were destined for the Palau Islands, which lie southwest of Guam on the lower fringe of the Philippine Sea. This group, a bastion in General Tojo's defense line and headquarters of Admiral Koga since the fleet left Truk, was well fortified, heavily garrisoned, and had excellent air facilities.

Admiral Spruance's fleet, with TF 58 in the van, swooped upon Peleliu and Babelthuap at dawn on 30 March. Just before their coming, seven subs were positioned around the islands to sink escaping ships and rescue downed aviators. Koga was caught napping, an em-

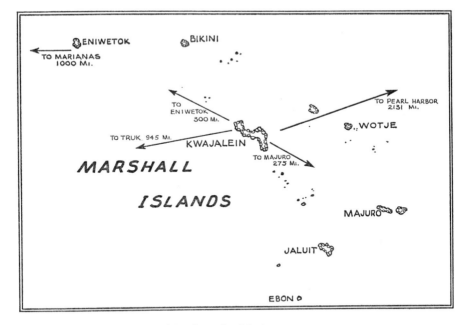

*Some 3,000 miles from Pearl Harbor, the Marianas were
prime targets of Operation Forager, to then the biggest
naval enterprise of World War II. In between lie the
enormous lagoons of Majuro, Kwajalein, and Eniwetok
atolls. Almost overnight these lagoons became fully
equipped advance bases for amphibious assaults that broke
Japan's hold on islands along the eastern rim of the
Philippine Sea and eventually blasted a road to Tokyo.*

barrassment he could have escaped had he interpreted an early
snooper's sighting of the fleet as the warning it was. While he sent
Admiral Kurita to sea with what remained of the Second Fleet, excepting *Musashi* and a few DDs, the admiral mistakenly believed that
the Americans had turned south because subsequent reports were to
that effect. True enough, the fleet went on a southerly course, but
only as a feint. At nightfall on 29 March it headed for the Palaus at a
speed that would place it within striking distance at daylight. Alas,
when the pilots roared in for the kill the Second Fleet had vanished.
Still, there were enough targets to go around. Koga suffered crippling
losses that day and the next. Some sixty ships—several destroyers,
large and small oilers worth their weight in black gold, and many

cargo vessels—were either sunk or damaged. The total score was 104,000 tons of shipping.

United States fliers reported 93 enemy planes destroyed and 29 probables; 39 aircraft were wrecked on the ground or in the water, with 20 probables. These heavy plane losses were very bitter to Admiral Koga. While wrack and ruin struck ground installations of all kinds, the ample garrison forces suffered few casualties because the troops, literally, took to the hills, where they found cover in caves prepared by the Army.

Submarines did not do so well at sinkings off the Palaus for the simple reason that naval aviators had shut off escape to the sea by mining the channels. After pioneering in radar-directed night operations at Truk, CV *Enterprise* pilots, who usually launched torpedo runs, now chalked up a new mark for initiative and efficiency. They had mastered the difficult trick of dropping mines in narrow channels. Some ships, however, evaded the mines.

One big fish that got away, despite mines and all, was the *Musashi.* Still, as she emerged from Tuagel Mlungi Passage, the 63,000-ton Grand Dame of the battle line was sighted by the SS *Tunny* (Commander John Scott) at maximum torpedo distance; a spread of six tin fish produced two hits forward, but the battlewagon brushed them off as if they were mosquito bites and sailed out of sight. Worse than low sinking scores, one of the U.S. subs, the *Tullibee,* was sunk by a circling torpedo from one of her own tubes. She went down with all hands but one, a lookout who was picked up by an enemy destroyer. Air and sub lifeguards united in plucking 26 airmen from the sea; 25 planes were downed and 18 fliers were lost.

During the afternoon of 31 March the fleet left the area, Admiral Spruance having accomplished his purpose to give the Palaus a haircut, which, like a GI trim, left very little standing. The islands had been neutralized to a point where they could not interfere effectively, by sea or air, with General MacArthur's drive to the Philippine Sea or Admiral Nimitz' assaults on the Marianas. As TF 58 set course for its next targets—Ulithi, Yap, and Woleai—Admiral Koga made his future plans, prompted by the belief that the attack on the Palaus, coming on the heels of those on Truk and Saipan, forecast strong amphibious thrusts to the southwest toward the Philippines by the combined forces of General MacArthur and Admiral Nimitz. In other words, he anticipated the single road to Tokyo that the general favored. In line with that reasoning, Admiral Koga decided to move his

Combined Fleet HQ to Davao on Mindanao, some 500 miles across the Philippine Sea from the Palaus.

To replace wrecked planes on the islands, aircraft would be transferred down the lifeline from as far north as Iwo Jima; supplies and ground personnel would be ferried in aboard submarines. That night two huge Kawanichi (4-engined flying boats) left Babelthuap, where Koga had established his headquarters after he sent the *Musashi* out of striking range. As Admiral Yamamoto did on his last and fatal flight, Admiral Koga occupied one plane with part of his staff; his C of S, Vice Admiral S. Fukodome, occupied the second plane with other staffers—in case of accident. Koga knew his plans by heart; Fukodome carried them on paper. From the time it took off, Koga's plane was never seen again. Fukodome's, driven off course by a violent storm, sank after a rough water landing off Cebu Island in the Philippines. The C of S was captured by Philippine guerillas, who released him a week or so later when local Japanese Army commanders threatened reprisals if they did not. As for Koga's treasured war plans, they were sped to Brisbane via submarine and aircraft by James Cushing, an American mining engineer who had become a guerilla commander. Their vital information was quickly encoded and flashed to Pearl Harbor and Washington. Now all top commands knew the latest trend in Japanese planning.

The Japanese High Command made Admiral Koga's disappearance top-secret information and hoped against hope that he, like Admiral Fukodome, would reappear. Execution of his plans was sidetracked as high-ranking generals and admirals marked time. However, the heavy assaults on the Palau Islands—more damaging than those inflicted on the Marianas in February—gave further proof to the Japanese admirals that ultimate American aims were to stage an all-out attack on the Philippines from the south. They therefore planned to use the steadily dwindling means at their disposal to block those aims.

Chapter Three

PRELIMINARY THRUSTS

LIKE HIS COLLEAGUE AND OPPOSITE NUMBER at Pearl Harbor, General MacArthur did not mark time in Brisbane waiting for the JCS to clear all channels and to issue their 12 March directives to himself and Admiral Nimitz. The working outline of his westward thrust along the north coast of New Guinea, with Hollandia as the first target, was crystal clear in his head before Rabaul was wrapped up and the Admiralties in the bag. It was a long, difficult, and challenging road, but the general proposed to take it swiftly with his vastly expanded amphibious forces. Between Saidor—his present New Guinea base at the eastern end of the northern coast of (excepting Greenland) the world's largest island—and Sansapor, on Vogelkop Peninsula at the western end, were a rough 800 miles which he proposed to take in a series of amphibious jumps. He would leapfrog some 400 miles to his first beachheads at Aitape and Hollandia. In doing that, he would bypass Japanese Army garrisons and air installations at Madang, Hansa Bay, and Wewak. From Hollandia he would swoop upon Wakde Island and Sarmi some 125 miles away, jump another 190 miles to Biak Island in Geelvink Bay, make a quick hop to nearby Noemfoor Island, then head into the homestretch of 150 miles to Sansapor. All these mileages are air, not shoreline, distances. Possession of the bases named would give General MacArthur's forces full control of air and harbor facilities on New Guinea's entire north coast. His drive on Hollandia was to seize and occupy anchorages in Humboldt and Tanahmerah bays and to expand them into supply bases and minor naval facilities. The airfields would become major acquisitions. Landings would also be made at Aitape, east of Hollandia, mainly to hold in check what remained of the 18th Japanese Army garrisons at Madang, Hansa Bay, and Wewak. Estimates (on the low side) of strengths in the various garrisons were: Aitape, 2,000; Hollandia, 9,000 to 12,000; Wakde, 3,000; Biak, 10,000; Noemfoor, 2,000; and Vogelkop Peninsula, 15,000.

The Hollandia-Aitape project, named Operation Reckless, was conceived and executed on a grand and daring scale. The twin targets were located in areas of which little was known beyond the fact that narrow strips of open shorelines were hemmed in on one side by the sea and on the other by the dank green hells of malarial jungles. Good land maps did not exist, and all information about the terrain had to be obtained by aerial photo reconnaissance missions, a very inadequate method for acquiring detailed information about the lay of the land. Into this unknown and hostile area it was proposed to dump some 74,000 troops from the sea on the three separate landing beaches at Aitape, Humboldt Bay, and Tanahmerah Bay.

According to plan, Admiral Kinkaid's Seventh Amphibious Force, composed of American and Australian surface ships and commanded by Rear Admiral Daniel E. Barbey, would be expanded by the loan of many types of vessels from Admiral Nimitz' command. In addition, three task groups of Admiral Mitscher's Task Force 58 and their formidable shell-belching screens, would be assigned to support the Hollandia landings. Originally, the carriers' primary mission had been to deal with any surprise appearance of enemy fighting ships intent upon disrupting the landings; their secondary task was to neutralize enemy airfields and to give air support as requested. But by the end of March Admiral Kurita's Second Fleet had been shunted out of the Palau Islands and Vice Admiral Yoshikazu Endo's Ninth Fleet, assigned to defend New Guinea, had dwindled to a conglomeration of small vessels such as patrol boats, subchasers, lighters, and barges. No reinforcements were in sight, because the razing of defense installations by Admiral Mitscher's fliers in the Palaus had convinced Japanese naval leaders that the Combined Fleet had to be reorganized and readied to defend the Philippines.

As early as mid-March, General Kenney set out to perform a two-purpose bombing and strafing program with heavy bombers, escorted by P-38 fighters whose range had been lengthened by increasing their fuel loads. From Wewak, east of Hollandia, to Wakde Island, west of Hollandia, the bombers staged an almost continuous schedule of bombing runs and fighter strikes. It did not take the Japanese long to conclude that action was in the offing, but knowing where it would strike was another matter. It could be at any one of those points or somewhere in between. On Vogelkop, Lieutenant General Fusataro Teshima, commander of the 2nd Army, had his eyes on Wewak, the eastern flank of his command. As a protective measure, he ordered

Lieutenant General Hatazo Adachi to march his 18th Army into the Hollandia area. But General Adachi had other ideas. Clever tricks by longheaded Barbey and Kenney planners had persuaded General Adachi that Wewak was the invasion target. This was done by continuous bomber and fighter sweeps; by parachuting dummy paratroopers into the area; by letting life rafts drift to the beach from submarines at night, so that when they were discovered after daylight the inference was that snoopers had gone ashore; by occasional destroyer bombardment runs; by PT boats roaring offshore at night; and, of course, by flocks of bombers dropping their deadly sticks all over the area most of the time. In view of these activities, the Japanese general deduced that Wewak was the bull's eye and he decided to stay there, orders or not. If he had followed orders and marched his 16,000 men at Madang and 36,000 men at Hansa Bay to Hollandia, the taking of Hollandia would not have been as easy as it turned out to be for Lieutenant General Walter Krueger and his 6th Army.

In April the short- and long-range haircuts imposed by the Army fliers rivaled any performed by Admiral Spruance's big guns. What remained of the 18th Army was thoroughly isolated from moving in any direction by air, land, or sea. To check General MacArthur's move on any target, the airfields and strips around Hollandia were suddenly covered by enemy plane reinforcements. These virtually put all of the planes in the 6th Air Division in the Hollandia basket, where they were crowded like fowl in a farmer's crate. There General Kenney's fliers found them, and there they left them—some 200 planes—like so many plucked and gutted birds. The few that got off the ground were gunned down by the P-38s. This blow reduced the 6th Air Division to a feeble shadow of its former self. Long-range operations against enemy air installations west of Hollandia prevented the Japanese from bringing in massive reinforcements.

To insure surprise, the three amphibious task groups in Admiral Barbey's force united at a rendezvous north of the Admiralties and steamed northwest, as if they were Palau bound, to mislead any Japanese snoopers who might be around. The force elements held that course until 0900 on 21 April, when they turned toward their targets to the south. Before that hour, Admiral Mitscher's fast carrier task force of three groups, totaling a dozen carriers, had launched their planes to attack Hollandia airfields and those at Wakde Island and Sarmi, some 100 miles to the west. They also searched for targets of opportunity, such as small craft, ground installations, fuel and ammunitions dumps, and stores. But the pickings were slim. General Kenney's fliers had left very little to bomb. On the following day, when General Krueger's men hit the beach, they supported the landings and troop deployments ashore, mainly by keeping the airfields neutralized. Despite the vigorous sweeps by 5th Air Force bombers, the Japanese capacity to make planes reappear where none had remained created impressive results. Of these newcomers, 13 were shot down near TF 58 and about 20 over the target area. On the ground, the destruction of 67 planes was claimed at Hollandia; 21 were reported wrecked and 17 damaged at Wakde and Sarmi. Task Force 58 lost 10 planes in combat. The claims, with respect to destruction on the ground, were disallowed by the U.S. Strategic Bombing Survey (Pacific), which contended that "damage to grounded planes was difficult to assess because of prior heavy destruction."

Even at dawn on 22 April, when the amphibious forces prepared to lower landing craft offshore, Major General Kitazano, the local commander, believed that Wakde Island was the invasion target. This belief had become solidified during the night when Rear Admiral L. T. DuBose led a bombardment group of cruisers and destroyers within point-blank gun range of Wakde and Sarmi to slam away with every piece he had till first light of day. No salvos were fired by the defenders of Hollandia. Their hoaxed commander was blasted out of his complacence when the first volley of the pre-invasion cannonade thundered from Admiral Barbey's fighting ships. By then it was much too late to take precautions or even to improvise defense positions. The shelling was so fierce that defenders took to the jungles in droves. The same situation held true at the Aitape beachhead, where invading troops met only negligible opposition. Beachheads were secured in the two bays near Hollandia by noon. Hollandia town was captured on D-day plus one; two days later Hollandia airdrome was occupied, and on 26 April the cratered remnants of Cyclops and Sentani airfields were also in American hands.

At Aitape, the only real resistance was encountered during the advance on Toji airstrip. It was quickly and effectively scrubbed by tanks and automatic weapons. Compared with the fierce duel-to-the-death opposition at Tarawa, Betio, and Roi Namur, these landings had been a breeze, mainly because of saturation bombings and clever deception, plus an unusual (for the Japanese) lack of will to fight. To be sure, bloody contests were staged somewhat later when the enemy deployed from the jungles and sniper fire became common. One of the largest deployments occurred when General Adachi drove against Aitape from Wewak in a futile effort to chase the invaders into the sea. One wonders what the score might have been had the general marched his troops to Hollandia as ordered. It is quite possible that he might have stalled General MacArthur's push to the Philippine Sea long enough to help his superiors in Japan gain some of the time they so desperately needed. To be sure, Operation Reckless lived up to its name because of the many hidden dangers that might have been encountered. But it is hard to argue with gamblers who win. As General Krueger observed in his report: ". . . the operation proved the soundness of a scheme . . . so patently daring."

On the way home Admiral Mitscher's fast carrier task force sideswiped Truk. Much to their surprise, the attackers found that the atoll's defenses were not so depleted that it could not put up a show of tenacious resistance. It was learned later that air defenses had been built up to 104 aircraft. Of these only 11 remained when the carrier fliers got through. Ground positions of AAs and other artillery maintained steady and strong firepower, and the gunners handled their weapons so effectively that they knocked down 20 of the attacking planes. With seven planes lost in aerial dogfights, this made a total TF 58 loss of 27 planes. Only 18 airmen died; 28 were saved by plane-sub rescue teams, who had hectic work on very choppy waters. The SS *Tang,* commanded by Commander Richard O'Kane, picked up no less than 22 wet and grateful aviators. Of these, Lieutenant (jg) John A. Burns—pilot of a rescue floatplane off the BB *North Carolina*—contributed 8 survivors garnered by him. For a round 10, Lieutenant Burns and his gunner boarded the *Tang* because their plane, damaged during rescue operations by heavy seas, could not take off.

On 3 May Admiral Soemu Toyoda succeeded the late Admiral Koga as commander in chief of the Combined Fleet. Short of stature, he appeared to be even shorter because of a plump body topped by a moon face, which was as blandly urbane as that of an ancient god. Behind this facade was a quick incisive mind, a stout heart, and complete devotion to the emperor, Japan, and the Navy. A naval officer of wide administrative experience, he had been chief of Naval Procurement before the war. In 1944 he was commandant of the Yokusa Naval District. Like most Japanese naval officers, in contrast to many Army officers from General Tojo down, he had never joined the warmongering pressure cliques; in fact, he had been opposed to making war on the United States. This was for various reasons, but mainly because he had not believed that Japan had the resources adequate for a war which, as General Tojo had predicted, could be won in a year.

It seems rather ironical that Admiral Toyoda, who had seen disaster so clearly ahead, should now be called upon to pick up the pieces of what remained of Japanese naval air and striking power, without which the Japanese would never be able to stave off the might and offensive power of America's Pacific fleets. His position was much like that of a man called upon to make bricks without straw.

During the seven months that had passed since General Tojo's new War Direction Policy and its "absolute national defense line" were adopted, its do-or-die provisions had caused little doing but much dying. Outposts on which this line depended for security had—from the Marshalls to Hollandia—crumbled much sooner than had been anticipated. And while the line itself had not been broken, American carrier forces had demonstrated that the Marianas and the Palau Islands, once regarded as immune to attack, were now as exposed to assault as were the bypassed islands in Japan's original defense perimeter.

While Admiral Toyoda, in his heart, may have regarded his job as hopeless, he resolutely set about doing what he could to improve Japan's position and snatch the offensive from his enemies. His first act was to prepare the fleet for full-out action within the last ten days of May. His authority for this was an Imperial Headquarters directive issued on 3 May. That same day the new commander of the Imperial Navy issued a secret operations order from his flagship *Oyodo* anchored in Tokyo Bay. It was a masterpiece of wishful thinking.

> The Combined Fleet will direct its main operations in the area extending south of the Central Pacific to the north coast of New Guinea. It will concentrate decisive strength in this area and will cooperate with friendly forces [i.e., land-based Japanese aircraft]. It will destroy the enemy offensive strength, in particular the enemy task forces, and thus frustrate the enemy plans for resistance.

It is apparent from this that the Japanese still believed American forces in the Pacific would unite in a drive from the southeast. It is significant that in staff discussions only a very junior commander is reputed to have held to the belief that the Marianas were the logical invasion targets. To be sure, the recent participation by Admiral

Nimitz' carrier task forces in the taking of Hollandia could have given extra credibility to the erroneous assumption.

The strategy of the admiral's plan, which was to become known as A-GO, was to lure the enemy into a battle situation similar to that proposed by Admiral Koga. Island-based air and shuttle bombings by carrier planes would unite to wreck the American task force, which, as the order said, ". . . will be attacked and destroyed for the most part in a day assault." The order added that the decisive battle areas "roughly prearranged" were the Palau Islands and the western Carolines (Yap, Ulithi, and Woleai).

But the order hardly mentioned the Marianas, the very islands that Chester W. Nimitz and his admirals were preparing to attack and invade. These islands were dismissed with the casual reference: ". . . when the enemy maneuvers in the Marianas . . . the enemy will be attacked by base air forces in that area."

To lure the Americans into the predetermined area, Ulithi or Palau would become traps baited with small naval forces designed to trick the United States into underestimating Japanese naval strength in the area. Assuming that the bait would be taken, it was further arranged that Admiral Jisaburo Ozawa's First Mobile Fleet would be lurking secretly west of the Philippines. On proper signal, it would leave its hidden anchorage and enter the Philippine Sea "without leaving a trace." When the moment was right, Admiral Ozawa's armada, which included nine carriers and some hefty gunpower, would pounce upon the luckless Americans.

As for land-based aircraft, Admiral Toyoda expected to have 598 assorted combat planes in the Marianas, on Yap, and on Peleliu in the Palau Islands. He depended on them to account for at least one-third of American losses.

The day after the order was issued, the new Japanese C in C sent a letter to all commanders in his Combined Fleet in which he said in part:

> Our Combined Fleet in several engagements has crushed the main enemy forces with lightning speed. In the two and one-half years since, together with our armies, we occupied the areas essential to the Greater East Asia, officers and men of the fleet have voluntarily sacrificed their lives and inflicted great damage on the enemy. The fate of the enemy was nearly sealed, but in the midst of this period the enemy recovered his

fighting strength, and taking advantage of our supply difficulties, moved over to a full-scale counterattack.

The war is drawing close to the lines vital to our national defense. The issue of our national existence is unprecedentedly serious, an unprecedented opportunity exists for deciding who shall be victorious and who defeated. This autumn we will make this great task our responsibility.

By giving all possible thought to basic plans, by utilizing opportunities for advance or retreat, and by placing faith in the great fighting ability of our officers and men, we will carry out the decisive operations which mean certain enemy defeat.

We must achieve our objectives by crushing with one stroke the nucleus of the great enemy concentration of forces, thereby reversing the war situation, and, together with our armies, shifting directly to the offensive . . . the decisive battle force [must] in one decisive battle, determine the fate of the Empire.

Officers and men guarding important areas will exert themselves to the utmost, using all possible ingenuity to complete bases immediately. They will endure hardships, strengthen unity, and devote every effort to building an iron wall of defense for the homeland.

Officers and men of forces guarding islands in the Marshalls and important points in the Southwest Area must defend the main bases and fight back. They will wage decisive battles and will execute raids and pursuit attacks. Every effort will be made to create strong points for pursuit attacks. Thus our entire forces, united in our noble cause, fighting to the death, will destroy the enemy who enjoys the luxury of material resources.

Realizing the gravity of responsibility for the fate of our Empire, with its history of more than 2,600 years, full of reverence for the glory of the Imperial Throne and trusting in the help of God, I will endeavor to comply with the Emperor's wishes.

The desire of officers and men of the entire fleet must be to respond wholeheartedly to this great honor and duty.

In compliance with this program, Admiral Jisaburo Ozawa issued orders for his somewhat scattered carrier divisions to assemble at Tawitawi, in the southwestern Philippines, not later than 16 May. As matters then stood, the D-day signal could be expected anytime after 20 May. Japan had many able and courageous military and naval

leaders; among the best was Admiral Ozawa. Like his American opposite, Admiral Mitscher, he was a flattop sailor and had brought distinction to himself and his vessels by his excellent employment of
carriers in combat. He was rather tall and on the thin side. The skin
on his long, narrow, high-boned face was drawn as tightly as yellow
parchment stretched over the head of a drum. He was affable, considerate, and well-liked by all ranks throughout the Imperial Navy.

To reduce fuel consumption in the oil-poor Empire, Admiral
Ozawa's First Carrier Division—with its main body of battleships,
cruisers, and destroyers commanded by Admiral Kurita—had taken
station at Lingga Roads near Singapore, where the proximity of oil-
fields on Borneo and other nearby areas assured a plentiful supply of
fuel. Then it was discovered that the refineries could not work fast
enough to meet the combined demands of the fleet and the homeland.
Undismayed, Admiral Toyoda took a big gamble and ordered the
Mobile Fleet to use a certain type of Borneo oil so pure that it could
be taken right out of the wells and poured into fuel tanks. The only
trouble was that in its natural state it contained gasses that ignited
easily and burned furiously. But that risk had to be taken. Fuel for
ships and gas for carrier planes were, in fact, among Admiral
Toyoda's greatest concerns. Japan produced only 5 percent of its oil
requirements, and the stock piles built up over many years before the
war had long since vanished. Armies may, as Napoleon said, march
on their stomachs; modern fleets, along the same line of reasoning,
sail on oceans of oil.

Still, easy access to fuel did not solve all of Admiral Ozawa's problems. The flying skills and fighting proficiency of his aviators were
still substandard from lack of proper training. His planes, type for
type, stacked up well against American aircraft; in fact some out-
reached the latter in range. But maintenance was difficult because
parts were scarce. As for Admiral Kurita's fleet, that salty mariner
had good reason to feel proud of the equipment and training in all
departments of his ships. His principal handicap was caused by
Japan's failure to improve radar designs and to expand production of
radar sets. The wide use of radar in American surface ships, submarines, and aircraft constituted an advantage that even the best marksmanship and finest navigation could not counteract. Admiral Ozawa,
however, might have regarded his two 63,000-ton superbattleships
—*Yamato* and *Musashi*—as a brace of very effective equalizers. These
heavily armored and well-compartmentized ships were regarded as

torpedoproof and unsinkable, assumptions that were to prove as wrong as similar views, held decades earlier, with respect to the *Titanic*. From turrets, 18-inch rifles—the largest in the world—poked their impressive steel snouts. With nine such guns on each ship, these battlewagons could deliver some 50,000 pounds of high explosive projectiles in one broadside salvo; enough to scuttle any ship afloat if directed at a single target.

As planned, the admiral's entire fleet was assembled at Tawitawi by 16 May. But his hopes of being able to extend the training of carrier pilots were destroyed when he found that the land that ringed the anchorage was unsuited for airstrips. Greater disappointments were in store for Ozawa; his troubles had just begun.

On the night of 14 May, the submarine *Bonefish* (Commander T. W. Hogan) caught and sank the Japanese destroyer *Inazuma* in the Sulu Sea. The next day Hogan discovered and approached, while submerged, a large enemy fleet unit, which included a carrier guarded by screening destroyers. Careful as his approach was, the enemy was alert because of the sinking the night before. Commander Hogan was discovered. He had to go deep and stay deep during several hours of depth charging. Darkness was falling when he finally surfaced and delivered his contact report to ComSubSoWesPac in Australia. Ralph Christie's reaction was quick and to the point: Track the Japanese warships; report and continue tracking; do not attack or reveal your presence.

In line with orders, Commander Hogan hastened to catch up with the enemy, who had been headed south. He did not have far to go. He found a large Japanese fleet holed up in Tawitawi anchorage, which lies in the southwestern Philippines opposite the northeast coast of Borneo. The news that the Imperial Japanese Navy was out in force was made known immediately in Brisbane, Washington, and Pearl Harbor and passed on to all force commanders concerned. From SubSoWesPac, submarines were sent to the Tawitawi area to stand constant vigil; other subs were placed on guard by Admiral Christie in the Celebes Sea and off Luzon's west coast.

Realizing that the demands for the services of his submarines would be extensive, ComSubPac created Submarine Task Force 17 to support Operation Forager. Because of the great distances involved, destroyers did not have the range required for scouting or picket duty. In this instance only subs could do the job of serving as the eyes of the fleet in the Philippine Sea.

To do this adequately, ComSubPac had stationed subs in Luzon Strait southeast of Formosa, off San Bernardino Strait south of Samar Island, and off Surigao Strait south of Leyte Island, the last two in the Philippines. Watchers were also placed off the Bonin Islands to the north of the Marianas and off the western Carolines to the south of them.

In planning his sneak attack, Admiral Toyoda had failed to figure on his opponent's submarines and the tight, though invisible, net they had drawn around Admiral Ozawa.

Early on 19 May Japan's High Command received a radio flash from Marcus Island, 999 miles southeast of Tokyo. It reported that the island had been subjected to a predawn sweep by carrier fighter planes and that it was now under heavy air bombardment. So far as could be ascertained, the planes came from a group of three flattops. This set Tokyo strategists to speculating on where the rest of the fast carrier fleet could be. Their thinking led them to believe that Marcus was being attacked—first, to draw attention from the rest of the carrier fleet's real target; second, to neutralize the island so that its planes could not interfere with the mission (actually there were only two planes on Marcus). The target, they concluded, was Tokyo. Without delay, Operation TO, for the defense of Japan, was set into motion. All aircraft in Japan and the few warships that still remained in homeland waters were alerted to stand by. Long-range search planes were dispatched to scan the seas for approaching enemy ships. Operation TO was cocked and ready to be triggered. These activities were kept secret at very high levels. The warlords did not want to stir up memories in the public mind of the Doolittle fliers who hit Japan in 1942.

For several days the high and the mighty waited for word about the approaching enemy fleet. But no word came; no ships were sighted. It had been a frightening false alarm. Operation TO was dismounted, and those in the know sighed with profound relief. The strike-and-scram operation they feared had only been a hideous nightmare.

The truth of the Marcus strikes on 19–20 May and those that followed three days later on Wake, 764 miles to the east, was that they were routine affairs to which a dash of combat seasoning for new and untried carrier air groups had been added. The task group was commanded by Rear Admiral A. E. Montgomery. In 373 sorties on Marcus, the fliers dropped 148 tons of bombs on air installations; ammunition and supply dumps were destroyed and many structures damaged. All in all their work, for "learners," had been satisfactory. While they met no air opposition—one medium bomber was shot down, another sieved with bullets on the ground—there had been real tests of courage and skill in penetrating the terrific volume of antiaircraft fire put up by ground batteries. American losses were four planes and three fliers. One was lost when he ditched at sea. More than 20 percent of our planes were hit by bullets or shell fragments.

At Wake, where no enemy planes were sighted, 150 tons of bombs were dropped in 354 sorties. This meant a total of 727 takeoffs and landings, great training for newly hatched flattop fliers. In addition they also had to run the gamut of AA shells. Despite this, the attackers inflicted satisfactory damages. No planes or personnel were missing when, at sunset on 23 May, Admiral Montgomery issued orders to shape course for Majuro. He was well satisfied with the results of his mission; but the furore it had caused in Japan did not become known until the war ended.

At the very time Admiral Montgomery was giving his training course on the invisible line of latitude 25 degrees north, a slim little fighting lady began her career as a submarine killer some 20 degrees of latitude to the south. She was the DE *England,* and being a destroyer escort she measured only 306 feet from bow to fantail and tipped the displacement scales at 1,400 tons. On her narrow deck were three 5-inch guns, nine smaller automatic weapons, and depthcharge tracks from which her deadly ashcans could be plunged into the sea to wreak harm upon submarines. She could turn up 23 knots, and into her scant spaces were crowded the 6 officers and 180 men who called *England* their home. Brand new, she had joined Admiral Halsey's South Pacific Fleet in April 1944 after shakedown cruises at San Diego. These included one short week of antisubmarine exercises. The DE was named after Ensign John C. England, who was killed at Pearl Harbor while serving aboard the BB *Oklahoma;* she was commissioned on 26 December 1943, with Commander Walter B. Pendleton as skipper and Lieutenant Commander J. A. Williamson as executive. Since she arrived in the South Pacific, *England* had been assigned to convoy escort duty.

Before the air-raid scare hit the Japanese High Command, Admiral Toyoda was confident that the forces of Admiral Nimitz would try to capture the Palau Islands from the south. That done, he believed, they would effect a junction with General MacArthur. As a blocking movement, Toyoda issued orders to Vice Admiral Takeo Takagi, commander of the Sixth (submarines) Fleet. Takagi ordered a flotilla of subs into the region south of the Carolines to intercept and decimate the U.S. Fifth Fleet. A scouting line, designated NA and covering a stretch of 200 miles of sea would be established between Truk in the Carolines and Manus Island in the Admiralties. In conformance with this, a net of seven subs, intended to catch and kill enough big American steel sharks to frustrate any attempt at invasion, was set along the NA line. But as luck would have it, U.S. Naval Intelligence learned of the plan, located the net's approximate position, and took countermeasures.

At Purvis Bay, near Guadalcanal, DE *England* was impatiently awaiting another set of convoy orders. All around her a war was going on, and all hands aboard hoped to get into it before it ended. Pendleton and Williamson were both eager for combat instead of riding herd on cargo vessels. Finally, on 18 May, orders came for *England* to join the DEs *Raby* and *George* and, under the tactical command of Commander Hamilton Hains, go find and sink an enemy submarine seen lurking near the southern tip of Bougainville. At 1330 the following day, all hands aboard *England* learned that sound contact had been made with a submarine. Captain Pendleton, with the aplomb of an old hand at sub sinkings, made five depth-charge runs over the target. On the fifth, his ship was almost hoisted out of the water by an explosion. Soon debris and oil floated to the surface. *England* had made her first kill.

During the next three days, Commander Hains' DEs steamed northward in quest of the NA line. At 0350 on 22 May all three sub hunters picked up sound contacts from the same target. Going to flank speed, to box the sub in, the *George's* searchlight caught an RO-boat in the act of diving. She made a depth-charge run over the target but missed. Commander Pendleton, believing that he had contact, made two runs. Again *England* scored a hit, as proved by the splintered planking and the steady spread of oil on the sea.

On the morning of the 23rd, *Raby* stumbled upon a contact but lost it before she could make a run. Next, *George* tried her luck and drew a blank. Now came *England's* turn. The first run was unsuccessful. On the second run, a wave-tossing eruption came from below. *England* had made her third kill. Just to make sure that the sub was not sneaking off after leaving a time bomb to throw off pursuit, Hains ordered a pattern of depth charges laid around the spot. The flotsam they brought up told their own story. The sub commander had not been hoaxing.

Another twenty-four hours had passed when *George* reported a radar contact 7 miles dead ahead. The three DEs approached it gingerly in the predawn dark. Evidently the sub commander smelled trouble. When the DEs approached within 3 miles, the sub battened down hatches and pulled the plug. At full speed, they were on his trail. Soon *England* picked up sounds that spelled submarine. To Pendleton it seemed that the boat below was wriggling like an eel in its erratic movements to escape. Presently, the DE located the escapee at 186 feet. On the third run, after a rumbling noise, the usual display of oil and debris appeared. Kill number four for the *England.*

England scored a fifth kill toward the end of day on 26 May while the DEs were en route to Manus to replenish their supply of depth charges. Radar picked up a surface contact at 16,000 yards. At full speed, *Raby* streaked toward the target, an RO-boat on the surface. Before she reached torpedo range, the sub had slipped under. To throw off his pursuer the skipper took her straight down the course over which *Raby* was approaching. By chance, *England* caught the sub on her fathometer at 250 feet. Swift action brought a salvo of depth charges rumbling down her tracks. Several explosions followed in about 20 seconds; they were followed by the gruesome sounds a submarine makes in her death throes. At the time she launched her ashcans, *England* had only enough depth charges left for one more run. But one was enough and the fifth kill was in the bag.

As the DEs headed for Manus they left a very depleted NA line behind. Of seven subs, only two remained. After a quick turn about at Manus, where the trio was joined by the DE *Spangler,* they were nearing the NA area when a call came from the DD *Hazelwood*— which was screening a carrier—for two DEs to take over the search for a hostile submarine. *Raby* and *George* answered the summons while *England* and *Spangler* continued toward the NA line. With an ear glued to the TBS radio, Commander Pendleton overheard the chatter between the two sub-chasing DEs. He asked if they needed help. No offer could have been more promptly and firmly rejected. Suddenly the excitment of the chase between *Raby* and *George* died. They had lost contact with their intended victim.

Somewhat later, searchlight beams knifed through the night not far from where *England* and *Spangler* were cruising. The sub sought by the absent pair of DEs had evidently surfaced and was trying to locate her tormentors. For one brief moment a beam pointed straight in the sky, which gave *England* and her companion perfect bearings. As they sped in the sub's direction, Pendleton flashed the news to Hains, who directed that no attack should be made until daylight and not to close nearer than 5,000 yards. With daylight came *Raby* and *George*. The latter made the first run over the target, which had been kept in continuous contact by *England* and *Spangler*. Result: zero. *Raby*, next at bat, swung wide and wild. Now *Spangler* was called up by the OTC. She, too, missed. In the meantime, *England* had edged into a position some 2,000 yards from the center of the zone, eager for a chance. When the OTC gave it to her, she crossed the area and let go a salvo of depth charges. All four DEs heard the explosions and stood by waiting for results. The seconds dragged past—30 . . . 45 . . . 60—a whole minute and nothing happened. . . . 70 . . . 80 . . . 90 seconds. Then came sounds of a submarine breaking up. In time, an expanding sheet of oil appeared, along with flotsam, to give mute testimony to what had happened many fathoms below.

Commander Hains, who had hoped to nail that last sub himself, grabbed the TBS and shouted in mock dismay, "God dammit, Walter—how do you do it?"

When news of the feats of *England,* the submarine killer, reached the CNO in Washington, Admiral King sent the message:

"There will always be an *England* in the United States Navy."

Aboard the DE, Pendleton shook hands with Williamson. Both men had enjoyed their vacation from convoy duty. For her gallantry and skill, the *England* was awarded a Presidential Unit Citation.

But there were no citations issued in Admiral Toyoda's headquarters in Tokyo as May drew to a close. On 27 May a message from Biak arrived at the admiral's headquarters announcing that that very day an amphibious assault had been launched on the island by General MacArthur's forces, following a devastating air and sea bombardment and shelling of beaches and inland positions that began at dawn. The invasion was now a solid reality that had to be dealt with promptly. Although it is true that a few weeks earlier the Imperial Headquarters had shifted the absolute defense line westward to Sorong, on the western tip of New Guinea, Toyoda intended to hold Biak as long as possible in an effort to gain time. The three airfields on the island were strong defense factors for the Japanese that would become menacing possessions in American hands. The Navy Section, Imperial Headquarters, agreed with Admiral Toyoda on this. On 28 May the buildup of air strength in the Biak area began. Within three days 118 fighters and 40 bombers had been drawn from the Philippines, the Carolines, and the Marianas for distribution at airfields on

Vogelkop and in the Moluccas. About 12,000 soldiers on Biak commanded by Colonel Naoyuki Kuzume were to be reinforced. For that, sea transportation was needed to transfer 2,500 troops from Mindanao to Biak; since no other means were available, cruisers and destroyers would be used. The enterprise entailed the use of a transport and screening force of one battleship, one light and three heavy cruisers, and eight destroyers, commanded by Rear Admiral Naomasa Sakonju and hastily drawn from Admiral Ozawa's fleet at Tawitawi. It was called Operation Kon. Besides the troops, the Army also strengthened the hands of the area air commander, Rear Admiral Ito, by sending sixty land-based planes from the Marianas to Menado on Celebes. Japan could move fairly fast if prodded by emergencies.

At Biak, General MacArthur's forces encountered even greater opposition than at Wakde and Sarmi, a few weeks earlier, where the defenders had shown the fighting spirit displayed in former engagements. To begin with, the strength of Colonel Kuzume's garrison had been estimated at about one-sixth of the 12,000 troops he had on hand; second, defense positions were excellently planned and prepared; third, the well-equipped troops included many units of seasoned combat soldiers. It soon became obvious that weeks, not days, would be required to subdue defense positions in the deep limestone caves that overlooked and covered Biak's three airfields. Unfortunately, when on 2 June Admiral Ito's fliers attacked shipping off Biak, not a single U.S. plane was there to meet them. All General Kenney's fliers were grounded by weather at Hollandia and Wakde. Amazingly enough, only one vessel was damaged. Despite a heavy overcast, however, our antiaircraft fire accounted for twelve Japanese planes. (This success may be laid to the new proximity fuzes already described. They were, incidentally, equally effective against ground and sea targets. Our subs used them to good effect against antisubmarine vessels in surface encounters.)

Operation Kon failed dismally. On the morning of 3 June, as Admiral Sakonju's fleet approached Biak a sharp-eyed lookout sighted a submarine's periscope; alert radio operators in the admiral's flagship, by guarding all potential channels, were presently rewarded by hearing the submarine send a contact report. Soon long-range Army and Navy reconnaissance planes hove into view, and cautious Sakonju raced for Sorong, where he disembarked his troops and left for safer parts.

The next effort to reinforce Biak came a few days later when the

Japanese embarked 600 men in three destroyers, escorted by a similar number of other DDs. They were spotted, and an Australian-American cruiser-destroyer force, under Rear Admiral V. A. C. Crutchley, RN, was sent to meet them. Rather than expose his cruisers to torpedo fire, and because his Small Boys were faster than the Big Boys, the admiral sent seven destroyers out to engage the now-fleeing enemy flotilla. Abandoning all hopes of landing troops, the Japanese headed westward. The stern chase began at a distance of 24,000 yards. It was, from a destroyerman's point of view, one of the most exciting in the war. But, aside from frustrating troop landings, little was accomplished beyond a thrilling chase that demonstrated the superior speed of Allied destroyers. Torpedoes, fired into their own wakes by the Japanese, were avoided by the pursuers. Shells, occasionally sent their way, fell short. On the other hand, because of the long gap between them—never less than some 13,000 yards—American fire scored only one hit, which did not stop the Japanese DD which received it. It was a good show on both sides, and the pursuers were gaining slightly when, according to previous orders, they broke off the three-hour engagement to return to the cruisers and resume their roles as screening vessels. All hands aboard felt that, if given more time, they would have come within accurate shooting range of the fleeing DDs.

One cannot assert that the Japanese overevaluated Biak as a point of major resistance; but it can be said that the drastic withdrawal of planes from such critical areas as the Carolines and the Marianas had fatal consequences. The day would come, and soon, when Admiral Toyoda would give everything within his power to have those planes back at their original bases ready for combat over the Philippine Sea. But by then, many Japanese airmen had been killed in action over the Wakde–Sarmi–Biak areas; most of the survivors were so plagued by tropical diseases that they could neither fight nor fly.

June had begun most inauspiciously for the Japanese High Command. On the first day of the month a wolf pack commanded by Captain L. N. Blair, and known as Blair's Blasters, began a series of attacks on four different convoys. The attacks, which occurred on the Ryukyus-Marianas track north and west of Saipan, involved nipping at the heels of frightened marus and sinking more than a few. The first convoy got away by the skin of its teeth; the second lost a 4,700-ton maru, thanks to *Pintado* (Commander B. A. Clarey); the third convoy lost a maru of the same tonnage when it was sunk by the

Shark (Lieutenant Commander R. H. Close), which also damaged another. On 3 June a fourth convoy came into view. The first three had all been homeward bound in ballast; but this one was evidently headed for Saipan, and the vessels in it were so loaded that the Plimsoll mark was well awash. The Blasters were unable to catch up with the rather speedy convoy until midafternoon of 4 June. *Shark* and *Pintado,* first into firing position, sank seven vessels for a total of 24,000 tons. They wrought more damage than they knew. This convoy carried 10,000 of the troops being transported from Siberia to reinforce lifeline garrisons. That such transfers were poor insurance risks was proven on this occasion when 10,000 men badly needed in General Saito's army were reduced to 4,000 by torpedo action. Equally unsettling to the general was the discovery that most of the surviving troops were without arms, artillery, ammunition, and supplies, because vessels that carried these essentials were now at the bottom of the Philippine Sea.

There may have been several troopship sinkings other than this. For instance, after the war it was learned that *Trout* (Lieutenant Commander A. H. Clark)—reported lost in mid-April, 1944, and never heard of again—was probably destroyed by the enemy during or after an attack she made on a convoy off Formosa on 29 February 1944. But before she went down, *Trout* sank the 7,100-ton cargo-passenger *Sakito Maru,* along with some 4,000 soldiers who were her passengers.

Submariners could not always judge success by the tonnage of their victims. The cargo, not the displacement, is the main point. But submariners never knew the importance of cargoes destroyed. The *Trout's* and the Blasters' feats were cases in point, as was the sinking of an unknown and lowly little freighter off Guam in 1943. Chances are that the submarine skipper who tossed torpedoes at the rusty little tramp felt that the game was not worth his costly candles. But what his victim lacked in size, she made up for in her cargo of scarce and essential radar controls for the enemy's AA guns on Truk. Had this equipment—according to a post-war declaration by Captain Tamura of Truk's air staff—reached its destination, the AA batteries on that island would have displayed better fire control than they did during Task Force 58 strikes in February and April 1944.

On the other side of the Philippines, the *Puffer,* on 5 June, added to her score by sinking two of Ozawa's irreplaceable tankers. On 6, 7, and 10 June the *Harder,* according to her log, sank three and damaged two destroyers. On the 10th, as well, Commander Dealey, her skipper, saw three battleships, several cruisers and about eight destroyers depart Tawitawi and steam southward over the Celebes Sea. This was Admiral Ugaki's task force peeling off from the main fleet to help Admiral Sakonju reinforce Biak's hard-pressed garrison, an operation for which Admiral Ito would provide a sheltering air umbrella. Commander Dealey's prompt report won him a warmly worded commendation by radio from General MacArthur. He was also awarded the Medal of Honor for this epoch-making patrol, but did not live to receive it personally.

Things were on the move at Tawitawi, and the Japanese, more than ever, believed that the main threat was a joining of the forces of Admiral Nimitz and General MacArthur in the south. At that time Admiral Toyoda and his colleagues knew that Spruance's fleet had pulled anchor at Majuro. A daring young Japanese navy pilot flew over the Majuro anchorage a few days after the fleet steamed out. There was no sign anywhere of the fast carrier task force. He returned to report aboard the submarine from which he had taken off in a floatplane whose parts had been uncrated and assembled on the sub's tiny deck. In Tokyo an obscure officer on Admiral Toyoda's staff hoped against hope that his predictions with respect to the Marianas being the invasion target would prove incorrect. Admiral Toyoda himself was more than slightly miffed by the irony of things. In the South Seas Japanese submarines had been sent to the bottom by American warships, while elsewhere American submarines were sinking Japanese cargo marus and warships.

In Europe General Dwight D. Eisenhower had sent his huge invasion force across the Channel on 6 June. In the Pacific General Mac-Arthur exerted a relentless invasion pressure against Biak; and farther north Admiral Nimitz was poised to strike at some, as yet unknown to them, invasion target. The Japanese High Command was bewildered by the capacity of America to wage offensives in widely separated areas at one and the same time.

Chapter Four

OPERATION FORAGER
BEGINS

ACCORDING TO SCHEDULE, D-day on Saipan was 15 June and H-hour was at 0800; W-day (another letter for D-day; on carriers D-day was called Dog-day) on Guam was 18 June. J-day on Tinian would depend upon the time consumed in taking Saipan and Guam.

Although it had become known on 14 May that the Imperial Japanese fleet was concentrating on Tawitawi, most United States commanders still believe that Admiral Ozawa's fleet would not go into battle unless security of the Japanese homeland was at stake. At any rate, orders issued earlier by Admiral Nimitz to the Fifth Fleet Commander were not amended to change the purpose of his mission—namely, "to capture, occupy, and defend the Marianas."

Meanwhile ships had been assembled, troops had been trained, and dates for departures had arrived. On 25 May the slowest vessels in Admiral Turner's Joint Expeditionary Force departed Honolulu. Other units left Pearl on succeeding days. By 9 June all were moored in Eniwetok anchorage. Here they were joined by Admiral Conolly's Southern Attack Group, which was to seize Guam with the 3rd Marine Division, the 1st Provisional Marine Brigade, Corps artillery, and the 77th Infantry Division's 305th RCT under the over-all command of Major General Roy S. Geiger, USMC. These, added to Admiral Turner's Northern Attack Group of 2nd and 4th Marines, plus the 27th Infantry Division—to take Saipan and, later, Tinian—totaled 127,571 troops.

During the two days required for topping off fuel and supplies there was no liberty to go ashore for the cramped Marines and soldiers. Some of the Marines who were to form the initial attack waves on Saipan were transferred to LSTs to be ready to make for the beachheads. Others were put aboard LSDs (landing ships, dock), whose submersible decks could take aboard, house, and set afloat amtracs and other amphibious craft. The 1,000-mile voyage in such vessels was hardly to be envied, especially when one considers the reception that awaited the men at the end of the journey on Saipan's red, green, blue, and yellow beachheads—red and green for the 2nd Marines, blue and yellow for the 4th Marines. The 27th Infantry would be held in reserve to land wherever they might be needed. Admiral Conolly's Southern Attack Group would mark time for W-day Guam by shuttling back and forth in the Pacific about a hundred miles from the target island.

Task Force 58, with Admiral Spruance in the *Indianapolis* and Admiral Mitscher in the *Lexington,* weighed anchor at Majuro on 6 June, the very day General Eisenhower's European forces crossed the Channel. TF 58 was followed on 11 June by Admiral Turner's command. For a few days the Marshall lagoons had been the most cluttered and busiest anchorages in the world; now, all that remained were the supply and repair ships of Carter's ServRon 10, the local base garrisons, a hospital, and the few palm trees that had survived the Spruance Haircut administered in February, plus the weird-looking windmill laundry machines set up by inventive sailors in residence.

According to schedule, Admiral Mitscher was to start a two-day strike on the morning of 12 June. Although these explosions would reverberate in Tokyo, they would not be the only sounds of fury to register in Japan on 10–11 June. From the Kuriles down to New Guinea and throughout the Marshalls and Carolines, bombs would burst on Japanese possessions. To the north, long-range Army bombers and a North Pacific cruiser squadron would bombard the Kuriles. In the south, General Kenney's bombers would strike at Mindanao and give Yap and Peleliu a good dusting. Admiral Hoover's land-based planes would attack the Carolines and the enemy-occupied Marshalls. From China, new B-29 superbombers would pay their first visit to the Japanese homeland. This elaborate and effective program of offensive action went according to script—except for the B-29s. Their end of the show had to be scrubbed because of conditions that prevented takeoffs.

Back at Pearl Harbor, satisfied that Operation Forager was well under way and on schedule, Admiral Nimitz prepared for the execution of a plan that would put the Fifth Fleet on a two-shift basis. To accomplish this, he had obtained the services of Admiral Halsey, whose South Pacific Fleet (now the Third Fleet) was about to be dissolved. The South Pacific Theater, once crammed with exciting action, was now dark and silent. Bill Halsey had, so to speak, worked himself out of a job. The Third Fleet was to be divided between Admiral Nimitz and General MacArthur, whose fleet, under Admiral Kinkaid, was now the Seventh.

Admiral Halsey was eager to continue sea duty. He would be accommodated in that respect by Admiral Nimitz, who had a unique plan: When Admiral Spruance had completed Operation Forager, his Fifth Fleet would be turned over to Admiral Halsey. It would then become known as the Third Fleet. The ships and their personnel would remain unchanged; only the fleet number and the commander would be different. While the Fifth Fleet took the Marianas, Admiral Halsey would plan for action that would take carrier warfare across the Philippine Sea to Formosa, the Philippines, and other islands in Japan's inner defense perimeter. Then, while Admiral Halsey was at sea Admiral Spruance would plan for operations beyond Halsey's and, in time, execute them with his old Fifth Fleet. All very simple, highly efficient, and bound to confuse the Japanese into thinking that the United States had not one but two fleets waging war upon them.

"It was like relay stage stations in the old West," Admiral Nimitz once explained, "only instead of changing horses, the stages changed drivers."

Some may conclude that this was pretty hard on the horses—the officers and men who served in the fleet—and hard on the ships as well. And in some respects that was the way it worked out. Back in the days when the fleet was based at Pearl, there were attractions galore for men on leave or liberty. But as the fleet moved westward so did facilities of entertainment and recreation. USO units of famous performers came in fairly steady streams to forward bases and were as welcome as manna from heaven. The men of the silent service still speak of how Eddie Peabody and his banjo helped to relieve monotonous days between patrols.

At all new bases officers clubs and white-hat clubs were established almost as soon as the fleet moved in. Also, at nearly all bases, men famous in the sports world served as recreation officers and did a lot to keep the men occupied with ball games and such. Also, personnel was transferred back and forth to shore duty, and despite the wonderful work done by service squadrons, ships had to head Stateside to enter Navy yards for overhaul and repair. Still, most of the fast task force seldom saw anything but Japanese beaches from August through October 1944.

Close-in and far-ranging combat air patrols spread a huge umbrella over the carriers and screening ships of TF 58 on the morning of 11

June as they sped toward the target islands. At dawn on the 12th, Operation Forager would begin when the first deckloads of fighters and bombers took off to dump their tons of destructive hardware. After a day of that, Admiral Lee's battle line would subject Saipan and Tinian to heavy bombardment from daylight to dark. There would be another day of the same on 14 June from the guns of Admiral Oldendorf's pre-Pearl Harbor battleships.

The seascape was cluttered that 11 June by flattops as well as by battleships, cruisers, and destroyers whose propellers left long, white 20-knots wakes over an area that seemed to stretch from horizon to horizon. Widely separated and surrounded by their massive gun-support screens were Pete Mitscher's carriers with their huge complements of planes and pilots. Ahead, less than 300 miles away, lay their targets. In order that readers may come to know the ships and air groups that were to play such important parts in the events to occur, the roster of TF 58 follows:

Fifth Fleet: Admiral Spruance commanding, riding in the screen of TG 58.3 (CA *Indianapolis*).

Task Force 58: Admiral Mitscher commanding, riding in the hub of TG 58.3 (CV *Lexington*).

Task Group 58.1: Rear Admiral J. M. J. Clark commanding. CV *Hornet*, Capt. W. D. Sample commanding; Air Group 2, Lt. Cdr. J. D. Arnold commanding.

> CV *Yorktown*, Capt. R. E. Jennings commanding; Air Group 1, Cdr. J. M. Peters commanding.

> CVL *Belleau Wood*, Capt. John Perry commanding; Air Group 24, Lt. Cdr. E. M. Link commanding.

> CVL *Bataan*, Capt. V. H. Schaeffer commanding; Air Group 50, Lt. Cdr. J. C. Strange commanding.

> Screen: CAs *Baltimore, Boston, Canberra;* CL-AA *Oakland* and 14 DDs.

Task Group 58.2: Rear Admiral A. E. Montgomery commanding.

> CV *Bunker Hill*, Capt. T. P. Jeter commanding; Air Group 8, Cdr. R. L. Shifley commanding.

> CV *Wasp*, Capt. C. A. F. Sprague commanding; Air Group 18, Cdr. W. C. Wingard commanding.

> CVL *Monterey*, Capt. S. H. Ingersoll commanding; Air Group 28, Lt. Cdr. R. W. Mehle commanding.

> CVL *Cabot*, Capt. S. J. Michael commanding; Air Group 31, Lt. Cdr. Winston commanding.

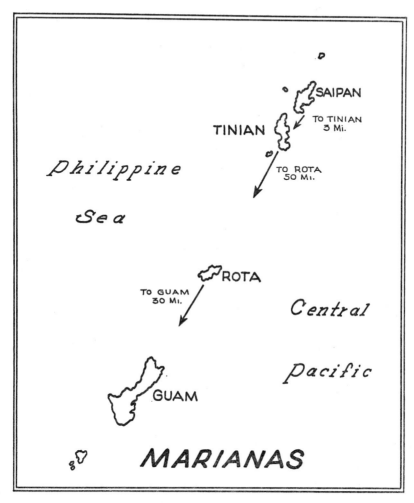

The lower Marianas formed a formidable barrier that Admiral Nimitz had to crash before his Central Pacific Fleet could enter the Philippine Sea. The Japanese, expecting attacks farther south, were taken by complete surprise when pre-invasion air strikes were launched against all four islands on 11 June 1944 by Admiral Mitscher's Fifth Fleet fast carrier force.

Screen: CLs *Biloxie, Mobile, Santa Fe;* CVL-AA *San Juan* and 12 DDs.

Task Group 58.3: Rear Admiral J. W. Reeves, Jr., commanding.
CV *Enterprise,* Capt. M. B. Gardner commanding; Air Group 10, Cdr. W. R. Kane commanding.
CV *Lexington,* Capt. E. W. Litch commanding; Air Group 16, Cdr. E. M. Snowden commanding.
CVL *San Jacinto,* Capt. H. M. Martin commanding; Air Group 51, Lt. Cdr. C. L. Moore commanding.
CVL *Princeton,* Capt. W. H. Buracker commanding; Air Group 27, Lt. Cdr. E. W. Wood commanding.
Screen: CA *Indianapolis;* CLs *Birmingham, Cleveland, Montpelier;* CL-AA *Reno* and 13 DDs.

Task Group 58.4: Rear Admiral W. K. Harrill commanding. CV *Essex,* Capt. R. A. Ofstie commanding; Air Group 15, Cdr. D. McCampbell commanding.
CVL *Langley,* Capt. W. M. Dillon commanding; Air Group 27, Lt. Cdr. E. C. Outlaw commanding.
CVL *Cowpens,* Capt. H. W. Taylor commanding; Air Group 25, Lt. Cdr. R. H. Price commanding.
Screen: CLs *Houston, Miami, Vincennes;* CL-AA *San Diego* and 14 DDs.

Battle Line Task Group 58.7: Vice Admiral W. A. Lee, Jr., commanding.
BBs *Alabama, Indiana, Iowa, New Jersey, North Carolina, South Dakota, Washington.*
CAs *Minneapolis, New Orleans, San Francisco, Wichita,* and 14 DDs.

One may be certain that any Japanese snooper would have given his eyeteeth for a glimpse of this armada. As a matter of fact, opinions differ among historians as to whether one did or not. Some maintain that reconnaissance planes sighted were shot down by alert CAP pilots. Others, that at least one saw the fleet and roared off to spread the tidings. Be that as it may, Admiral Mitscher, in CV *Lexington,* communicated with Admiral Spruance, whose flagship, CA *Indianapolis,* steamed in the screen of Mitscher's own Task Group 58.3 He proposed that, instead of waiting for dawn of 12 June to launch strikes, he would send his warbirds over the Marianas that afternoon when visibility was expected to improve. Admiral Spruance, also eager to jump the gun, endorsed the idea. In short order, crews on hangar and flight decks were readying the 225 planes—fighters and a few torpedo planes—that were to take to the air.

At 1300, when CAP observers reported increasing visibility to westward and when TF 58 was some 200 miles from Guam and 225 miles off Saipan and Tinian, carriers and screens turned eastward into the wind and plane engines roared into life. Soon aircraft zipped off flight decks and rose into the sky to assemble into divisions. Over the islands the visibility was from 10 to 15 miles under a ceiling of some 12,000–13,000 feet, which meant that the Hellcats had to zoom in fairly low for fighter tactics. The sweep was so nicely delivered that the four targets were hit simultaneously. The airborne opposition, what there was of it, was neither well organized nor effective. There were a few hot dogfights but not as hot as the flak the attackers had to dodge on strafing runs on planes parked near runways. This fire, quick and close, produced an unpleasant number of near-misses. Of the Zekes that rose to give battle, 81 plunged to earth and 13 more were probables. In addition, 29 planes were destroyed on the ground, including many Betty bombers, and 24 more were damaged. In return, we lost 11 Hellcats, 5 of whose pilots were rescued.

The Japanese air defenses of the Marianas were rather weak, probably because men and machines had been transferred to the Biak area and few replacements had arrived from Japan. The largest bag of the day was a convoy out of Tanapag Harbor in ballast for Japan. It was attacked by dive-bombers, who sank five cargo marus, one tanker, and four escorts. As it happened, they missed an even larger convoy somewhat ahead of this one. Since there was keen competition among air groups for collecting the largest numbers of meatballs, the Hellcatters of CV *Hornet's* VF-2 squadron (Lieutenant Commander W. A. Dean commanding) crowed lustily that night over the 24 victories scored by four 4-plane divisions of their squadron that day.

On being debriefed by ACI (air combat intelligence) officers after returning to CVL *Monterey,* fighter pilots of VF-28 reported that their planes could not turn or climb as rapidly as the Zekes. On the other hand, Japanese pilots were not as good as U.S. pilots in handling their planes, in team work, or in defensive maneuvers.

After recovering all returning fliers, the main force set course for Tinian and Saipan while TG 1, commanded by Admiral Clark, steamed toward Guam, which lies some 100 miles south of Tinian.

At about 0300, radar in the main force discovered bogeys, which turned out to be about a dozen Bettys coming up from the south, probably Truk. They proved much less aggressive than the sister bombers that attacked Admiral Mitscher's task force during the February strike. The strong AA fire put up by carriers and screens held them off and eventually drove them away, all but one, which, mothlike, flew too near the flame and splashed burning into the sea.

By June 1944, rescues by submarines of carrier pilots downed at sea had become strictly SOP. In fact, as Rear Admiral Jackson D. Arnold—commander of Air Group 2 aboard CV *Hornet* at the time of the battles for the Marianas—recently observed, "About one fourth of my air group at one time or another put in a tour on a submarine, and our affection for those boys was without bounds.

"I happened to be present during a strike on Guam when one of the most unusual rescues by submarine took place. Ensign Donald C. Brandt of VF 2 was flying on my wing as we strafed the field at Agana, when he was hit by antiaircraft fire. He bailed out and landed in Agana Harbor. I immediately notified the rescue submarine, which was submerged several miles off the harbor entrance."

Actually this sub, the *Stingray,* commanded by Lieutenant Commander S. C. Loomis, was off southern Guam, about 40 miles from the downed pilot. Despite the possible presence of enemy planes, Loomis took a chance on making a surface run in broad daylight. At 21 knots and surface battle stations, he made for the harbor, where the ensign had just been given a rubber raft by a TBF.

Meanwhile at Agana, Admiral Arnold established a strafing circle of dive bombers over the beaches that enclose the harbor in order to silence shore batteries that were taking Brandt under fire. The latter was floating on his inflated life jacket in the center of the harbor. The strafing operation was kept going for several hours with changing attack groups, and Admiral Arnold was beginning to wonder if the "damn sub would ever come."

Had he been endowed with depth penetration vision he would have seen the *Stingray,* now submerged and with Captain Loomis at the periscope, steal into the harbor at slowest possible speed. Had he been close enough he would also have noted that the sub's periscope made several passes at Ensign Brandt, in fact it nudged the raft three times as if trying to say, "Come on, grab me." It was all in the book and the aviator should know it. At long last, Ensign Brandt remembered his rescue briefings and hitched the raft's bow line to the scope.

Greatly relieved, Captain Loomis made a soft retreat from the harbor. His first approach was made at 1303, his last at 1516.

"Just as my patience was getting thin with the no-show submarine skipper," continued Admiral Arnold, "it suddenly appeared as if Don was making a new world record swimming toward the harbor entrance. I peeled off from the strafing operation and flew several feet over the water to see what was going on and found that he had lashed himself to a sub's periscope and was being towed to sea."

After about an hour of slow towing, Captain Loomis surfaced. No man was ever more happy to see the inside of a submarine than was Donald Brandt.

During the small hours of 12 June, Task Groups 2, 3, and 4 swung south of Tinian and headed north to the west coast of Saipan. TG 1, having done its job on Guam, took a heading that brought it east of Saipan. The sun was barely over the eastern horizon when all four task groups released deckloads of planes to deliver a double-edged assault that covered the coast lines and the interior of the island. This was the start of four days of dawn-to-dusk maximum bombings and strafings as well as air participation in bombardment operations on Saipan and Tinian. The prime objectives were to destroy all remaining aircraft, to make airfields temporarily unusable, to knock out antiaircraft and other gun positions, and to clear away by burning all underbrush and cane fields that overlooked and gave cover along beachheads. In order not to disclose the actual landing beaches, all potential beachheads were given identical singes.

During these attacks, a far-ranging search plane discovered, about 220 miles northwest of Saipan, the convoy of 21 large and small vessels that had escaped detection the previous day. A speedily organized bomber attack caused the sinking of 11 vessels, including 8 of the larger ships estimated at 26,000 tons.

Air opposition over the islands was negligible. Admiral Kakuta was husbanding his few remaining planes to engage in dusk and night nuisance missions until reinforcements, en route from Japan, could reach him.

From intelligence interrogations aboard TF 58 carriers on 12 June it would appear that the bombing strikes, though over-all results were satisfactory, could have been better if more targets could have been identified. Despite excellent, extensive, and up-to-date photo coverage, positions of mortars, mountain guns, and other mobile weapons were hard to identify. This was because lively ground fire usually forced photo planes to rather high altitudes and clouds hid many gun positions.

On 12 April a unit of Avenger planes off the *Lexington,* led by Lieutenant Commander Robert E. Isely, put the theory of airborne rockets to the test. They had been used extensively across the Atlantic by RAF submarine hunters and had been tested, with promising results, by U.S. Marine aviators. The trick was to make a shallow dive approach, release rockets half a mile or so from the target, then climb fast as the long slim missiles, propelled by their own fuel, dashed toward their goals. On that day the Tiny Tim rockets were used chiefly against mortar batteries, and they performed as well for our fliers as they had abroad for RAF sub killers. One exuberant Avenger rocketeer declared that from then on, Tiny Tims were his friends for life.

Unhappily, another story was to be told the next day when Lieutenant Commander Isely, spearheading a three-plane Avenger formation armed with rockets, attacked Aslito Airfield on Saipan. As they nosed toward their launching points they ran into heavy flak at about 4,000 feet. One plane was damaged but escaped, but Rob Isely's and the other Avenger flamed, crashed, and exploded. This tragic event, which could be ascribed to the dangerously low flying required during rocket runs, threw a very wet blanket over the fires of Tiny Tim enthusiasm. In honor of Robert Isely, Aslito Airfield was eventually renamed after him.

Another tragic incident occurred on 13 June when Commander William I. Martin, boss of VT-10 torpedo squadron on the *Enterprise,* was hit by flak at 3,500 feet over the lagoon on Saipan's west coast. A few seconds and 500 feet later, Commander Martin and his two crewmen were hurtled out of the disintegrating and burning plane. The two crewmen, probably unconscious, did not open their chutes and were killed on impact with the sea. Bill Martin hit the silk only to discover that due to a long rip, the chute did little to reduce his rate of fall. He had the great presence of mind to press his legs and feet firmly together in the manner of circus stunt divers who plunge from tall poles into shallow canvas pools.

When he reached the sea, he went in feet first, cleaved the surface like an arrow, and emerged uninjured except for a few bruises. He had barely had time to realize that the lagoon was only four feet deep when rifle bullets, fired by soldiers on the beach, began to buzz around his head. Gathering his chute and dragging his one-man raft in its seat pack, Bill Martin made for the security of the reef. While he crawled across it to seek shelter from missiles on the seaward side, he saw two boats setting out from shore. At almost the same time he heard an air strike come thundering in. As the planes peeled off to hit their targets, the men in the boats scrambled ashore. Concluding that he would have a better chance of being discovered by friendly eyes at sea, Commander Martin released the charger cartridge on his raft, slipped into it, made a jury rig of his paddle and parachute, and was presently buzzed by two carrier planes. A little later he was picked up by a floatplane catapulted off the CA *Indianapolis,* which took him to the fleet flagship where he reported to Admiral Spruance on his experiences and observations. Soon a destroyer, bound for a close-in bombardment mission, picked him up for later delivery to CV *Enterprise.* Before he reached base, Bill Martin had the satisfaction of helping to reduce to dust the AA battery that had downed his plane.

While bombers and fighters ruled over Saipan and Tinian, Admiral Lee's streamlined battleships, each with nine 16-inch guns in their main batteries, swung gracefully into battle line. They were flanked by Big and Small Boys armed in proportion. For hours—from ranges of 10,000 to 16,000 yards—great guns boomed and smaller guns barked while shells of all sizes tore through the air toward their targets. On Saipan, the bombardment men-of-war made the dirt, dust, and debris fly with the earnest intent of ridding the surface of the island of guns, emplacements, redoubts, and the soldiers who manned them. The cloud cover thus created obscured everything. Later, there were critics who maintained that Ching Lee should have drawn closer to the island and wrought more damage on definite targets. Exception to this attitude is taken by Vice Admiral Theodore C. Ruddock, a veteran battlewagon skipper, whose commands in the Pacific included Battleship Division 4 (*Maryland* and *Colorado*) in Olie Oldendorf's fire-support group of seven grand old girls of the battle line who shot themselves to enduring fame. After the Gilberts and the Marshalls, where he captained *Massachusetts,* he was promoted to Rear Admiral and given BatDiv 4, which he commanded from Saipan to Leyte and way stops in between. Before the war Admiral Ruddock served in the Bureau of Ordnance. This gave weight and value to his opinions on the subject of the Saipan bombardments.

> As I remember the general plan for Saipan, the bombardment by the new BBs, was more in the nature of a preparation strike to soften it up for the older ships to finish off. I am of

the opinion that the preparatory bombing of Saipan by the
new BBs accomplished all that could reasonably be expected
of such an operation and was conducted at proper range for
maximum effectiveness of an area bombardment.

On the other hand, the complexities of shore bombardment and
AP vs HC are too great to be covered in a paragraph, according to
Rear Admiral E. M. Eller, also a battlewagon sailor and ordnance
expert of wide experience. In a letter, dated 4 February 1966, he
wrote:

> AP projectiles are suitable and were used from North
> Africa to Okinawa. They had to be against heavy concrete
> fortifications. We did develop reduced charges for high-angle
> fire that enabled relatively close range. Naval gunfire is so
> accurate, relatively, such heavy sustained volume is so fear-
> some, that it was a major factor in the success of most
> assaults.
>
> However, as all of us remember from bombings in England,
> the radius of destruction of even the most powerful bomb or
> projectile is small. There are roughly thirty million square feet
> in a square mile. Most people who talked about saturation
> bombarding did not know what they were talking about or did
> not stop to think. A few thousand yards do not make a large
> difference in precise heavy gunfire. There are always some
> duds and ricochets. One reason for the heavy ships to come in
> close was the great volume of fire that could be delivered from
> 5-inch and 40mm batteries at less well protected defenses.

On that 13 June it was strongly suspected in the Navy that the
shallow shelf between the invasion beaches and deeper waters had
been mined. Certainly, Admiral Lee could not be blamed for not risking men and ships by entering such a highly suspect area. In fact,
under cover of his bombardment, six minesweepers combed it for
mines but their paravanes did not produce a single one of those "we
never surrender" monsters. Contrary to expectations, the shoal was
not mined. Why not? No one knows. After the Marines took Saipan
they discovered stacks of mines, ready for use but never planted.

Promptly at 0530 on 14 June Admiral Oldendorf and his venera-
ble gun-toting ladies stormed into the shelf area, swept by minesweepers the day before, brandishing their eighteen 16-inch and
eighty-four 14-inch rifles. In their broad wakes followed a swarm of
cruisers and destroyers, as well as the UDT units, which promptly

went to work. Admiral Oldendorf subjected Saipan to a day-long pounding from distances of 3,000 to 1,000 yards. At such close range, it would seem that destruction of beach and secondary defenses should have been complete; that, however, was not the case. But as Ted Ruddock described the situation:

> As I review what I experienced the next day (14 June) upon taking up the bombardment with BatDiv 4 at very close range, 2,000 yards or less, I recall that there was no resistance to our gunfire from shore and that such emplacements as were shown on our target maps appeared unoccupied. . . . The amphibious people in the Pacific required that we close in at point-blank range to shoot up objects on the shore prior to landing. These were ineffective. On Saipan, duds fell all over the place and ricochets endangered ships (our own) on the other side of the island. I, for one, had a frantic call from another flag officer to quit trying to sink him.

There were two main reasons for the ineffectiveness of the naval shelling: First, with major-caliber shells, only direct hits do damage; second, the fuses of the bombardment ammunition were not designed specifically for naval use. Before the war heavy ships depended primarily upon AP (armor piercing) shells to destroy their adversaries. These were not suited for shore bombardment. Our needs in that direction were met partially by new thin-skinned projectiles with maximum high-explosive capacity for all major and intermediate-caliber guns. The Army fuse then in use was adopted to save time in developing and testing a new one. The exploder of this missile, however, required a down angle of 15 degrees or more to explode on impact. Otherwise the shell would behave like a skip-bomb and either end up as a dud or go ricocheting all over the place. To develop a sufficiently high angle of fall, ranges from 8,000 yards up were required or the missile's trajectory would be too flat for the exploder to detonate the filler.

Thus, the surface Navy found itself in an exploder problem similar to the one that plagued the submarine force during the first eighteen months of the war. In those days submariners would return to Pearl from patrols heavyhearted because their torpedoes much too often failed to explode when they scored hits. In time, misfiring causes were eliminated.

At Saipan, where Admiral Oldendorf's bombardment gunners

vainly tried to lure the defenders into answering their fire, enemy batteries showed great reluctance to enter into tit-for-tat exchanges that would pinpoint their locations. They would be heard from when their chances of longevity were better. While the cannonading went on, carrier and escort pilots did their stuff aloft, bombing, strafing, and dropping marker bombs on targets that were invisible to gunners at sea. After sunset the destroyers took over. Throughout the night they dashed close inshore and fired on charted positions and at targets of opportunity, as revealed by fires or the faint light of the moon. The idea was to give the enemy the smallest possible opportunity to creep out of the typhoon cellars to mend his fractured defenses.

The former U.S. Navy anchorage at Tawitawi, meanwhile, was not the peaceful and secluded place that Admiral Ozawa had expected it to be. This was revealed later in a special report in which he wrote:

> In accordance with orders . . . the Task Force was standing by at Tawitawi since 20 May. During this time, because of enemy submarine activities and lack of training fields, the ability of the air personnel constantly declined. Therefore it became necessary to speedily move to Guimaras or Manila.

There were other reasons why the admiral wanted to leave Tawitawi: submarines. In a running commentary he notes (c. June 10):

> Between the 6th and the 9th, four destroyers were damaged by enemy subs in spite of our antisubmarine operations by ships and planes. Due to lack of sufficient destroyers for decisive action [and] . . . in temporary recognition of need to bow before enemy submarine dispositions . . . decided to move anchorage to Guimaras on 13th.

Admiral Ozawa was in constant touch with Admiral Toyoda, in Tokyo, who tried to keep him up to date on highly confusing war events and interpreted them as he saw them develop. This is revealed in the following text from the same source:

> [On] 11 June we received reports of the enemy task force attack on Saipan. The Fleet Headquarters [Admiral Toyoda's] estimated that this was a diversionary operation of the Biak operation, but on the following day, the 12th, learning that the enemy was in great force, that it had 12 to 15 aircraft carriers as its nucleus, it was thought possible that this was a forerunner of an invasion operation. Having previ-

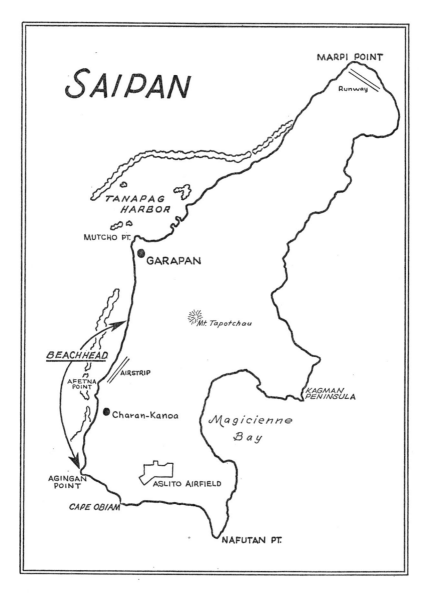

*Saipan, then the strongest Japanese bastion in the
Marianas, is a dozen miles long and less than half that
in width. Yet its rugged terrain, hostile jungles, and
determined defenders retarded occupation until 9 July,
far beyond the U.S. Navy's time schedule.*

ously estimated that the advance to Guimaras was advantageous to air operation, the entire force proceeded to Guimaras anchorage as [previously] scheduled at 0900 on the 13th. Receiving reports on the 13th that the enemy had commenced shelling operations in Saipan, the belief that landings would take place there gained credence.

At 1727 on 13 June, after having steamed for more than eight hours northwest across the Sulu Sea, Admiral Toyoda's signal to "prepare for A-GO operation" was received by Admiral Ozawa. Five minutes later he was notified that Operation Kon against Biak had been "temporarily suspended" and that Admiral Ugaki had been ordered to stand by to return to the First Mobile Fleet. Admiral Ozawa, after a staff conference, noted:

> It was decided to destroy in daytime the enemy regular carrier groups in accordance with Combined Fleet Operation Plans and in cooperation with friendly [land-based] air forces and Advanced Expeditionary Force. This was to be followed up with an all-out attack aimed at the annihilation of the enemy. The daytime attack was scheduled for the 19th.

As the First Mobile Fleet crossed the Sulu Sea, those in it were blissfully unaware that part of their fleet had been sighted that morning by the SS *Redfin*. In keeping with orders, Lieutenant Commander M. H. Austin held off firing in order to report his highly fortunate sighting. Since he had to surface to do this—and wisdom dictated that it would be an error to do that before nightfall—Commander Austin did not get his message off to ComSubSoWesPac until after sunset. From there it was sped to Brisbane and Hawaii and on to Admiral Spruance in the CA *Indianapolis,* who relayed the news to his two force commanders. It did not cause a great flutter of excitement. Whatever Admiral Toyoda and Admiral Ozawa had in mind would not be revealed until, or unless, the latter's fleet entered the Philippine Sea by going around or through the Philippine Archipelago. There was nothing to do but to wait watchfully and stick to the program for the invasion and capture of Saipan. It was up to the submarines, at their various stations, to keep watch on the movements of the First Mobile Fleet. Going by their records so far, that watch would be well kept. But as a safety measure, Army and Navy long-range planes at SoWesPac bases, as well as Fifth Fleet seaplanes based on tenders stationed west of the Marianas, were ordered to stretch their search patrols as far as their fuel capacities permitted.

Till sunset on 13 June, Admiral Nagato and General Saito had believed that the invasion would be staged in commodious Magicienne Bay on the southeast coast of Saipan. But that conclusion began to change on the morning of 14 June when cannonading started all around Saipan, and Tinian as well, with Admiral Oldendorf setting the pace off the west coast. The appearance of mine sweepers the previous day, coupled with the fact that the heaviest fire was concentrated on the west coast between Charan-Kanoa and Agingan Point, were two items of evidence. A third appeared on the morning of the 14th when scores of half-naked Yanks, looking like zebras, invaded and explored the lagoon that ran along a 4-mile stretch of beach well suited for landing purposes.

In accord with this change of mind, General Saito transferred his mobile artillery from the Magicienne Bay region to elevated positions that commanded the west-coast invasion area. The latter was already well prepared to challenge an invasion. Aside from fixed coastal guns, batteries of light and heavy artillery were hidden on forward and reverse mountain slopes. The reverse slopes, completely out of sight from the sea and difficult to locate from the air, would be hard to silence. Other guns were emplaced in pillboxes and blockhouses; guns, carefully hidden in mountain caves, were aimed at the beaches and used flashless powder that did not reveal their positions. For further support there were mortar units, machine guns, and men with other automatic weapons concealed in well-selected positions or in camouflaged trenches. Could be that General Saito felt himself so secure behind this breastwork of guns that he had not felt it necessary to mine the sea or the lagoon, or even cover the bottom of the latter with barbed wire. After the battle, stacks of spooled barbed wire and mines were discovered, as well as numerous heavy guns that never had been emplaced.

According to Admiral Spruance's assault arrangements for 14 June and after, fire-support units of the Fifth Fleet would operate generally within a circle that completely embraced Saipan and Tinian. This circle was divided into seven fire-support sectors to which fighting ships would be assigned. This meant that the total firing power of the fleet was concentrated on these targets from every point of the compass. To help direct this fire, planes from the two carrier groups that Admiral Mitscher had on hand aided pilots from Admiral Turner's escort carriers, under Rear Admirals G. F. Bogan and H. B. Salada.

Promptly at 0530 on 15 June the cannon ball was reopened when

Olie Oldendorf's battleships reappeared with their cruisers and destroyers.

Air resistance had been wiped out on Tinian and Saipan. True, planes occasionally sneaked out from cover on Rota or Guam to stage nuisance raids; however, they usually accomplished nothing but the demise of their aviators. But prospects that planes fresh from Japan—and staged in the Bonin and Volcano Islands 600–700 miles away—would interfere with the landings hung like a menacing cloud on the northern horizon. To remove it, Admirals Spruance and Mitscher agreed that since the Japanese fleet, even at constant flank speed, could not come within launching distance of Saipan for several days, it would be timely and profitable for Admiral Jocko Clark's TG 1, accompanied by Admiral Harrill's TG 4, to rush north, do a job of cloud removing on the three Jimas—Iwo, Haha, and Chichi—and return post haste.

Chapter Five

D-DAY

A NARROW STRIP OF BEACH runs north-south for about four miles along Saipan's west coast. Halfway up, on a slight forward bulge, stands Afetna Point, a stubby, jungle-clad hill with a truncated top. Just south of this point lies Charan-Kanoa Village, a collection of ramshackle huts, which by June 1944 were crumbled by gunfire and seared by flame. Near the village were the ruins of a sugar mill dominated by a tall slanting smokestack. On the waterfront was a decrepit boat landing. Back of the northern two miles of beach, the tall sugarcane had been partially destroyed by incendiary shells. The southern half of the beach is one of natural desolation covered by bush jungle, grass, and occasional clumps of trees. At the extreme southern end of the beach stands another hill, Agingan Point. It is larger and with denser jungle cover than Afetna Point. Behind the beaches, a flat country, slashed by ravines, rises gradually for about a mile until it reaches the first level of foothills at an elevation of 100 feet, back of which other hills rise in shallow tiers to Mt. Fina Susu.

This stretch of real estate, 4 miles long and 1 mile wide, was the D-day objective. It was expected that the early assault waves, assisted by heavily armored amtracs and tanks, would advance the entire distance along the 4-mile front. Succeeding waves, totaling 20,000 Marines, would occupy the entire area by nightfall. On the following day, with more troops and equipment arriving in swelling numbers, three blitz prongs would shoot out from the beachhead perimeter, one to seize Aslito Airfield, another to capture Magicienne Bay, a third to march north toward Garapan. With that much of the island in their grasp, the invaders hoped to make short shrift of capturing the remainder. To insure strong initial assault waves muscled with armed impact, their components would consist of two combat teams and four assault battalions from each of the two participating Marine divisions, the 2nd and 4th, both composed largely of combat veterans. The 2nd Marines would take the green and red beaches north of the boat landing; the 4th would tackle the blue and yellow beaches south of it.

Spearheading the landing tanks would be a number of heavily armed and armored amtracs, mobile fortresses that were equally at home on land or sea. Their armament, aside from numerous machine guns, included a 75mm howitzer turreted in the top of each vehicle. Behind them, other landing craft would follow with cargoes of combat teams and assault battalions; after them would come continuous waves of troops, artillery, ammunition, and communication and medical units, plus supplies.

All day long Big and Small Boys would stand in close support along the entire length of beachhead, crowding as near to the barrier reef as practicable. Other gun-support vessels would take stations on the flanks. Air spotting and combat assistance would be provided mainly by Admiral Turner's own escort carrier planes. Such was the over-all landing program.

At midnight on 14–15 June, ships' bells throughout Raymond Spruance's fleet sounded the start of D-day. On most ships the bells were heard only by men who changed watches, but in the eighty landing ships, tanks, and docks, cooks were already at work in the galleys preparing the traditional invasion breakfast of steak, fried eggs, and steaming black coffee. This was to be served at 0200 to the Marines in the early assault waves. Then the men would proceed to the parking decks in their vessels in full combat gear and await orders to enter their amphibious vehicles.

While the assault troops of the 2nd and 4th Marines breakfasted, the crews of their LSTs and LSDs prepared for the moment when they, with the rest of the Admiral Turner's TF 51, would set course for the Philippine Sea. Their planned route was to go around Marpi Point on the northern end of Saipan—but so far to the north of it that they would not be sighted. The ships were well under way before day dawned clear and bright. The Force was well to seaward of Saipan when the BB *Colorado,* on signal, departed station in line, as did a string of transports. Landing nets were draped along their sides, landing craft were ready to be lowered, and Marines, armed to the teeth, were lined up behind them. In the wake of *Colorado,* the transports headed toward Mutcho Point, which stands between Garapan and Tanapag Harbor, a few miles above the actual beachhead. As the battleship's guns roared, landing craft were lowered, men filled them, and the entire flotilla of LCIs made for the beaches. The reaction ashore was quick and violent. Strong artillery and mortar fire slammed into the sea in the path of the oncoming landing craft, which presently began to scatter. After a while, they re-formed and headed shoreward again, only to break up in confusion and turn away to escape the shells that burst all around them. After a third attempt, with equally humiliating results, the boats pushed toward their transports, the would-be invaders re-embarked, and soon steamed away, as did *Colorado*.

The landing attempt had, of course, been a deliberate diversion. And Saipan's commander swallowed it and proclaimed its repulsion a great victory. Overstating the outcome, he radioed Tokyo that would-be invaders had been driven off with heavy losses, a battleship sunk, several carriers damaged, and some 140 planes shot down. This report would certainly make naval authorities in Japan conclude that the setup was tailor-made for Operation A-GO's basic plan of pinning the American fleet between carriers and shore, and pounding it with air attacks from both sides.

At Guimaras, Admiral Ozawa had begun, but not completed, refueling operations on 14 June. Resumed on the morning of 15 June, they were disrupted when the admiral, at 0717, received orders to activate Operation A-GO, along with information that the enemy had begun landing operations on Saipan. In less than an hour, all ships in the fleet had pulled anchor and set course for San Bernardino Strait by way of Guimaras Strait and the Visayan Sea. Admiral Ugaki was ordered to steam north at his best speed for a rendezvous at sea on 16 June. Similar orders were issued to the 1st Supply Force at Davao. The 2nd Supply Force, its oilers fully loaded, was already waiting east of the Philippines, with part of the 3rd Supply Force, for the First Mobile Fleet to enter the Philippine Sea "without leaving a trace," as ordered. According to the schedule, Admiral Ozawa would attempt this feat at 1730 that very afternoon.

At 0542 on 15 June, less than two hours before Admiral Ozawa received the A-GO action signal, Admirals Oldendorf and Ainsworth's fire-support ships were at their stations off the beachheads and commenced firing. At about the same time, Admiral Turner's transport and tractor groups hove into view and headed for their predesignated areas. Soon after that, from the admiral's flagship came the order to prepare to land the landing forces. The operation was time consuming and complicated, but it had been carefully rehearsed.

At 0700, planes from TGs 2 and 3, together with escort aircraft, delivered intense strikes on and around the landing area. During this time the gun-support ships moved closer for an intense pre-assault close-range naval bombardment, which began at 0800. With precise care, the great and small guns walked their shells, step by step, over the entire sector. Special attention was given Agingan and Afetna points, which, because of their thick green cover, could shelter hidden defense positions.

Just as the guns elevated their fire inland to clear the beach, a low-level flight of about seventy planes clobbered the beach area again with a strafing attack that ranged from bullets to rockets. When this sortie ended—and considering all the hardware that had fragmented before—it seemed that nothing could have remained alive in that region of devastation.

Now the jumping-off point, as well as the boat lanes to the beaches, had shaped up under the keen eyes of Commodore Paul S. Theiss. From his flagboat the commodore directed the various control and guide units assigned to make sure that the proper boats reached their proper beaches by way of the proper lanes. There was one lane for each of the eleven beaches. Back of the starting point, the LSTs stood in line while their self-propelled cargoes wallowed out in the sea and headed for positions. On the quarter staff of all landing craft waved white flags with red, green, blue, or yellow stripes to denote which beach they were headed for. Each of the four colors represented from two to three beach sectors. The number of stripes on each flag indicated the particular beaches they were headed for. Thus, a landing craft with a flag showing three red stripes was headed for Red Beach Three. In the glitter of the morning sun on the calm sea, the scene looked much like a colorful water carnival. From the starting line, which ran about two miles from shore, moved a flock of Elsies (LCIs) transformed into gun and rocket boats. Their automatic guns and rocket launchers pointed shoreward, ready to down any enemy effort to make good on General Saito's promise that he would destroy all invaders on the beaches. In moments, the Elsies were followed by the first long wave of armored amtracs and LVTs. Ahead, nothing stirred.

The amtracs reached the coral reef and clawed their way to the coral top so that they could cross it and slide down into the lagoon. Suddenly, a withering artillery fire, combined with mortars and guns of smaller caliber, fell upon the entire length of reef from hidden, pre-sighted batteries on Agingan and Afetna points and other flanking positions. Heavier guns boomed from the reverse slopes in the hills and other points. Machine guns and assorted automatic weapons chattered. One particularly menacing weapon was a big-bore antiboat gun that fired from surface level at point-blank range against the slowly crawling amtracs on the reef and literally bowled them over.

Although the reception was hot and wholly unexpected, amtracs that were able to move kept moving. They reached the beach, where bullets ripped through the air and mortar and artillery shells burst all around in precise patterns.

Many guns, whose firing revealed their whereabouts to spotters aloft or observers at sea, were blown up by counterfire or bombed by aircraft. But others, positioned in caves, were as invulnerable as they were accurate. Therefore, although the volume of fire was considerably reduced, it diminished slowly and continued despite the efforts of Navy gunners to stifle it. And yet, in the face of this determined opposition, long lines of landing craft discharged their passengers and turned back for more. Many vehicles were wrecked and many more were damaged. Many men were killed and many more were wounded. To give an idea of the massive flow of well-disciplined, courageous Marines onto the beachhead, more than 8,000 had been landed by 0900 with nearly 150 LVT(A)s operating as light tanks in support. Despite great difficulties, initial beachheads were established. Concentrated and constant enemy fire piled up casualties, as did a few less determined enemy counterattacks. Efforts to expand the beachhead one mile inland on D-day made very unsatisfactory progress.

Agingan Point, which took a heavy toll among the 4th Marines, was taken that afternoon soon after 4th Division tanks came ashore. Another daring tank drive by the 4th—to take Mount Fina Susu, the day's planned objective—failed when it was found that the tanks could not negotiate the steep mountain sides. Due to heavy fire, the hole where the Marines sought shelter was found untenable, so they retreated to a better one a good quarter-mile nearer the beachhead. Meanwhile, the 2nd Marines were also making progress, storming part of Afetna Point with bazookas, flamethrowers, and grenades. Other D-day objectives captured by the 2nd included the airstrip north of Charan-Kanoa and the radio station to the east of the village; also, they pushed a good half-mile inland.

By sunset some 20,000 men, the day's quota, had been landed; and about 2,000 casualties, many more than anticipated, were taken off the beachhead. This, too, was one of Admiral Turner's new departures and instigated by Major General H. M. Smith. On previous landings the wounded had been cared for under crude combat conditions on the invasion beaches until the shooting died down. There would be no more of such inhuman treatment "Terrible" Turner and "Howling Mad" Smith agreed. Though it would be no picnic for wounded men to be transported from Saipan, they would benefit—if they could get back to the transports—from better medical care and comfort pending the arrival of fully equipped hospital ships. Credit must be given here to coastguardsmen who manned most of the landing craft on which the wounded were evacuated from Saipan, as well as the transports that carried them to the island.

Among the dead and wounded were a larger than usual percentage of officers. It has been said that D-day on Saipan caused more casualties among Marine lieutenant colonels and majors than were incurred on any other day of battle in the annals of the Corps.

Off San Bernardino Strait, about 1,260 miles west of Saipan, cruised Commander R. D. Risser in SS *Flying Fish.* Careful to avoid being seen by enemy surface vessels or plane patrols, he looked westward for the Japanese fleet and to the east for a sister submarine, *Cavalla* (Lieutenant Commander H. J. Kossler) who was to relieve him. After weeks of patrolling, *Flying Fish*'s oil was running low. Then, from the west, Ozawa's Mobile Fleet—carriers, battleships, and all—emerged from the Strait. The ships were too numerous, the light too dim, and *Flying Fish* too far away for her skipper to make a real count, but it was obviously a carrier-battleship fleet in full strength. He watched as the stately vessels plowed away on a course slightly north of east, turning up about 20 knots. As soon as he dared, Risser surfaced and transmitted the much-awaited news to Pearl. The date was 15 June 1944.

ComSubPac wasted no time in relaying the message to CincPac, who alerted Admiral Spruance. That same night the *Seahorse* (Commander Slade Cutter) sighted smoke and masts some 200 miles east of Surigao Strait and about 300 miles south of San Bernardino Strait. These were Admiral Ugaki's ships coming up from Batjan. Not risking a closer look for fear of discovery, Commander Cutter put enough distance between himself and the fleet to allow him to surface in safety and to transmit the following message: "Task force in position 10–11 N(orth); 129–35 E(ast). Course north-east. Speed 16.5 knots. *Seahorse* trailing." The flash reached Pearl without delay, but in forwarding it to Admiral Spruance it was found that the Saipan area was saturated by enemy jamming of such intensity that the admiral did not receive the information until 0400 on 16 June. Topping that bad break was *Seahorse*'s inability to keep up with the enemy because of engine trouble.

Now the basic picture was clear, although several vital details were lacking. The two enemy fleet components would rendezvous, but when and where? Would they be delayed by refueling and for how long? Would they approach the Marianas in one solid unit or would they, in line with Japanese naval tradition, split up, so that while one group made a head-on charge the other made a flanking turn?

After reading the signal from *Seahorse,* Admiral Spruance had good reason to congratulate himself on the foresight he had shown the night before when he initiated orders for Admiral Clark to strike the Jimas on 16 June and return at once. Jocko Clark's task groups had made better time than expected. On 15 June there was plenty of daylight left for a surprise strike when he reached launching distance to his three targets. On all seven carriers pilots boarded planes, became airborne, and soon disappeared in the distance. On their return it was found that the day's score included 10–12 intercepting Zekes and 28 planes wrecked on the ground. During the night a young typhoon howled into the region. On the morning of 16 June, winds were too high for flying, but after lunch they abated to a mere gale. Planes took off and the pilots took their objectives by complete surprise. Nobody on those islands had believed it possible that aviators would, or could, fly on a day when even flying fish remained submerged. Their reward was some sixty planes reduced to scrap; airfields and fuel dumps so thoroughly blasted that it would take many days before planes from Japan could be staged south through the Jimas again. After a harrowing time recovering planes on the windy carrier decks, the task groups turned south to rejoin TF 58. Their mission had been accomplished with a loss of only four U.S. planes.

At Saipan, the night of 15–16 June had its share of excitement, tensions, and dissatisfactions. At sea, TF 58 was attacked after dark by a formation of fighters and torpedo-bombers sent out from Guam and probably based in the Palaus. The Zekes were detected by radar and intercepted by night fighters and Hellcats in the CAP. Eight of the Zekes were downed. But the torpedo-planes, by flying below radar level, approached unseen. Sighted when within torpedo distance, they ran into heavy AA fire. Though they made a determined attack and sent some torpedoes dangerously close to some of the carriers, not a single fish hit anything. Our task-force gunners, however, knocked out seven torpedo-planes of the brand-new Francis type.

On land, the Marines had lots of work and little sleep in guarding against and blocking night attacks, of which at least three were of major caliber. But the Marines, with occasional help from gun-support vessels lying offshore, beat them back. Both the 2nd and 4th Marines were targets of these attacks. An outrageous masquerade was staged during the night by Japanese infantry to hoodwink the 4th Marines. The enemy soldiers advanced behind a shield of Saipan natives—men, women, children—who piteously offered to surrender. Discovering what was afoot, the Marines lobbed some well-placed howitzer shells into the tightly clustered mass of soldiers behind the civilian shield. And the masquerade was over.

In the flag-plots of Admirals Spruance, Mitscher, and Turner staff discussions ranged till far into the night, from how to deal with Admiral Ozawa when he was located to critical comments on the inability of air strikes and naval gunnery to silence Japanese batteries on Saipan before the Marines landed. It was felt by some that more time should have been allowed for pre-invasion air attack and naval bombardment. These had been planned on the premise that after four days of air attack and two of naval cannonading Japanese gun resistance would be smashed. On the surface, and without applying the wisdom that comes with hindsight, this seems reasonable. The carefully preserved silence of batteries in more or less invulnerable positions was largely responsible for this survival of gunpower. As for Admiral Ozawa, it was estimated that he might be in launching position as early as 17 June but certainly by 19 June. What troubled Admiral Spruance most were the methods Admiral Ozawa would employ if he took the offensive.

One thing seemed certain: There would be a showdown with the Japanese Fleet. To prepare for it, the invasion program underwent some swift changes. Admiral Turner was informed that air support for the Marines would have to be limited to his own escort carriers. The screens in TF 58 would be beefed up by vessels from TF 51's gun-support groups; also Admiral Turner's battleships would be withdrawn from Saipan to take station 25 miles to seaward to deal with enemy task groups if they should attempt to attack the American beachhead. To speed the hour of Saipan's surrender, the 27th Division would be landed that day (16 June) and Admiral Conolly's in-

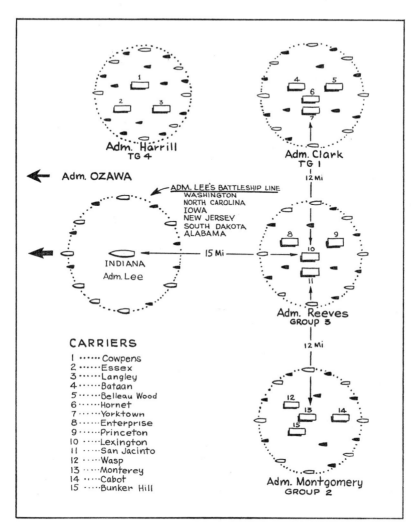

CARRIERS

1 ······Cowpens
2 ······Essex
3 ······Langley
4 ······Bataan
5 ······Belleau Wood
6 ······Hornet
7 ······Yorktown
8 ······Enterprise
9 ······Princeton
10 ······Lexington
11 ······San Jacinto
12 ······Wasp
13 ······Monterey
14 ······Cabot
15 ······Bunker Hill

*Task Force 58 in formation for the first battle of the
Philippine Sea, also known as the Marianas Turkey Shoot:
In the lead is Admiral Lee's force of battleships, cruisers,
and destroyers, flanked by Task Group 4, whose planes
provided Lee with air cover. Astern are three carrier task
groups with Flagship Lexington (10) in the center. The
circular battle "wheels," with carriers in their hubs and
fire-support ships on their rims, provided the best defense
against air attack.*

vasion fleet, cruising off Guam, would not land troops on 18 June as planned but stand by as a force in reserve. On 17 June, transports would break off unloading operations and return to waters east of Saipan for safety.

Meanwhile on Saipan, resistance would flare up, die down, and flare up again, which did not hinder the continuous flow of Marines to the beachhead. That afternoon, when all Marines were ashore, the 27th Infantry followed far into the night, until the GIs, too, had reached the beachhead.

At his headquarters on Hill 500 near the center of the island, General Saito had brewed a dish of double trouble for the Marines. He served it just before dawn of 17 June in the shape of a tank attack on land and a counter landing assault at sea. The latter was composed of infantry who were floated down on barges from Garapan and inside the coral reef that flanked the entire coast. This enterprise died aborning. It took more metal and muscle to drive back the general's attack, but 28 of the 44 tanks he sent into action were destroyed. From that point on, major resistance at the beachhead was a thing of the past. But much blood was still to flow on rough and rocky Saipan before the Japanese would be beaten.

During this time—from 15 to 17 June—Admiral Spruance looked vainly for Admiral Ozawa's fleet. By day, submarine officers swept the ocean with with their periscopes. By night, on the surface, bridge personnel and lookouts scanned the sea while overhead radar probed farther than eyes could see. Seaplanes and long-range patrol planes extended their search patterns almost to the point of no return. But the Japanese fleet was not sighted.

Then, about midnight 17 June came word by way of Hawaii. Earlier, *Cavalla,* sailing on her maiden patrol to relieve *Flying Fish* at San Bernardino Strait, had sighted and reported Japanese fleet oilers, which she had been ordered to track, attack, and sink. But she never caught up with them. Commander Kossler continued his patrol, hoping that he might strike oil again. He struck something much bigger than that. At 2015 the sub's radarscope indicated the approach of a large force. Soon the boat's sound gear heard their fast screws. Kossler was on the spot. He had been ordered to hit the oilers. Did this new situation call for attack and report, or vice versa? The commander decided that at this stage a report of the enemy's position was of paramount importance. He quickly submerged to safe depths. Shortly, he was literally run over by a huge fleet. Those aboard the sub tried to estimate the size of the force by counting and classifying the sounds made by heavy, medium, and light propellers as they drummed past overhead. The count was 15. Later, Commander Kossler surfaced to report, and soon all American commanders concerned knew the size, course, speed, and position of one enemy unit. Putting these bits of data together, they figured there would be a lapse of about twenty-four hours before Admiral Ozawa could be in a position to strike.

At Pearl Harbor, Admiral Lockwood looked at his chart and speculated on an invisible trap placed by him some 500 miles due west of Saipan. It covered a square area of 60 miles to each side, each of which was patrolled by four "invisible" submarines, *Albacore, Stingray, Finback,* and *Bang.* Acting on a hunch endorsed by his staff, ComSubPac moved his trap about 250 miles southwestward to a similar area, nearly 600 miles due west of Guam. The submarines that formed the trap had instructions to shoot on sight. The whereabouts of the enemy was no longer a mystery.

One of the weakest parts of Operation A-GO was the belief that the Americans would never suspect that it was, to a large degree, built upon strong support from land-based aircraft.

Just why Admirals Toyoda and Ozawa did not anticipate destruction of land-based aircraft and air facilities by TF 58 planes is not known. But whatever the reason, it was not a good one. As already noted, Admiral Spruance took planes and installations in the Jimas off the active list on 16 June. On that same day, despite vigorous AA fire, TGs 2 and 3 gave airfields on Tinian and Guam another of the many poundings that began on 11 June. So far as Aslito Field on Saipan was concerned, though not in American hands until 18 June, it could not be used after 11 June as a base for Japanese fliers.

The heads of the Combined and Mobile fleets were well aware of these interdictory measures, which posed a serious threat to Admiral Toyoda's concept that land-based planes—of which he had fewer as each day went by—would account for at least one-third of American losses. Perhaps he depended too heavily on planes from Truk, Yap, and the Palaus, perhaps even the Jimas. He may also have depended heavily on Japan's amazing ability to restore cratered airfields to useful status in next to no time. There were two reasons for this: plenty of manpower and a handy and good supply of dirt. Owing to the light construction of Japanese planes, they did not require strongly surfaced runways as did America's much heavier planes.

Admiral Kakuta, on the evening of 17 June, staged two air counterattacks. One, out of Truk, hit and damaged slightly a tractor group in Admiral Conolly's attack group off Saipan. Another, from Yap, bombed some of Admiral Turner's service vessels and escort carriers. Although there were thirty U.S. casualties, no irreparable damage was done to the escort carriers; but the hull of one landing craft was so holed that she had to be scuttled.

It could be that the inflated victory reports sent in by Admiral Kakuta—three or four task-force carriers sunk—helped distort estimates of the situation in Tokyo and aboard the CV *Taiho*. At any rate, no changes in operational plans were suggested. Admiral Ozawa made his rendezvous with Admiral Ugaki in the afternoon of 16 June, as planned, and refueled his fleet on that and the following day. At that time he was not quite certain that his entrance into the Philippine Sea had been accomplished "without leaving a trace."

While this was taking place east of the Philippines, Admiral Spruance prepared for action west of Saipan. On the afternoon of 17 June he announced his plan of battle, which was (1) to dispose of Admiral Ozawa's carriers; (2) to destroy the enemy's battle fleet. The exact procedures were left in abeyance pending further information. When the information arrived from *Cavalla*, it became obvious to the admiral that the Japanese fleet was not in a solid unit but divided into two sections. Not forgetting the Japanese tendency to use a straight lead to cover a flanking attack, the admiral had to ditch his personal desires for a naval slugging match. His orders expressly provided that his primary responsibility was to capture and control the Marianas. If the Japanese wanted a fleet-to-fleet showdown, they would have to start it.

Hence, when Admiral Mitscher proposed that TF 58 should go out, find the enemy, and confront him in a night gunnery engagement—followed at daylight by an air attack—the Fifth Fleet commander vetoed the proposal. In this Spruance was supported by Admiral Lee, who, with reasonable caution, said that he was opposed to night action because his personnel lacked training in night tactics.

The attitude was wholly different among Pete Mitscher's air admirals. To a man, they wanted to come to grips with the enemy. However, their enthusiasm did not budge the cautious Spruance. He knew that *Cavalla*'s estimate of 15 ships meant that she had encountered only part of a fleet believed to number about 40 ships. Until the missing 25 vessels were located, the fleet commander must anticipate a two-pronged attack.

On 18 June increased Japanese snooper activity from Guam and Rota gave evidence of significant events to come. TF 58 search planes, venturing some 300 miles out, came near the enemy fleet, although some 60 miles short of sighting it. About noon TGs 1 and 4 returned from the Jimas and Admiral Mitscher, pursuant to orders issued by Admiral Spruance, made his battle dispositions. The program was for TF 58, with heavily reinforced screens, to stand out to sea on west-southwest bearings. At sunset, it would reverse course toward the Marianas. At sunrise on 19 June, the task force would once again turn about to see what contacts the day would bring forth. The reason for this shuttle arrangement was that Raymond Spruance did not want to give the enemy a chance to slip past him under cover of night. That was the way he wanted to play the waiting game until better information about the enemy was at hand.

Warfare is somewhat like a chess game in which the adversaries try to anticipate each other's moves. In this particular case, the admiral held his chessmen so ready and mobile that he could block his opponent no matter what his opening gambit might be.

The task force disposition consisted of five groups, the fifth being Ching Lee's TG 7 of battleships, cruisers, and destroyers. Like the carrier TGs, Admiral Lee's vessels were in a circular formation about 6 miles in diameter. In the center was his flag aboard BB *Indiana.* About 15 miles east of TG 7 was the wheel of Admiral Mitscher's TG 3, some 4 miles in diameter. Approximately 12 miles to the north of Pete Mitscher was the wheel of TG 1, and, 12 miles to the south was TG 3. This line of carrier groups ran north-south for a distance of 36 miles. TG 4, assigned to provide air and antisubmarine cover for Ching Lee's TG 7, was 12 miles north of the latter. Admiral Spruance, aboard CA *Indianapolis,* rode in the screen of Admiral Mitscher's task group within easy voice-communications reach of the latter's flagship, CV *Lexington.*

With all groups holding station and all personnel ready to respond to the call of battle stations, the armada held course at west-southwest. But as the sun went down no calls had been heard, and the Mobile Fleet had not been sighted by search planes ranging 300 miles southwestward. There was, therefore, little chance of Admiral Ozawa meeting up with TF 58 during the night. With the neat precision born of good seamanship, the Force reversed course for the Marianas.

Some 3,500 miles away at Pearl Harbor, Admiral Nimitz had kept his sensitive fingers on the pulse of events. To aid him in that, he had powerful Huff-Duff radio direction-finder stations in Hawaii and elsewhere. They listened incessantly for and to radio signals. The head-quarters of the CincPac came alive that 18 June evening when the sharp ears of the HF/DF system caught a signal from the Philippine Sea. The source was determined to be the Mobile Fleet, and its cause a radio message from Admiral Ozawa to Guam. The exact spot of the radio emanation was learned, and a quick check on charts revealed that it was about 300 miles west-southwest of TF 58's last known position, namely the point where it reversed course.

Admiral Nimitz notified Admiral Spruance at 2200 about the HF/DF finding. When informed of this, Admiral Mitscher, following a staff conference, called the Fifth Fleet commander by TBS radio phone and proposed to turn about at 0100 and launch planes at daylight. Saying that he would think it over, Admiral Spruance discussed the matter with his staff.

Meanwhile, radio operators aboard CA *Indianapolis* had intercepted a message from ComSubPac to SS *Stingray* asking Commander Loomis, her skipper, to repeat a message garbled by what appeared to be jamming. Keen-nosed staffers, knowing that *Stingray* was one of the four submarines in ComSubPac's "invisible trap" and knowing the trap's location, assumed that *Stingray*'s message dealt with the sighting of the enemy; next they determined that the submarine's position was about half the distance from the Mobile Fleet of the 300 miles estimated by Huff-Duff. In other words, chances were that the enemy fleet, or elements of it, were much closer than realized. If that were the case, Pete Mitscher's plan for heading toward the enemy at 0100 to reach attack position at dawn posed a grave risk that should not be taken. In advising Admiral Mitscher of this decision, Admiral Spruance concluded with: "End run by other carrier groups remain possibility and must not be overlooked."

And thus a 1,500-ton submarine unwittingly influenced the action of TF 58. Who can say what would have happened if the interception of a message to her had not muddled up the situation. The sad truth was that a fire in *Stingray*'s superstructure was the subject of Captain Loomis' message. Later, he woefully noted that while he was gum-shoeing around for the Japanese the *Stingray* stood on the surface lit up in the night like a lighthouse.

About the time that Admiral Mitscher would have turned to meet the enemy, a PBM search plane, far to the southwest, counted forty pips on its radar screen—a ship for every pip. A radio message was flashed at once to base, 600 miles away, but it was never received.

Only when the search pilot, Lieutenant H. F. Arle, returned to base at dawn did his discovery become known. But by then his news was stale, because the early phases of battle were developing.

By dawn, TF 58 was from 150 to 175 miles southwest of Saipan. Standard patrols—search, antisub, and combat air—were launched early. The Force stood westward again at 0619 at 22 knots, but although every vessel in it made good speed, the Force virtually stood still. The lack of progress was the result of frequent reversals of course to launch or recover planes. This disadvantage, brought about by the east wind, was a modern version of not having the weather gauge, as it was known in the days of fighting under sail, when being upwind of the enemy was a vital factor.

The Mobile Fleet, after refueling from tankers on 16–17 June, was divided into a van force, headed by Vice Admiral Takeo Kurita, who had 3 light carriers, 3 battleships, 5 cruisers, and 10 destroyers. The remaining two carrier divisions, consisting of 6 carriers, 2 battleships, 8 cruisers, and 15 destroyers, were in the main force. The Mobile Fleet's air arm totaled 430 carrier craft, exclusive of 43 floatplanes.

During the night, Admiral Kurita's van force broke away from the rest of the fleet; at sunup 19 June, Admiral Kurita was 100 miles to the northeast of Admiral Ozawa. Several hundred miles away, Task Force 58 was steaming on its westward leg when it was discovered by search planes from Admiral Kurita's van. Some of these tangled with TF 58 dawn patrols and were shot down. The first contact had been made. After receiving dawn reports from his search pilots, Kurita closed the gap between his unit and TF 58 to about 300 miles.

Admiral Kurita knew that the distance between the opposing forces gave Admiral Ozawa's main force a great advantage; 300 miles was beyond maximum combat range of American carrier planes, whereas Japanese planes could cover it easily. This differential in performance did not mean that the Japanese had superior planes. It was due mainly to the extra weight of American planes by the addition of such protective features as self-sealing fuel tanks, bulletproof canopy glass, and built-in armor.

At 0830, on orders from Admiral Ozawa, the first attack wave—45 Zekes with 500-pound bombs, 8 torpedo Jills, and 16 Zeke fighters—was launched from CarDiv 3 in Admiral Kurita's van force.

Chapter Six

THE MARIANAS TURKEY SHOOT

ALERTED TO THE ENEMY'S PRESENCE on the morning of 19 June, TF 58 was making 24 knots to westward, striving to come within 200 miles' striking distance. At 1000, Admiral Mitscher's radars showed pips of approaching bogeys—distance: 150 miles. Throughout the Force, squawkboxes bleated standby for battle. Deciding that he would rather have his fliers spend gasoline in combat than in flying far out to engage the foe, the admiral's order remained "steady as you go" for the next twenty minutes. Then he went about and nosed his flattops into the wind.

This, however, was not the first activity of the day. About 0600, DD *Stockham* of Ching Lee's TG 7 was the target of a bomb-carrying Zeke, probably based on Guam. The bomb missed, but the gunners aboard DD *Yarnell* scratched one Zeke. Soon after this, a bogey was discovered over Guam. Four planes were vectored out of *Belleau Wood's* CAP. On arriving at the scene the Hellcatters found that the bogey had become bogeys, which sprouted into numerous Japanese planes taking to the air from Orote Field. "Hey Rube" calls for help were sung out by the Hellcats. But before reinforcements could reach them, the four fighters had either shot or driven the enemy planes to the ground. But that was not the end; Guam was destined to be a center of mass Hellcat and bomber attention throughout the day. Next event was ushered in when a number of bogeys came in from Truk or Yap. Three dozen Hellcats formed a reception committee that knocked out 30 fighters and 5 bombers. The battle might have lasted longer, but the sighting of Admiral Ozawa's first attack wave on radar screens made it mandatory to deal with first things first. Fighters were recalled from Guam, others were launched from all carriers. Bombers of all types, loaded with fuel, were sent aloft to circle to eastward. Later they were vectored against Rota and Guam. In the carrier groups, decks were cleared for the backbreaking task of taking fight-

92

ers aboard, refueling, and rearming those that could continue to fight; damaged aircraft were lowered to the hangar deck to await repairs or to be tossed into the sea if beyond repair. Deck crews, made up of blue-clad plane handlers, catapult men in green, and fire fighters in asbestos suits, were at their stations.

Upstairs, Hellcats were scurrying for ceilings of 25,000 feet. About 50 miles out, enjoying full advantages of altitudes above the enemy and with their backs to the sun, American fliers began the biggest show yet staged in the Pacific. Pete Mitscher's fighters plummeted upon the Japanese airmen in the first wave. The attacking formations were split apart; violent multi-plane and individual dogfights were staged between Hellcats, Hamps, and Zekes; bombers went down in flames, but a few succeeded in slipping past the Hellcats and roared toward the fleet to lay their explosive eggs. Some of these intruders were shot down from above by CAP fighters; others were shot up by gunnery ack-ack from below. Within a half hour 27 Zekes and Jills had been destroyed. So much for the first wave.

Wave number two came rolling in about 1140, a big one of 47 Zeke fighters riding shotgun for 61 Judy dive-bombers and Jill torpedo-bombers. It was halted by a withering fire of .50 caliber bullets. Fliers returning to CV *Taiho,* Admiral Ozawa's flagship, were shocked to see heavy columns of smoke rise from their carrier and were directed to land on other flattops.

While Admiral Ozawa's Carrier Division 1 was launching its second attack wave, his ships had, unknowingly, barged into Admiral Lockwood's invisible submarine trap. At 0750, *Albacore* was running at full speed submerged, trying to close on a group of ships that included a carrier, which she had sighted at long range on the horizon. Suddenly her skipper, Commander J. W. Blanchard, discovered a second group, also containing a carrier, approaching. This second force was headed so as to pass the submarine at an ideal firing range of about 1,500 yards at a speed of about 27 knots. Captain Blanchard, determined to get that carrier (which was the 31,000-ton *Taiho*), managed to avoid a cruiser and a destroyer that nearly got in the way. At 0808, he upped periscope for a final sighting and issued orders to stand by number one tube.

At that instant, it was discovered that the very important Torpedo Data Computer was out of order. With the target moving at 27 knots there was no time to make manual corrections, so the skipper did the only thing he could do—fired all six bow tubes hoping that at least one would hit. The first four streaked harmlessly astern of Admiral Ozawa's flagship. The fifth was seen by a Japanese pilot, who swiftly tipped his dive-bomber into a suicide plunge that ended when the plane hit the torpedo. Thus Ensign Sakio Komatsu became one of Japan's unscheduled Kamikaze pilots. But his sacrifice was in vain. The sub's sixth torpedo hit the *Taiho* well forward, but the *Albacore,* hard-pressed to escape the destroyers that rushed upon her, did not linger to observe results. Instead, she went deep and did not see the fires that broke out on the carrier.

While *Taiho* was fighting fires and hunting subs, the attacks upon TF 58 continued. Wave number three was trimmed down to 7 Jills and 40 Zekes; 25 of the latter carried 500-pound or lighter bombs. They were discovered about noon. Because of confusion brought about by changes in orders, about half the planes turned back. The rest tangled with a batch of Hellcats, lost 7, and ran for base.

The fourth wave—40 Zekes and Tony fighters, 27 Vals, 9 Judy dive-bombers, and 6 Jills—came in at 1306. It split into two groups, neither of which did very well. Six Judys attacked TG 3 and did little damage; one got away. Hellcats reduced 14 Zekes to 7. Some 40 Vals and Zekes that had mislaid their target tried to land on Guam, where they tangled with 27 Hellcats. Nineteen Japanese planes landed but were too shot up ever to fly again. The rest were gunned out of existence.

Unhappy landings also awaited the pilots of the CV *Shokaku.* Five minutes after she had sent her fourth wave fliers away, an unseen submarine delivered a load of fish that stopped the carrier. The torpedoes came from Commander Kossler's *Cavalla,* which had sighted, reported, and lost a unit of fleet oilers, and later reported the speed, course, and numbers of an enemy force while she remained discreetly submerged. On each occasion Commander Kossler had had to forego the pleasure of taking torpedo action. But this time things were different.

Twice that morning Commander Kossler had sighted planes. And, out in the middle of the Philippine Sea, where there were planes there had to be carriers. After a careful search by periscope he sighted a 30,000-ton *Shokaku*-class carrier at about 1100 while she was sending planes aloft. Because of this, the carrier—escorted to port by two cruisers and one destroyer to starboard—would have to hold a steady course.

After taking a second swift look, Captain Kossler lowered his periscope and instructed *Cavalla*'s Talker to pass the news about the target topside. Showing as little scope as possible, Herman Kossler made his approach. The cruisers remained to port and out of the way, but the destroyer was still on vigilant patrol between *Cavalla* and the carrier. At 1,500 yards, Kossler started a spread of six torpedoes. Four were on their way when the wake of the first was discovered by the destroyer, which instantly came barreling down on *Cavalla* at flank speed. To avoid being sunk, the sub's skipper went deep, but as he started down he fired the last two forward torpedoes in quick succession. Seconds later, depth charges exploded around the submarine, but above their detonations could be heard the louder ones made by three torpedoes that reached their mark. Of the 105 depth charges counted, fully half were near misses, which—as any submariner knows—is too close for comfort. When he contacted Pearl that night, Commander Kossler reported the attack and the damage caused to *Cavalla,* and added laconically, "Believe that baby sank."

He was right. She did.

When the battle started, Admiral Ozawa had 430 carrier planes, including 222 fighters, 113 dive-bombers, and 95 torpedo-bombers. Admiral Mitscher had 891 carrier planes, including 475 fighters, 232 dive-bombers, and 184 torpedo-planes. Mitscher's air arm outgunned the enemy in quality as well as in quantity. According to an official action report:

> The Zeke can outclimb the F6F-3 (Hellcat) and is more maneuverable, but the F6F-3 is considerably faster, being able to out-dive the Zeke and catch it or out-run it in level flight. The F6F-3 is more rugged and the six .50 caliber m/gs seem to deal a more fatal blow to a Zeke than the 20mm cannon and 7.7 mg (on a Zeke) do to a Hellcat.
>
> The quality of enemy pilots engaged in this action seems to run from very good to very bad. Some Zeke pilots combine daring and good judgment with proficient flying technique while others appear to be confused or frightened.

Because many of the enemy pilots were inexperienced, the Japanese air strikes were poorly executed and coordinated. Although the Japanese launched four major attack waves during the day, together with numerous smaller raids, most interceptions took place some 50 miles west of TF 58. Of the hundreds of planes hurled against Pete Mitscher's ships, about 40 got as far as the task force.

For the American pilots, who defended their vessels so well, the long day was a kaleidoscope of individual duels and combat incidents.

In the ready rooms of Air Group 10 on CV *Enterprise,* aviators waited for the squawkboxes to sound the call: "Pilots, man your planes." Suddenly they heard the click that announced circuits were open and someone was going to speak.

" 'Morning men! Here's some news!" The voice belonged to Commander Thomas L. Hamilton, air officer of the Big-E and one of the most popular men in the Tailhook Navy. "We are going to give the Japanese emperor half of the Pacific Ocean." Another pause. Confused murmurs in ready rooms. Then: "Yes, boys, we'll give him the bottom half!"

The outburst of cheers and laughter that greeted this was stilled moments later when the squawkboxes clicked again and a sonorous voice droned: "Pilots, man your planes."

Three smart fighter pilots of AG 31 CVL *Bataan* were on submarine patrol in the early forenoon when the first enemy raid was heralded by radar. Over their intercoms they heard scramble flights being launched on all 15 carriers. Their requests for permission to join the interceptors were granted. Led by Lieutenant (jg) D. R. Rehm, Ensigns C. G. Miller and W. A. McCormick climbed to 25,000 feet from their 500-foot patrol level and headed out on the vector given for the bogey. About 40 miles from base, they saw what seemed to be 100 enemy planes about 10 miles away at 23,000 feet. Already on hand, or coming up fast, were other Hellcats. Watching the approaching enemy closely, Lieutenant Rehm saw three Zekes pull out of the formation to port, and the trio went for them. Rehm picked and downed the left Zeke, Miller did the same to the right Zeke, but McCormick was unable to get a clear shot at the center Zeke.

There was a big dogfight in the making, and the sight of burning planes attracted other Hellcats. Suddenly the sky seemed full of F6s chasing Zekes or vice versa. None of the three *Bataan* pilots wanted any of that Donnybrook. Instead of dogfighting, they sat on top of the heap and picked targets as they came along. At any rate, that was the basic idea.

After having been squeezed out of firing position on his run on the center Zeke, Ensign McCormick picked out and hit a Judy. That done, he returned to the top of the heap, took a look around, and saw a flight of six Judys being harried by several F3s. One Judy pulled out. Quicker than a flash, the ensign dived, fired, and saw it flame. Seeing another one 1,000 feet below, he swooped upon it to discover that only three of his guns were firing. Even so, he saw his tracers go in and watched the plane go down.

Back on the top of the hill after his first run, Lieutenant Rehm saw three Zekes at 23,000 feet. He dropped on their tails, flamed one, pulled out sharply, and climbed above the melee. Seeing two Zekes below, he swept at them in a wide turn. One pulled up; the other plunged down in flames. The first Zeke started down on the Hellcat's tail, but seeing the danger in time, Lieutenant Rehm nosed over and outran him. Since he was low on gas, he headed for base.

After his first run, Lieutenant Miller also climbed to 25,000 feet again. The closest plane he saw was a Zeke 3,000 feet below and half a mile away. Doing a wingover to port, he tailed in behind the Zeke and fired from 800 feet. The Zeke did S-splits, but Miller, going too fast to follow this dodge, rolled over on his back and saw the Zeke in a vertical dive trailing heavy black smoke. Climbing once again, he presently saw three Zekes dash out on the other side of the dogfight. Pulling over on them, he came in astern of the port wingman. In so doing, he lost track of the starboard wingman but saw the leader pull up in a loop. Not liking the looks of things, he fired a short burst at his original target and dived away. At 15,000 feet he was joined by another F6, which turned out to be Ensign McCormick. Both were low on gas and headed home.

"The interesting part of these incidents," observed Lieutenant Commander J. C. Strange, commander of CVL *Bataan's* Air Group 50, in his report, "is that the three pilots, although they were split up during almost the entire action, had the presence of mind to pull out above the free-wheeling battle and pick their targets from the top layer. This probably had more than anything else to do with their coming off unscathed with six sures and at least two probables to their credit."

A four-plane fighter division, led by Lieutenant L. W. Abbott from the *Bataan's* Air Group 29, also saw plenty of action. At 0945, while standing CAP watch, Abbott's division was vectored out to check on a bogey some 30 miles away, found it to be a Zeke, splashed it, and returned to the humdrum job of CAP circlings. Within minutes they were vectored out again to intercept bogeys. An hour later and 45 miles from base, Lieutenant Commander Strange recalled the division

because they were getting low on gas. From 25,000 feet, in wide diving turns, Lieutenant Abbott led his Hellcats back. All were down-
hearted because they had not flushed a single enemy.

Suddenly, at about 10,000 feet, Lieutenant Abbott saw several
planes burning and hitting the water to starboard. A second look revealed two bandits at 2 o'clock below and evidently headed toward
Admiral Lee's battle line. Signaling his pilots, Lieutenant Abbott
peeled off to starboard. The two enemy planes, seeing the Hellcats
coming, parted company. One, a Judy, dived about 2,000 feet; the
other, a Zeke, kept altitude but turned to port. Chances are that the
play was to lure the F6s to hit the juicier Judy and ignore the Zeke,
whereupon the latter would dive upon them from above.

But if it was a trap, the *Bataan* fliers avoided it. As Abbott and his
wingman, Ensign F. V. Smith, went down to flame the Judy, Lieutenant (jg) P. C. Thomas and his wingman, Ensign E. R. Tarleton,
rushed toward the Zeke. Seeing what was coming, the Zeke pilot
nosed over and started to run. Down, down the trio went and soon
they were almost on the deck. The enemy pilot began a set of skillful
maneuvers. Whenever Lieutenant Thomas would get into firing position, the Zeke would pull up in a right or left wingover, then duck for
the water, but only for a second. Then he would come zigzagging up
again and go into a violent turn.

"It was," said Lieutenant Thomas, "like trying to catch a flea on a
red-hot griddle."

The Zeke's wing-dingings might have enabled him to escape except
for the arrival of four Hellcats. Now, everywhere the Zeke turned, he
found an F6 ready to make a run on him. The quarry thus hedged in,
Lieutenant Thomas delivered a good burst dead astern. The Zeke,
burning, tumbled toward the water.

A look at his fuel gauge told Lieutenant Thomas that unless he
headed for the hangar pronto he, too, would splash. But when he saw
a Zeke pursued by four Hellcats, he joined the party and became an
interested observer in an exhibition of aviation acrobatics that made
the first Zeke look like a novice. At 300 feet the pursued pilot executed fifteen slow rolls in succession; next he dived to about 50 feet
above the water and then jinked up and down between that level and
within 5 to 10 feet of the surface. It was precision flying of the high-
est order and probably the Japanese flier was hoping to lure one of
his tormentors into diving on him and falling into the sea. He would
occasionally pull into half-loops, fly on his back a brief instant, and

then pull up in an outside loop. Finally, he made the mistake of doing a full loop under 300 feet. He was caught by a burst of fire that flamed him just as he pulled out of the loop. It had been a good show, and when Lieutenant Thomas, nearly out of gas, landed on the nearest carrier, he learned that Lieutenant Abbott had downed the Judy and had barely made it to the same flattop.

It was after 10 o'clock when pilots from the CV *Essex* became involved in the battle. Commander David McCampbell, boss of Air Group 15 aboard the carrier, had ordered Lieutenant Commander C. W. Brewer at 0910 to take 11 of the 36 Hellcats in his VF 15 squadron aloft on combat air patrol over Task Group 4. Three of Lieutenant Commander Brewer's planes were vectored out 27 minutes later to find a bogey. Much to their disappointment, the pilots made a Tallyho at 0950 on a friendly TBF whose friend-or-foe signal had gone haywire.

Within the narrow spaces of the radar room, Commander McCampbell kept a watchful eye on the screen, which suddenly disclosed a faint and tightly packed bunch of dots. Admiral Ozawa's boys were on the way. The time was 1013, the bearing was 250 degrees, and the distance was 118 miles. Lieutenant Commander Brewer was instructed to take his remaining eight planes to 24,000 feet and stand by. Word was passed to the squadron's ready room for all available Hellcats aboard to prepare to take off. At 1025 the radar pips clearly showed a big batch of bogeys; it was designated Raid #1. Brewer and his two 4-plane divisions of fighters were vectored out to intercept the raid. At the same time Commander McCampbell had 4 Hellcats catapulted off the flight deck to fill the CAP gap left by Commander Brewer's departure.

At 1024, Commander Brewer and his 8 planes, circling overhead at a height of 4 miles, were sent out to intercept Raid #1, whose planes were now less than 100 miles from TF 58. Ten long minutes later came a shout from Brewer over the voice radio:

"Tallyho! Raid #1 bears on 255 degrees. Distance from disposition (the task force) 55 miles. Estimate 24 rats, 16 hawks, no fish at 18,000." In carrier jargon these identifications meant 24 fighters and 16 dive-bombers but no torpedo planes. Although outnumbered 5 to 1, this did not trouble the VF 15 fliers. Commander Brewer led the 4 1st Division Hellcats; the 2nd Division was headed by Lieutenant (jg) G. R. Carr.

The two divisions swiftly bracketed the enemy formation of the 16 dive-bombers, all Judys, still at 18,000 feet with 4 fighters (Hamps) on each flank. From 1,000 to 2,000 feet above and somewhat astern of this formation, a flight of 16 or so fighters (Zekes) weaved in very loose formation. The two Hellcat divisions started their runs almost simultaneously. (The Hamps, incidentally, had originally been dubbed Haps by our aviators as a goodwill gesture to AAF Commanding General Hap Arnold. They became Hamps when Hap Arnold declined the honor.) For his initial target, Commander Brewer selected the Judy that led the formation, disdaining the Zekes and the Hamps.

The dive-bombers were prime targets because their bombs posed a greater threat to carriers than did fighter bullets. Swooping down in a hawklike dive, Brewer held his fire until within 800 feet of the target. He then squeezed a carefully spaced burst from his six .50 guns. The target disintegrated in a swift, eruptive flash. Making better than 300 knots, the Hellcat was in and through the debris in seconds; its pilot pulled up shooting at another Judy. He saw his target lose half a wing, then flame and nose steeply into the sea. Spotting a Zeke from a corner of his starboard eye, Commander Brewer gave chase, overtook it, got on its tail, and closed to 400 feet as he fired. Hit in the wing roots, the plane blazed like a torch and spun down.

Commander Brewer blessed the water injection apparatus recently installed in F6F-3s to soup up their engines and add extra zip to their speeds. In very short order, he had reasons to bless it again when he matched performance with another Zeke which dived on him. They tangled in a dogfight that ended when the Hellcat climbed on the enemy's back and started clawing. With each burst from the Hellcat's guns, the Japanese pilot would maneuver violently—go into half rolls, stay on his back briefly, and either pull through sharply or gyrate into barrel rolls, wing overs, or cartwheels—all intended to shake the Hellcat off, but the F6 held on. Always alert against the chance that any one of these movements might terminate in a reverse that could put the Zeke into a position of attack, Commander Brewer sprayed bullets whenever his target was steady enough to hit; his tracers showed that he was placing shots into wings, fuselage, and cockpit, but the Zeke seemed to bear a charmed life. Finally, with vast relief, Commander Brewer saw flame lash out from the plane; the engine stopped and the Zeke, in a tight spiral, dived into the ocean.

While Commander Brewer's 1st Division rolled up a neat score,

Lieutenant Carr went Judy hunting on his own. The first Judy he shot at exploded into flame. Like Commander Brewer on his first kill, Lieutenant Carr was going so fast that he had to flash through fiery flotsam before he could pull into a wingover, at the top of which he spotted another Judy. A short, loud tattoo from the Hellcat's six heavy machine guns, caused the Judy to burst into flame and enter a corkscrew from which it never recovered.

Lieutenant Carr was suddenly aware that he had a Hamp on his tail. Before the enemy pilot could get into position, the Hellcatter went into a cyclonic 90-degree dive. As he watched his speed rise to 430 knots, Lieutenant Carr's windshield fogged badly, although the heater and defroster were on. When the ocean seemed to rise up to meet him, he pulled out. The Hamp was no longer in sight.

At full throttle he climbed and spotted another Judy, which he downed with a short burst into its engine. But just before his plane exploded, the enemy pilot got the range on the Hellcat's windshield. Had it not been bulletproof, Lieutenant Carr would have been a goner. Pulling up to avoid the debris, Carr saw two more Judys stealing off to drop their bombs on Pete Mitscher's carriers. They were well ahead of, and some 2,000 feet above, the Hellcat. He gave his engine all it could burn, reached a good spot, and let go all six barrels. Result: the leading edge of one enemy plane's port wing flamed. Carr skidded left, hit the other plane, and started a blaze just abaft the engine. The pilot, taking evasive action, dived, whereupon Lieutenant Carr followed with lightning speed. But the Judy exploded before he could get it into his sights.

By now, Lieutenant Carr was fairly close to the sea again. As he started to climb, the Hellcatter saw the first Judy splash. During his climb, Carr, with five Judys to his credit, counted 17 splashes and oil slicks on the water.

It was a happy homecoming for the men of CV *Essex*'s VF 15. The total score of the eight pilots was 21 planes—11 divebombers and 10 fighters. But before nightfall they had some sad news: Commander Brewer had been killed in combat over Guam.

What with so many Japanese and American planes in the air, ship's gun crews had some difficulty in telling them apart. This put a great strain on gun-control personnel.

At noon, forward antiaircraft gun controls aboard CV *Wasp* trained optically on two targets on the starboard bow at 20,000 yards. Sky Forward reported to Sector Control that they did not "look friendly." Sky Forward tracked the planes till they disappeared from view behind the carrier's superstructure. Another gun-control group picked the targets up. Now there were three, of which two were identified as friendly. Gun control was advised by sector control to keep their eyes on them and not to shoot unless they were sure that the planes were unfriendly. Suddenly, Sky Port Control uttered a wild yell and guns started slamming. The plane fell like a dead duck, but before that, its Japanese pilot had pulled his bomb release. A 550-pounder scored a near miss on the port bow just before the flaming plane hit the water 12,000 yards ahead of the ship. Aside from killing one man and wounding four, the fragments holed the carrier's hull in several places.

But more was to come. In midafternoon, seven to eight enemy planes scooted out of the blue and staged bombing runs toward the ship's starboard quarter. Their marksmanship was worse than their intentions. One small 125-pound bomb exploded about 200 feet off the port beam. Its spray of shrapnel injured four men. Fragments from other near misses hit the ship, and an incendiary cluster burst about 300 feet above the flight deck. The incendiary pellets danced all over the deck. Before those that exploded could do any damage, they were extinguished. But all afternoon deck personnel, as well as gunners, had to keep their eyes peeled for pellets lest they should step on one.

The officers and men in Admiral Lee's TG 7 also had a chance to show their mettle. During the first attack of the day, while steaming at 22 knots with the rest of the Force, the battleships and cruisers were targets that would tempt any bombardier until he ran into their heavy curtains of antiaircraft fire. A few got through, however, and dropped their bombs. One hit *South Dakota*, killed 27 men, and wounded 23. Near misses fell close to the cruisers *Minneapolis* and *Wichita*. Though attackers got into TF 7's wheel, they did not live to get out of it.

"The battle . . . was undoubtedly the greatest carrier action fought to date and the most one-sided." So observed Lieutenant Commander C. L. Moore, commander of *San Jacinto*'s Air Group 51 and its fighter squadron, in the action report. Almost all attacking aircraft were destroyed. Damage to the *San Jacinto* was nil; damage to our planes was negligible. For the most part, Japanese attacks were intercepted and broken up before the enemy could get into the screen. A few did penetrate and made attacks on the Force. TG 3 (*Enter-

prise, Lexington, San Jacinto, and *Princeton*) was attacked by at least six torpedo-planes. AA got four of them.

"Enemy planes, almost without exception, on receiving .50 fire in the vicinity of the engine, burst into flames," continued Moore. "At the height of the battle Commander Air Group 51 saw 12 planes burning on the water in a relatively small area while our aircraft circled overhead apparently without serious damage. Japanese pilots were reported to be inexperienced, inferior gunners and were inclined to separate and engage singly."

In order to give readers a running description of activities aboard a carrier under virtually constant combat pressure for hours on end, and the vital roles radio and radar played in finding and fighting the enemy, the following portion of the CV *Essex*'s Action Report is presented. Among other things, it reveals the close teamwork between carriers striving to sink the enemy before he came too dangerously close to the vulnerable carriers.

D Plus 4   19 June

0820 Several bogies 170°-75 miles on course 080°, evidently headed for Guam. Faded from our radars at 0829. Dispositions to south of us may have attempted interception, but no evidence.

1013 Large bogie 250°-118 miles—designated Raid One—closing.

1022 Eight *Cowpens* VF vectored to intercept Raid One—estimated altitude 22,000 feet now bearing 254°-93 miles.

1024 Eight *Essex* VF vectored to intercept Raid One, altitude 24,000 feet.

1035 *Essex* and *Cowpens* planes Tally-Ho on Raid One at 255°-55 miles. Estimated fifteen to eighteen Judy's—20,000 feet.

1047 Few bogies now 260°-20 miles and 220°-18 miles. Evaluated as few Bandits from Raid One and designated Raids 1A and 1B respectively.

1048 Vectored 4 *Essex* VF on Raids One A & B—low. Fighters fired upon by T.G. 58.7.

1050 Few scattered single bogies 210° to 250°, 15 to 30 miles.

1100 Screen clear of bogies.

1109 Large bogie 250°-112 miles presumed to be in momentary orbit. Designated as Raid Two.

1117 T.G. including *Essex* opened fire on one plane from south—no definite indication as enemy. Plane turned away.

1123 Raid Two closing—now 250°-108 miles.

1126 Vectored 12 *Essex* VF, at 24,000 feet on Raid Two.

1130 Raid Two—245°-88 miles—estimated twenty planes at 20,000 feet.

1139 Tally-Ho by twelve *Essex* VF on Raid Two at 248°-60 miles—reported 30–40 enemy planes, mostly Judy's at 18,000 feet.

1142 Vectored 14 *Cowpens* VF to assist against Raid Two, due to report of number of Bandits.

1146 *Essex* VF leader reports leader and wing-man of Raid Two, along with many others, already shot down. Does not believe any will get through.

1151 Few bogies, low, 230°-30 miles, evaluated as VT from Raid Two.

1153 Few bogies split and designated as Two Able at 245°-23 miles and Two Baker at 221°-30 miles.

1154 Vectored 3 *Essex* VF intercept Two Able—low. Vectored 4 *Essex* VF intercept Two Baker—low.

1156 T.G. 58.7 firing—evidently at Two Baker.

1158 Few bogies at 350°-35 miles designated Raid Three.

1159 *Cowpens* VF diverted from Raid Two to Raid Three.

1204 Raid Three faded from screens at 298°-28 miles and never materialized. *Cowpens* VF recalled after orbit and search.

1208 Single bogies reported—but all outside 25 miles.

1211 Screen momentarily clear of all bogies. All airborne VF recalled for landing.

1225 Large bogie 295°-110 miles designated Raid Four.

1238 Raid Four orbiting at 312°-100 miles. T.G. 58.1 vectoring VF toward it.

1239 Large bogie 275°-105 miles designated Raid Five.

1248 Raid Four in orbit at 325°-85 miles. T.G. 58.1 VF on vector towards it.

1300 Raid Four closing, now at 330°-53 miles. Vectored 12 *Langley* (low on fuel, at 22,000 feet) to assist VF of T.G. 58.1 if necessary.

1306 Raid Four Tally-Hoed by *Hornet* VF who attacked and presumably dissipated it. *Langley* VF, on vector, ordered to orbit.

1314 Raid Five now in orbit at 285°-63 miles.

1316 Four *Langley* VF and four *Essex* VF joined and vectored to intercept Raid Five.

1322 Raid Five appeared to open again—now at 270°-75 miles. Eight VF ordered to resume and orbit base—12,000 feet.

1340 Bogey at 287°-60 miles designated Raid Six.

1341 Vectored eight VF to intercept Raid Six.

1342 Raid Six showed momentary friendly indication.

1354 Raid Six identified as friendly by VF.

1449 Large Bogey 200°-135 miles designated Raid Seven.

1515 Raid Seven now 195°-55 miles, split with both parts on course east towards Guam.

1600 Possible bogey, single at 342°-27 miles crossing from West to East.

1601 Vectored 4 *Essex* VF to intercept above bogey—this target continued to cross and VF were recalled at 1617 with bogey at 305°-55 miles.

1606 Twelve *Essex* VF on sweep at Guam report many enemy carrier type planes being shot down—presumed to be Raid Seven.

1805 Many bogies 205°-85 miles designated Raid Eight on course for Guam. Indications of interception by T.G. 58.2.

1810 *Essex* VF on second sweep over Guam given range and bearing of Raid Eight from them and alerted for approach.

1825 Raid Eight Tally-Hoed by *Essex* VF over Guam—splashes reported.

2114 Snooper, single bogey 210°-65 miles on course 000°. Proceeded to 270°-35 miles and then turned west and faded at 290°-55 miles at 2200.

American pilots who were downed during the battle had a slimmer than normal chance for survival. In order that antisubmarine patrols from TF 58 would have no doubts as to the identity of submarine targets, ComSubPac had withdrawn all subs from the area surrounded by the task force. Thus, no submarines were on hand to help rescue downed American pilots and aircrews in that particular sector.

However, radiomen in the CIC watched the IFF emergency band with steady attention. IFF is a radio device that gives a steady signal identifying the plane that sends it as friendly. When such a signal comes steadily from a fixed position, it is easy to deduce that it comes from a plane no longer in flight. The next step is to determine its position and send a destroyer or floatplane out to the downed pilot and pick him up.

Unfortunately, in some cases, the IFF was shot up or did not function. In many instances fliers, later reported missing in action, were last seen on rafts by squadron mates, who flew down to the sea with them and radioed for help. They would circle over the downed flier to guide destroyers or rescue planes. In some cases this effort bore fruit; in other instances, guardian pilots, running low on gas, had to leave their comrades and return to base lest their tanks run dry. An act that was almost equal to a death sentence for the downed pilot.

The Japanese, however, suffered many more losses. There are many versions of how this, the greatest air battle of the war, came to be known as The Marianas Turkey Shoot. One has it that a Hellcatter from the deep South remarked to his plane captain as he returned from an interception, "Boy, this sure makes me homesick. 'Tis jest like a ol'-fashioned turkey shoot."

Ensign Wilbur B. Webb of CV *Hornet*'s VF-2, for example, bagged six "turkeys" within the space of a few moments over Agana Airfield on Guam. Ensign Webb caught up with a formation of six Zekes as they prepared to make a left turn to circle the field prior to landing. The Japanese pilots, who were in line, didn't bother to look behind them. Webb joined the formation, snuck up on the last Zeke, and fired. When the Japanese plane spun down, he moved into its position, and shot down the next plane. And so it went, plane by plane, until Webb sat right behind the leader. When that unfortunate pilot turned around to give the breakup signal, he looked straight into the six .50mm machine guns on Webb's Hellcat. Webb fired and the sixth Japanese plane followed the others.

Lieutenant W. E. Lamb, one of the high guns in Fighter 27 on CVL *Princeton,* also had a profitable day at the turkey shoot. Having already blasted one Zeke, Lamb was roaming the skies for more game, although only one of his .50 guns was able to shoot. He came upon twelve unescorted enemy Kates (torpedo planes), making for TF 58 and previously unreported. Lieutenant Lamb flew formation on the Kates while he reported their location, course, and speed to base. He knew it would be only minutes before a flock of F6s—a carrier term for the F6F-3 Hellcat—would be crowding in like buzzards

Left, at his headquarters in Australia General MacArthur points out his proposed route for reaching the Philippine Sea while Admiral Nimitz looks on. MacArthur favored an approach via the northern coast of New Guinea and the Moluccas; Nimitz preferred the Central Pacific route through the Gilberts, Marshalls, and Marianas. (U.S. Army)

Below, landing from the huge maws of an LST, U.S. Marines beach a jeep at Cape Gloucester on the northwest tip of New Britain. The 1st Division went ashore on 26 December 1943. From strategic points such as this, MacArthur hoped to leapfrog his forces to the Philippine Sea. (U.S. Coast Guard)

Photos courtesy of U.S. Navy unless otherwise indicated.

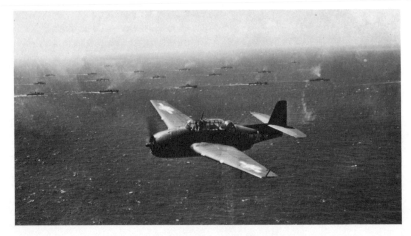

A carrier task force in Admiral Spruance's Fifth Fleet steams toward Tarawa in the Gilbert Islands on 14 November 1943. Tarawa was sought as an air base for further operations against the Marshalls and eastern Carolines. In the foreground a Combat Air Patrol plane watches for enemy planes and submarines.

On 31 January 1944, Task Force 58, under Admiral Marc Mitscher, invaded and captured Majuro Atoll in the Marshalls. Above, Mitscher's fleet is shown in the Majuro anchorage, some 2,000 miles west of Pearl Harbor.

Carriers of Task Force 58 at anchor off Majuro. In the foreground is the carrier WASP. *Behind her are* YORKTOWN, HORNET, HANCOCK, TICONDEROGA, *and Mitscher's flagship,* LEXINGTON.

Commodore W. R. "Nick" Carter headed Service Squadron 10, a mobile Navy base for repair, provisions, fuel, and ammunition. By establishing advance bases in the Marshalls, the distance to the Marianas was reduced by 2,000 miles.

*Marines approach the beach on Saipan, largest of the
Marianas, on D-day, 15 June 1944. (U.S. Coast Guard)*

Admiral Mitscher's attack on the Marianas began with a two-day air strike at dawn on 22 February 1944. Above, men aboard the carrier BELLEAU WOOD watch their gunners down a Japanese bomber.

Snipers' bullets down two Marines on the beach at Saipan. In spite of heavy mortar and artillery resistance, some 20,000 Americans landed there on 15 June. (U.S. Coast Guard)

A curtain of ack-ack is sent up to protect the amphibious attack force from enemy air raiders during Saipan invasion. (*U.S. Coast Guard*)

Strategically situated on the beachhead, this sugar mill smokestack became one of the landscape's deadliest features during the battle for Saipan. The Japanese used it as a spotting post to pinpoint artillery. (U.S. Coast Guard)

A lone fighter returns to the LEXINGTON *flight deck during the first battle of the Philippine Sea on 19 June. Known as the "Marianas Turkey Shoot," the battle was fought exclusively by carrier planes.*

Vice Admiral Marc A. "Pete" Mitscher, commander of Task Force 58, aboard the LEXINGTON off Saipan during the "Marianas Turkey Shoot." In two days Allied planes destroyed 400 Japanese planes and 2 carriers plus a couple of oilers. Allied forces lost 106 planes and no ships.

In mid-August of 1944 Admiral William F. Halsey (left), commander of the U. S. Naval forces in the South Pacific, took over Admiral Spruance's Fifth Fleet in the Central Pacific. Renamed the Third Fleet, it began to pave the way for the Philippine invasion by attacks on the Palaus. Halsey is shown here with Commander Joseph Clifton of the SARATOGA.

Rockets are launched against Peleliu, best defended of the Palaus, before American invasion. Twenty-five thousand Marines went ashore on D-day, 15 September 1944.

Amtracs, armed craft that can fight on land or sea, lead the invasion of Angaur Island, six miles south of Peleliu, on 17 September.

Top left, heavy guns on board the battleship IOWA *hurl tons of steel over the Philippine Sea during Admiral Halsey's campaign to soften up the islands for MacArthur's invasion.*

Top right, the fourth wave of GIs hit the beach on Leyte, the Philippines, on 20 October. By midnight of 21 October 132,000 American troops had landed on the island. (U.S. Coast Guard)

Bottom, soldiers build a sandbag pier from the Leyte beach to the landing ramps of two LSTs loaded with supplies and fighting equipment. (U.S. Coast Guard)

U.S. coastguardsman gives drink of water to GI wounded by shrapnel on Leyte beachhead. (U.S. Coast Guard)

On the afternoon of A-day, homeless but happy Filipinos swarm on to Leyte beach to greet their American liberators. (U.S. Coast Guard)

Probably shot down by the jeep carrier in the foreground, a suicide plane plunges toward the sea, dangerously close to the carrier it was intended to hit. This picture was taken on 25 October 1944, the day of the first Kamikaze attacks.

Commander in chief of the Japanese Mobile Fleet, Admiral Jisaburo Ozawa set to sea from Japan to lure Admiral Halsey away from the scene of action at San Bernardino Strait. This he managed to do, but only at great expense. On 25 October Ozawa lost all four of his carriers.

With secondary guns elevated for antiaircraft action, two of Admiral Oldendorf's battleships, PENNSYLVANIA *and* COLORADO, *escorted by cruisers* LOUISVILLE, PORTLAND, *and* COLUMBIA, *enter Lingayen Gulf to support the invasion of Luzon. In Surigao Strait, Oldendorf's six elderly battleships had crossed the "T" of the Japanese fleet under Nishimura, thus turning powerful broadside guns to the approaching enemy ships.*

Thick black smoke rises from fleet oiler MISSISSINEWA *in Ulithi anchorage on 20 November, two months after American forces had captured the island. The attacker, a two-man suicide Japanese submarine, was quickly torpedoed by a U.S. destroyer.*

Rescue boat of Admiral Kinkaid's Seventh Fleet gets under way to aid crew of ship hit during Kamikaze attack in the Mindoro invasion, 15 December 1944.

In a last-ditch effort to revive their air power, the Japanese sacrificed pilots and planes to crash 500-pound bombs onto the decks of American ships. This Kamikaze, shot off course by a stream of bullets, swerves to starboard astern the carrier SANGAMON.

on a dead horse. Deciding to seize the opportunity, he waded in with his single gun and knocked three of them down.

Ensign R. W. Matz of Fighter 1, *Yorktown,* had an even hotter time. With his VF division, the ensign was going into a starboard turn when he saw a Tony coming in a head-on dive. Doing what for him was the natural thing—intercepting the interceptor—he pulled up to meet the onrushing Tony with full engine power of 2,550 rpm. Aiming swiftly, he sent a bunch of tracers into the wing roots of the enemy plane. In a fraction of a second a blinding sheet of flame stood where the Tony had been. Ensign Matz' momentum carried him into and through the flames, which were so bright that he had to close his eyes. And because his canopy was slightly open, a wave of heat, hot as steam, poured into the cockpit. To cool off, Ensign Matz went into a glide. At 10,000 feet he saw three Zekes; two were being chased by a Hellcat. He dived on the third and hit the gas tanks. There was another hot explosion, which the F6 pilot narrowly dodged. A few minutes later, while Ensign Matz was under attack by two Zekes and a Tony, two F6s made a timely rescue by driving off the Zekes. The Tony, standing his ground, pulled up, rolled over the Hellcat from above, and attempted a head-on attack. Just before he dived to avoid it, Ensign Matz blipped a short burst that hit the Tony's engine; it flamed and fell out of control. Having had enough hot sessions for one day, Ensign Matz revved his engine and darted away just in time to avoid another encounter with an exploding plane.

While on CAP over the airfield at Gurguan Point on Tinian Island with two 4-plane Hellcat divisions, Lieutenant Commander R. W. Mehle, CO of Air Group 28, CVL *Monterey,* roamed the skies at 12,000 to 15,000 feet. Suddenly, he saw 7 Bettys and 1 Zeke circling to land on the field. He held off attack until all planes were down; then, by 2-plane sections, they came hurtling on them. As they neared the ground, the Hellcatters saw fliers and aircrews rush from their planes almost before they rolled to a stop. Seven Bettys and one Zeke were chalked up as kills.

Mehle, who doubled as boss of VF 28 as well as of Air Group 28, also had a busy day defending the *Monterey.* At one point, a formation of Jills came within fairly close range of TF 58. A few more miles and they would be able to drop their torpedoes. To deal with them, Mehle led three 4-plane divisions off the *Monterey's* deck. After a short run, Commander Mehle and his wingman, Ensign G. J.

Barnes, spotted two Jills about 150 feet apart. They swung into right-hand climbing turns to get astern of the Jill on the left whose gunner was strewing bullets in their path. A burst at 1,200 feet from Commander Mehle's guns silenced him. Seconds later, the Jill torched into a nose dive from which there was no recovery.

The other Jill took advantage of the attackers' pre-occupation to slide into a fast dive toward TF 58, now only 10 to 15 miles away. Gunning their engines to full speed, the Hellcats hightailed after the escaping Jill. Commander Mehle caught it in his sights in full dive and fired at 1,500 feet. While the plane flamed, two other Jills—more dangerously close to the Force than the two already downed—came into view on Commander Mehle's right. He made a fast side-run on the nearest, started shooting at 900 feet, and saw the Jill roll over in front of its own wingman's plane. They collided and fluttered toward the sea in a two-for-one splash.

While the boss was at work, the other Hellcats had disposed of two more Jills and one Zeke. There being no other enemy planes around, the torpedo threat had been eradicated, so Commander Mehle and his fighters made for their flattop.

One of the most valuable men that day was Lieutenant (jg) Charles A. Sims, who did not participate in the actual fighting. A member of Mitscher's staff, Sims was in close touch during the battle with Admiral Ozawa's air coordinator—without the latter's knowledge. Early in the day, radiomen on CV *Lexington* had located the channel over which the air officer issued orders to his various groups. A student of Japanese, Lieutenant Sims performed a valuable service by translating all the orders so that flag-plot was forewarned of Japanese moves. When, toward the end of fighting, a staffer proposed to the admiral that someone should go get Ozawa's coordinator, Pete Mitscher replied, "No, let him be. He did us a great deal of good."

The curtain fell on the last act at dusk when a large group of enemy planes tried to land on Guam, only to run into stiff opposition. Throughout the day, combat air patrols circled over airfields on Guam and made it hot for Japanese pilots, who perhaps hoped to make shuttle-runs according to schedule. They also acted as cover for bombers who blasted away at airfields at a fairly steady pace. All in all, the Japanese fliers accomplished little and hundreds of them paid with their lives. It is claimed that TF 58 fighters downed 366 enemy planes. To these, add 19 shot down by task group gunners and 17 destroyed on the ground.

The *Taiho* went down at 1532. Shortly before that, Admiral Ozawa had ordered his Mobile Fleet to head on a retiring course northwestward. Then he, with members of his staff, boarded a destroyer from which he later transferred to the heavy cruiser *Haguro*. In doing that, Admiral Ozawa virtually cut himself out of communication with the rest of his fleet. The cruiser had none of the *Taiho*'s elaborate command-communications equipment. One of his three remaining large carriers would have been better for that purpose, as would Admiral Kurita's command-cruiser *Atago*. But, for reasons known only to himself, the admiral boarded the *Haguro* instead.

Despite his losses, Admiral Ozawa was ready to resume the fight. But his combat information was either wrong or incomplete. Though he was aware that plane losses had been great, the admiral believed that many planes, then unaccounted for, had landed on airstrips. The loss of two huge carriers was, in his mind, offset by pilot reports of four TF 58 carrier sinkings and six flattops blazing like bonfires—all untrue. Moreover, Admiral Ozawa was confident that land-based bombers and fighters would reach the Marianas and be ready for action when, after refueling from oilers, the Mobile Fleet would resume battle on 21 or 22 June.

Full realization of the scope of his defeat did not reach Ozawa until a fleet-wide radio inventory disclosed that only 100 battle-ready planes were at his disposal. As night fell and search sweeps failed to reveal any pursuit, the admiral concluded that the Americans were licking their wounds and too weak to start a stern chase. Throughout the following day, he was uncertain as to when to refuel. In midafternoon, he decided to do it at 1645. But at 1615 Admiral Kurita sent him disquieting news. Radiomen in the *Atago* had intercepted a signal which indicated that an American search plane had sighted the Mobile Fleet. Admiral Ozawa canceled the refueling order; he also scuttled his program to resume battle and steamed at flank speed for Nakagasuku Bay, Okinawa. Had Admiral Kurita had his way, the fleet would have refueled earlier in the day and squared away for the homeland. That would certainly seem to have been a safer and better course to take in view of what was to follow.

Chapter Seven

MID-OCEAN STRIKE AT DUSK

OFF THE MARIANAS, after Admiral Mitscher had completed recovery operations and reported himself ready to be under way, Admiral Spruance had taken TF 58 in pursuit of the Japanese Fleet. Throughout the night the Force plowed steadily west and northwest at 23 knots. Realizing that Admiral Ozawa had a good head start, and loath to sacrifice time and mileage by turning into the wind to release and receive search planes, Admiral Mitscher sent up only a few night search planes and restricted day searches on 20 June. As the hours wore on, airmen and carrier deck crews grew increasingly eager to man planes and start engines. The air victory had been won at relatively small cost: 27 lives and 29 planes. The few enemy planes that had evaded fighters and succeeded in penetrating TF 58 gun curtains had inflicted no major damage on vessels, although they took 33 lives. To be sure, no one in TF 58 knew that the enemy had only 100 battle-ready planes; nor was it known that the *Taiho* and *Shokaku* had been torpedoed by subs and that some 3,000 men went down with them. The only American eyes that saw the Mobile Fleet that day were those of submarine commanders Blanchard and Kossler. But neither of them knew, until much later, that their torpedoes had sent both of these carriers to the bottom.

The tension of long waiting and wondering in TF 58 was shattered at 1542 when a signal from a search plane came in. Although it was badly hashed up, it conveyed the impression that the enemy had been sighted. On that assumption, Admiral Mitscher made plans to send planes aloft. At 1605 an intelligible report placed the enemy 275 miles to the northwest and a deckload of planes got rolling; at 1615 the distance was corrected to 370 miles. Even with belly tanks, installed during the night, this 740-mile round trip was more than short-legged planes could travel without reversible tail winds and angels stretching the fuel. By then, however, nearly 85 fighters, 77 bombers, and 54 torpedo-planes were aloft. In the *Lexington's* flag-plot, recall

110

was debated but vetoed. It was held that, by pushing the Force at full speed after the planes, enough distance could be gained to cut the return flight by 75 to 100 miles. Thus, if they spent twenty to thirty minutes over the targets, the airmen could just reach their carriers.

Admiral Mitscher's fliers zeroed in on the Mobile Fleet at 1840 with only twenty minutes of daylight left. This had to be a hit-and-run attack. There was no time for an organized mission. On the other hand, the enemy—although forewarned—was not too well prepared. A search flight was just landing on the *Zuikaku* after having failed to discover the Americans. Some Zekes were airborne. By dogged determination, the Japanese launched 75 planes from carriers whose decks were being swept by bullets and ricocheting bomb fragments. Attacking Hellcats were met by unexpectedly strong opposition. Meanwhile dive-bombers zoomed on carriers from above; torpedo-planes, swooping so low that they almost skimmed the sea, raced toward the sides of flattops to release their lethal fish. These targets, however, were far from stationary. They swished in S-turns or swirled in circles, and well-served guns produced torrents of fire.

The attack was delivered with blinding speed. A start-to-finish firsthand story of that eventful and dangerous mission is told by Admiral Arnold, who, as commander of Air Group 2 of CV *Hornet,* led his deckload of 14 dive-bombers, 13 fighters, and six torpedo-planes into the battle and home from it.

> At about 1600, all Task Group Commanders were directed to launch the first deckload. At this point, I was spotted on deck in the number one position and looked towards Primary Flight Control for the blackboard notation which would give us the last range and bearing towards the enemy. In place of range, a latitude and longitude were posted. As all pilots made the plot and measured the distance, they realized that with the speed of advance estimated for the enemy we would be pursuing them beyond the range of our aircraft and so far as our capability to return to our ships. We were under radio silence, but one could hear the microphone buttons click as various of the pilots apparently picked up the mikes to voice their surprise or objections—but not a single voice was heard. With the signal to launch aircraft, we looked at one another, gave a thumbs-up signal, and shoved off headed west.
>
> I throttled back immediately on takeoff, and gave the signal for a running rendezvous in order to conserve gas. With a slow climb, we headed due west and the Air Group was com-

pletely rendezvoused within about 30 minutes. After reaching
about 10,000 feet we leveled off, leaned our mixture out, and
I proceeded to move ahead with several fighters to scout out
the situation.

The flight to the target was probably unparalleled in the
history of naval aviation. Each pilot knew that the target was
beyond the combat radius of our planes. I had decided that if
the enemy fleet finally was discovered even further west than
originally plotted, it would be best to pursue and attack, retire
as far as possible before darkness set in, notify ship by key,
and then have all planes in the group land in the water in the
same vicinity so that rafts could be lashed together and mutual
rescues could be effected. When the target was found at about
300 miles it was decided that the best gamble was to have the
pilots in groups attempt to return to the ship in hopes of saving some few planes.

The approach towards the target was made with the *Yorktown* group in company. Transmissions from each of the
Group Commanders from the other task groups could be
heard approaching the target. It was apparent, as we neared
the target, that the Japanese Fleet was divided into three
groups. By listening to transmissions from the other group
commanders, I determined that they were going to attack the
southern group (3 AO, 3 GA, DD) and the western group (5
BB, 2 CV [*Hitaka* Class], 2 CVE [*Ryuho* Class], several CA and about 4 DD).

My primary concern was to avoid overlooking the third
enemy group of ships, so that no group would get away un-
damaged. This had happened in the battle of the Coral Sea to
old Air Group Two.

As our Air Group approached the Japanese Fleet Units,
our presence was acknowledged by an increasing array of
antiaircraft bursts, some white, some pink, but increasing to
the point where it appeared the planes were almost floating on
small white and pink clouds. The carriers and cruisers began
to maneuver circles and S turns making patterns in the sea below, while to the west the sun was setting.

By scouting ahead of our approaching group I had an opportunity to see all three groups, and immediately ordered the
attack on the northern group consisting of 1 CV (*Zuikaku*
Class), about 10 CA and CL, and about 14–16 DD. Since no
fighter opposition was in evidence our fighter-bombers were
first to attack. The bombers were all ordered on the large CV
as were the torpedo planes (VT).

It was a little disappointing that some VT had been loaded with 4–500# G.P. as all hands in the VT squadrons had been looking forward to the day they could put a fish in the *Zuikaku* or *Shokaku*. It is believed a better loading would have been fish for all VT planes.

The torpedo planes with bombs could not go in with the bombers because of steepness of the dive angle and so had to follow them. Since our primary mission was to knock out the enemy carriers, it would appear that torpedoes would have been more appropriate. Glide bombing a maneuvering ship is extremely difficult.

The attack executed by the bombing squadron was superb. Of the first six planes to dive, I observed one carrier hit in the center of the deck forward of the island structure and five near misses so close the splash could not be observed. The second division of nine planes came down so fast it was almost impossible to count the hits. I counted to seven and saw no splashes, so estimated the other two were either hits or very near misses.

Upon completion of the attack, and as darkness was setting in, I gave the rendezvous signal and proceeded on a dead reckoning course to attempt to intercept our carriers. My radio transmitter had been shot out, although my receiver was working. But, I was unsuccessful in attempting to turn the lead over to a young ensign who had joined up for the return flight. The young pilots always seemed to assume that the Air Group Commander would lead them home, radio or no radio.

As planes began to join up en route back to the carriers, I gave the close-up signal in order to attempt to count the aircraft accompanying me and to observe those that I was certain would go down for lack of fuel somewhere on our return trip. I gave a visual signal to my wingmen to lean back the mixture control, and then paid attention to my navigation and attempted to verify the intensity of the wind over the water to improve my dead reckoning track. Complete darkness was with us at this point and I received my first report of an aircraft making a forced landing in the ocean. I plotted his position, but was unable to acknowledge because of my transmitter and the same thing occurred many times that night.

In all, 7 fighters, 2 torpedo planes and 12 dive bombers from the *Hornet* Air Group splashed before we reached the carrier area. There appeared to be some confusion in the Task Force as signals were first given to the Destroyers to make smoke. This probably was because they felt we were lost. It would have been a fine signal in the daytime, but at night it only added to the intensity of the darkness and almost screened the ships from view.

Finally, much to our surprise, there were many searchlights flashing in the sky. As we flew overhead and identified our respective carriers, I noticed that my gauge was reading empty but decided that some of the boys were in a worse position. I gave the break-up signal and led the first group down into the groove, after which I waved off and let the others land and tried to lead some of the stragglers back to the carrier. After some time had lapsed, the carrier notified me that I could land aboard but that due to deck crashes, only one arresting cable remained intact. I approached for a straight-in approach, receiving the wands from the Signal Officer, and was told that I was the only aircraft in the air. Much to my surprise, a shadow of an aircraft appeared in the line of vision between the Signal Officer and myself. Immediately the Signal Officer appeared to give a wave off. I was not sure whether the wave off was for me or the unknown aircraft, but decided to take it and land in the water alongside.

As I applied the throttle the engine quit while I was some 50 feet in the air over the ramp. I pushed the nose of the Hellcat over and dived for the deck. At the same time I hit one brake in an attempt to loop the aircraft into the walkway to keep it from going up the deck into the parked aircraft. I was successful, and as the plane started over the side in a tail first position, the raised 40 mm gun mounts alongside the deck stopped the aircraft from going over the side.

Some 10 or 15 of the Flight Deck crew hung onto the wing while I climbed out of the cockpit up to the flight deck with chart board under arm. As I reached the flight deck, they let go of the plane and it went over the side—with my film of the battle! I proceeded to the bridge with my chart board and plot of aircraft down and delivered it to Admiral Jocko Clark. After a brief report, I went below for a sandwich and swig of "tea." It had been six hours since takeoff.

After rescue operations were completed the next day, our total losses were one bomber pilot and crew member lost in combat, and one bomber crewman lost in the water landings.

Although Arnold's group from the *Hornet* did not meet fighter opposition, other members of the attacking force did. In making a fast out from a brawling dogfight way up in the clouds, Ensign C. S. Beard of AG 50 on CVL *Bataan* found himself hurtling seaward in a spin. As he rotated he saw a Zeke zoom past him, pull up sharply, flip right around on his tail, and start down again in the ensign's invisible wake. Knowing that a Hellcat could outdrive a Zeke, Ensign Beard stopped his spin, nosed down to pick up speed, and pulled up straight toward the onrushing Zeke. Aiming at the spinner cone in the center of the Zeke's propeller, he held his trigger in a long, steady burst. As the Hellcat stalled out the Zeke whizzed past some three feet away. Feeling sure that his tracers went in, Ensign Beard nosed down to take a look. Another Zeke, boring in for a kill, started by shooting his radio aerial off. Instantly cured of all curiosity about that other Zeke, the ensign ran to take cover in a cloud.

The Zekes pounced upon the Hellcats with greater ferocity and determination than were shown by Japanese pilots during the battle the previous day. Lieutenant (jg) V. Christensen of VF 24, CVL *Belleau Wood,* tangled with one and scored a probable. However, his plane was so mauled in the process that there was nothing left for him to do but to run for home base and hope to reach it. His rudder cables, radio, and compass had been shot away; his right aileron was ripped and hydraulic system ruptured; his fuselage, tail, and wings were badly holed. But his crate seemed to hang together, and to compensate for Christensen's lack of navigational ears and eyes, Lieutenant (jg) P. C. Roger indicated that he would lead the crippled Hellcat home. After a grueling flight, Lieutenant Christensen limped into *Belleau Wood*'s landing circle. This is defined by a run along the length of the ship out beyond the bow, a turn across it, and a second turn to fly down the other side of the ship and beyond the stern; then a third turn to come in line with the center of the carrier's stern, followed by a fourth to slip into the landing groove that leads to the flight deck and the landing-signal officer.

What with rudder and ailerons gone, doing these turns would not be easy. But Lieutenant Christensen trimmed up plane with the rudder tab and found it worked reasonably well. Next he set full rudder tab as he entered the landing circle. Up one side of the carrier, across the bow, down the other side, toward the wake, and into the groove. He made it! Lieutenant Christensen watched the wand of the landing officer for the signal that would take him in. Instead, he received a wave-off. Again he weaved around the landing circle. Another wave-off. This was followed by a third and then a fourth rejection. On the fifth approach the LSO slashed a wand across his throat signifying "cut your engine and glide in." Christensen chopped his throttle and made a good landing. He climbed out, patted the side of his Hellcat gratefully, and headed for the island structure, debriefing, and chow. At the island entrance he turned just in time to see the deck crew rolling his Hellcat over the side.

It takes a lot of something or other to silence the guns, even temporarily, of a carrier that is fighting for its life during an air attack. That something or other was possessed by the members of a four-plane division of VT 28 off CVL *Monterey*. It was made up of Lieutenant (jg) P. G. Pennoyer, Ensigns R. W. Burnett and T. G. Dreis, and Lieutenant R. P. Gift, commander of AG 10's torpedo-bombers. Instead of torpedoes, each of these planes carried four 500-pound bombs.

Below them, three carriers were milling around, bow to fantail. A battleship and a cruiser circled around them, as did six destroyers. From 10,000 feet the quartet glided to 6,000 and pushed over to dive across the deck of the carrier. During their approach, the guns of the flattop had been tossing up a lot of hardware. But the Avengers came in so fast and dropped their bombs so accurately that their fragments must have driven all gunners under cover. At any rate, the flattop, which had been lit up by flashing guns a few moments earlier, suddenly went dark. Lieutenant Gift opened the show with three bombs that struck the flight deck just aft of amidships. Lieutenant Pennoyer also scored three hits on the deck; Ensign Dreis had two near misses and two hits near the stern; and Ensign Burnett's four bombs hit squarely on the after end of the flight deck. As the TBMs pulled out, all four turret gunners—and radiomen doubling at the belly stingers—drenched the entire topside of the carrier with a torrent of machine-gun bullets. Having performed their mission, the four planes retired in a southeasterly direction. The carrier was seen to burn fiercely under a plume of bloodred flames, apparently from a large oil blaze. All but Ensign Burnett put down on CVL *Monterey*. He ran out of gas while circling in the traffic pattern, made a water landing next to a destroyer, and was rescued with all hands.

During the action above the enemy fleet, Lieutenant (jg) R. C. Tabler and Ensign H. M. Barr, both Hellcat pilots in CVL *Belleau Wood*'s Fighter 24, were giving protection to each other after ending a dogfight at 14,000 feet. Suddenly, they found themselves attacked by another Hellcat whose trigger-happy pilot saw enemies at every hand. During this mix-up, a Zeke tried to get in on the action, whereupon Lieutenant Tabler took time out to splash him. Ensign Barr, having shaken off the F6, saw tracers going by and discovered a Zeke on his tail. As he pulled up and away, he noticed another F6 scoot out of a cloud with two Zekes crowding close. Waiting until the Zekes came within range, he gave them the works. Next, looking down, he saw Lieutenant Tabler with a Zeke getting into position behind him. Ensign Barr went into a steep dive, intending to blast the Zeke. Suddenly, an earsplitting crash and a trembling plane proclaimed that he had been hit.

Fire broke out in the Hellcat's cockpit. Out of a corner of his eye, Ensign Barr saw a plane a little bit behind him, but he was too busy to wonder whether it was friendly or not. Having no way to go but out, Ensign Barr went into a dive, leveled off at fairly high altitude, and made ready to go over the side with a fairly good chance of chuting into the middle of the Japanese fleet. He loosened his seat straps, opened the cockpit hatch, and swung one leg over the side.

The other leg was just about to follow when a flock of tracers rushed past. At that instant the fire in his cockpit flickered out. He climbed back into the plane, went into another dive that led from the battle area, and looked around. His wings and fuselage had been badly chewed up by heavy machine-gun blasts. The fire was out, but two or three inches of gasoline sloshed around in the cockpit, an open invitation to another blaze. The engine was percolating but missing. He gave it more throttle and it helped. Sparks were flying from under the port wing, which hung on by a hair. Barr was in a serious predicament, but found solace when he saw Lieutenant Tabler flying alongside. The latter flew wing to wing with him as Ensign Barr descended in an easy glide lest he lose a wing; getting his tail down, he landed on the water and stepped into the sea from the rapidly sinking Hellcat. Lieutenant Tabler saw his comrade inflate his small raft, crawl into it, and pull in his back pack. There being nothing else to do, Tabler returned to the wars.

After a benumbing and sleepless night, made miserable by chilling rain, Barr saw a large flight of American planes in search of Admiral Ozawa. They did not see him. Some time later, when the flight returned, they also failed to see him, although one F6 was within 500 feet. Barr waved, shouted, and swore at the plane. Then he put out a sea anchor, opened his fishing kit, baited a hook with pork rind and tossed the line into the water. Presently, he fell asleep.

In the early afternoon Barr was awakened by the throb of a Hellcat engine. He sat up and saw an F6 weaving along near the surface and almost up to him. The pilot spotted the raft and circled while four floatplanes came up. One landed, took Ensign Barr aboard, rejoined the rescue team, and headed for the now vacant scene of action. There they picked up seven survivors.

One thing had griped Ensign Barr throughout that long night. He got it off his chest in the report he made soon after he landed on his carrier.

"I am certain," he stated, "that the plane which shot me down was an F6. The damage done [to the plane] could only have been caused by .50 ammunition." Lieutenant Tabler, who was present, verified the statement. Ensign Barr also reported that he had seen fish, 6 to 8 inches long, near his raft, and added sadly, "But they would not bite on the pork rind."

Three Avengers from CVL *Belleau Wood*'s Air Group 24, with fish in their bellies, dived through the cloud layer that stretched over Admiral Ozawa's fleet. They streaked toward a *Hayataka*-class carrier (the *Hiyo*). In the lead flew Lieutenant (jg) George P. Brown. He was followed in close order by Lieutenants (jg) B. C. Tate and W. R. Omark. As they approached the target they widened out to give their torpedoes broader spreads. Ahead, behind, and around them, carriers, battleships, cruisers, and destroyers were staging a pyrotechnical display that was as spectacular as it was deadly.

Lieutenant Brown, making for the carrier's bow, was getting into torpedo-run position when a section of his port wing was torn away and shell fragments raked his plane from nose to tail. Flames leaped from his port wing-tank and shot toward the center section where Radioman E. C. Babcock and Gunner G. H. Platz were at their stations. The pilot ordered them to jump, and jump they did. With flame and smoke enshrouding him, Brown zipped toward the carrier. Perhaps his airspeed blew out the flames; at any rate, they died as he dropped his torpedo, which was seen to hit the target's bow. He pulled out and flew down the length of the carrier, over the blazing gun mounts and out of sight.

Seconds later, Lieutenant Tate dropped his fish, broke off to the left, and retreated between the carrier and a nearby battleship, both firing furiously. His torpedo exploded amidships. Tate's plane got in the way of a few near hits, but he escaped injury. Following Lieutenant Tate closely, Lieutenant Omark made his run through the increasingly vicious crossfire and dropped his torpedo, which found its mark about halfway between midships and the carrier's bow. After that Omark made a fast retreat.

Climbing from the target, Lieutenant Tate discovered that the trigger mechanism of his wing guns on the top of his control stick had been smashed; gunner J. R. Dobbs reported that the turret gun had jammed. At that awkward moment, Lieutenant Tate spotted a Zeke on station to port and slightly above him. The situation was exactly the same to starboard. Lieutenant Tate was well bracketed. A short distance off, but a good climb ahead, he saw a large cloud. Being a good poker player, Tate decided to run a bluff. Keeping wary eyes on the Zekes, he began to climb. When one Zeke would start to peel off, the Avenger pilot would turn toward him with guns that could not shoot. Unaware of this empty threat, the Zeke pilot would return to station. The other enemy flier reacted the same way when he became combative and Tate showed him his guns. The Avenger finally reached the cloud and gave the Zekes the slip.

Emerging from the cloud a few minutes later, Lieutenant Tate sighted Lieutenant Brown's plane flying low over the water, badly shot up and blackened by fire. Lieutenant Brown, looking dazed, seriously wounded, and bleeding profusely, sat grimly at the controls. All that Tate could do was to try and get Brown to follow him and head for base. But it did not work. Brown's Avenger could not keep altitude or stay on course. Finally, in the deepening darkness near the surface of the sea, the two planes lost contact. Unable to find his friend, Tate set course for TF 58, ran out of gas near his objective and made a water landing. He and his two crewmen were rescued by a destroyer.

Lieutenant Omark, after his run, had been attacked by two Vals. They were driven off by gunner J. E. Prince at the turret and radioman R. E. Ranes at the tunnel guns. When a Zeke approached, he, too, was driven off. In the half-light of the setting sun, Lieutenant Omark overtook a lone Avenger. It was George Brown's. With great patience, he led him until long after dark, but had difficulty keeping him in sight. Brown had no lights, could not maintain an altitude, and wandered. His Avenger finally disappeared while they were passing through a cloud. Lieutenant Omark ran for home base, was vectored to CV *Lexington,* where he made a perfect landing with one whole quart of gasoline in his tank. Lieutenant Brown was never seen again.

Radioman Babcock and gunner Platz, who had jumped from Lieutenant Brown's flaming Avenger, were left on the scene. Sticking close together, they bobbed on the flame-lit sea, kept afloat by their Mae Wests. They watched the tracks of, and heard, the explosions of the three torpedoes that hit the *Hiyo*. They had a front-row seat as the carrier burned, exploded, and disappeared—the only eyewitnesses to the torpedoing and subsequent sinking of the carrier by Avenger pilots from Air Group 24. After the *Hiyo* sank, after the standby ships had departed, sea and sky merged into darkness. All that claimed the attention of the two men afloat on the sea were speculations as to which would come first—rescuers or sharks.

Four floatplanes picked them up in midafternoon the following day. They were taken aboard the cruiser *Boston,* treated royally, and returned to their carrier. There their testimony clinched the claim that three Avenger pilots had sent an irreplaceable Japanese flattop to the bottom.

When the TF 58 fliers broke off their attacks, the carrier *Hiyo* was sinking, two oilers had already sunk, other carriers and ships were damaged. But, far more serious, Admiral Ozawa's total air strength had been reduced to 35 operational planes. So far 20 planes were downed. But American losses on this mission were not ended. No floatplanes or submarines were at hand to rescue returning airmen who crashed or ditched on the black sea.

Planes damaged by enemy fire or manned by severely wounded pilots were the first to crash. The unharmed men and machines headed homeward. Some fliers stretched their gas by running their engines at economical speeds; others throttled wide open, gambling that speed would improve their chances. But as every precious minute passed, more and more airmen, whose tanks had run dry, had to bail out into the water. Others ditched on the sea. All rode the waves on inflated rafts or life jackets. Eventually, those who remained airborne saw a great white glow on the far horizon.

The light, as the airmen concluded, came from TF 58. On orders from Admiral Mitscher, the carrier groups had spread out to ease and speed recovery operations. Fully aware of the risk he ran, the admiral broke the blackout rule. Landing, running, and truck lights were turned on; searchlights thrust towering beams into the sky; star shells blossomed high above the ships. This gallant and defiant gesture enabled pilots to converge on the Force.

As the fliers milled overhead, impatient to land while their engines were still running, the recovery patterns became a shambles and landing runs turned into races. Many planes had to ditch for lack of gas; many planes crashed on decks or smashed into each other. It was bedlam. Near and far on the sea's surface flashlights, waved by downed airmen, flickered like glowworms. Destroyers and floatplanes dashed hither and yon on rescue missions.

One of the worst problems that faced the pilots in the early part of the landing tangle was to find their own carriers. A helpful solution was provided by CV *Yorktown,* which coordinated her searchlight with her radio transmissions to pilots. *Yorktown*ers, milling above in search of home, would hear something like this:

"*Yorktown* planes, this is *Yorktown* base. When we finish this transmission, we will shine a searchlight straight up in the air for exactly one minute. Now!"

At that instant the straight white beacon would shoot up into the sky and any *Yorktown* pilot who had heard the transmission could readily identify home base.

In carrier warfare, pilots and aircrews naturally get all the attention, but the men who labor on hangar decks and on flight decks should not be forgotten. As for the night of 20 June, that was a night to try the stamina and skills of landing-signal officers and deck crews.

At 2033, CV *Bunker Hill* commenced landing aircraft. At 2056 she had her first serious landing accident when a Helldiver from CV *Hornet,* ignoring both a wave-off and a Very signal indicating a foul deck, flew in at considerable speed. The plane slammed into the safety barrier that crossed the deck amidships. Like a buzz saw, the propeller cut itself into the deck, held the plane up and on its nose. Miraculously, neither plane crew nor deck personnel were injured. The Helldiver was still gumming up the deck when a torpedo-bomber from CVL *Cabot,* also ignoring signals, roared in. As it veered to starboard it hit a gun mount, and a wing was torn off. Next, the TBF struck the Helldiver a terrific blow. Four men, including Commander W. O. Smith, Air Officer of CV *Bunker Hill,* were killed; four others were injured. The TBF then turned over on its back, crashed into the island structure, and caught fire. Luckily, the fire-fighting asbestos men put the blaze out in a jiffy. Ensign J. Jones, Jr., its pilot, suffered severe burns. Both planes were hastily jettisoned to clear the deck for other landings. The body of one of the dead men, Seaman J. J. Bieber, was so entangled in the wreckage of the TBF that it could not be removed. There being no time for ceremony, his body went into the sea with the TBF as its coffin.

Commander C. S. Cooper, exec of CVL *San Jacinto,* watched with admiration from the island's bridge as his flight-deck crew stashed away planes as fast as the arresting gear yanked them to a stop. Commander Cooper had been a little worried because this was their first night landing, and under pressure at that. But all hands acted with the coolness and efficiency of veterans. The exec was particularly impressed with the performance of Lieutenant Ralph M. Bagwell, fairly new at the trade of a landing-signal officer.

"He brought onto a crowded deck," said Commander Cooper in a report that recommended Bagwell for the Bronze Medal, "strange planes and strange pilots with no confusion and without delays. With the single exception of one forced landing, not a plane was damaged or a person injured. The Navy, the Nation, and the Sovereign State of Texas can well be proud of *San Jacinto,* the Baby of the Fleet."

Who has not heard of the *Flying Dutchman,* a ghost ship and harbinger of ill omen to seafarers who see it rush, under full sail, through towering seas?

But not many know about the *Flying Dutchman*'s airborne counterpart that appeared over the Philippine Sea. It supposedly emerged from the deep blackness on that moonless, starless, and hectic night of 20 July when scores of Pete Mitscher's falcons were having difficulty landing on their carriers.

This modern ghost ship was a Japanese Val, a large, outmoded torpedo-bomber. Time and again it joined the milling planes and tried to land. Over the years that Japanese Val has been the subject of heated discussions among carrier pilots who were there. Some insist it was real; others maintain the Val was a figment of lively imaginations. But according to official records, a Val did intrude in the area occupied by TF 58 that night and tried to land on the decks of two carriers.

"While landing nine strange planes on CV *Wasp,*" reads the action report of that ship, "a Japanese plane endeavored to confuse and disrupt the landing circle but without much success. It made approaches as if to land on board but was waved off by the landing signal officer."

Next, the wandering Val is heard from on the CVL *San Jacinto.* Wrote Commander Cooper in his report: "It is worthy of note that the refusal of a Japanese Val to lower his tailhook prevented this ship from capturing him. Three times the Val attempted to land on board.

In flashing a message to plane (about the tailhook) the light revealed a Val. The bandit departed but was tracked (by radar) to the *Bunker Hill* and beyond to a distance of 28 miles when it was lost."

But if that was a Val, why didn't someone take a shot at it?

The day of 20 June was like a bomb with a long, slow fuse set to go off at nightfall. And yet the first tallyho of the day was sounded by a search team of 8 VTs and 4 Hellcats, led by Commander William R. (Killer) Kane, boss of Air Group 10 of the *Enterprise*. Kane was the Eddie Rickenbacker of the carrier fighters, a deadly man with a row of six .50s. The 12 planes were sent aloft at 0500, and despite the early hour, Commander Kane returned to base with the scalps of one Jake and one Jill. Many hours later he led his fighters in strafing a carrier in Admiral Ozawa's fleet. After the battle and the hectic run to base ended, Killer Kane was not present or accounted for.

There was gloom aboard the *Enterprise*. Pilots only dabbed at their ice cream that night, and Big-E was famous for it throughout the fleet. The gloom deepened the next day when pilots who had landed on other carriers or had been picked up at sea had no word about Commander Kane. Then, in the late afternoon, a destroyer approached the carrier and by blinker signal asked how many gallons of ice cream they would give for Killer Kane. The DD had him aboard, ready for delivery.

Commander Kane, only slightly the worse for having landed in the drink, rejoined his ship. There was jubilation aboard the *Enterprise* that night—but no ice cream. Every scoopful aboard had been donated to the rescuers of Killer Kane.

Rescues continued during the night and into the next day as the task force, in broad formation, steamed toward the battle area of the previous night at 16 knots. On all ships, and from a host of search planes, eager eyes scanned the seas for the yellow spots that marked survivors. The last of these were recovered on the waters of the now deserted battle zone.

When it ended, the tally showed that of the 216 planes that had taken off on the afternoon strike, only 116 were landed safely. Twenty of the planes lost were shot down in combat or unaccounted for; the remaining 80 were lost in water landings (because of fuel shortage) or in deck crashes. Flight personnel killed or missing totaled 38.

The Japanese Fleet had been under continuous attack from 1820 to 1900. By sunset (1919) most of our planes had left the area. Damage to the enemy, as reported in Commander Kane's action report, follows:

Sank: *Hiyo* (XCV), *Genyo Maru* (AO), *Seiyo Maru* (AO).
Damaged: *Zuikaku* (CV), *Junyo* (XCV), *Ryuho* (CVL), *Chiyoda* (CV), *Haruna* (BB), *Maya* (CA), *Hayasui* (AO).

In addition, the attacking planes estimated that 22 Japanese fighters were shot down.

With the completion of recovery operations the task force resumed course westward, with the limited prospect of overhauling the main body but with the possibility of locating some damaged ships. During the night of 20–21 June, PBM patrol planes from Saipan made contact, but a scheduled night search and attack from the carriers was canceled because of the extreme range.

At about dawn on 21 June, deckload strikes were launched with enemy cripples designated as primary targets, but this had negative results. Equally unfruitful was a final afternoon search to the west. In the early evening, therefore, the retirement of Task Force 58 toward Saipan was directed.

At Okinawa, Admiral Ozawa suffered the pangs of great regret. Almost all of Japan's naval air arm had been liquidated and her carrier force had been critically mauled. Of nine carriers, only two remained seaworthy. As matters stood, Japan did not have a fully protected fighting fleet. Surface naval power could not function without offensive and defensive air cover. Succinctly, in the two separate encounters to be called the First Battle of the Philippine Sea, the emperor's Navy had been downgraded to a level close to impotency. Admiral Ozawa submitted his resignation. It was not accepted. A few months' time would show that, in Tokyo, Admiral Kurita's star was ascending, whereas Admiral Ozawa's was descending.

Chapter Eight

PAWN TO K-2

AFTER SPENDING PARTS of 22–23 June on mid-ocean refueling operations, TF 58 split up. Admiral Jocko Clark took TG 1 back to Iwo Jima; the rest of the Force turned toward Saipan, keeping CAP and ASP eyes peeled for enemy planes and subs. None of the latter were sighted, but an Avenger, flying ASP off *Princeton,* encountered a solitary Betty.

Ensign Warren C. Burgess sighted the Betty about 12 miles from TF 58 and caught up with it after a short stern chase that began some 50 feet over the sea and ended a scant 10 feet above the water. As he came up, Ensign Burgess fired his twin wing guns, which jammed almost at once. Meanwhile, the Betty's turret gunner did his best to hit the TBM. As Ensign Burgess pulled off to fix his guns, his own turret gunner, G. A. Hodgins, silenced the Japanese turret gun.

After some manipulating, Ensign Burgess got his port gun going and swooped toward his opponent. The tracers were boring in nicely, when the gun jammed again. Having no firepower, the pilot placed the Avenger squarely above the enemy plane, determined to crowd the Betty down into the sea. The Betty hit the water, but bounced up so hard and fast again that it almost knocked the Avenger for a loop. The ensign drew off, then tried the Russian technique of chewing up the wing of an enemy plane with the prop, but without success. Gunner Hodgins then opened his hatch and emptied his six-shot .38 revolver into the Betty. Fed up with the whole deal, Ensign Burgess withdrew about a quarter of a mile from the Betty. This time he tackled the starboard gun. He got it working and made a pass at the Betty. He held his fire until he was within easy range, then released a strong burst into the engine, which flamed the plane. The plane fell rather slowly into the sea, and a survivor climbed out and into the water. Burgess flashed the position to base, and shortly the enemy pilot was picked up by a Fifth Fleet destroyer.

Task Force 58 returned to Saipan waters on the afternoon of 23 June to resume its function of supporting the occupation of the island, to keep Guam, Tinian, and Rota under constant strike pressure, and to participate in the off-the-record discussions about the manner in which Admiral Spruance ran the air show. Aviation and surface forces were, in the main, divided on the issue. But the controversy never became more than that. Admiral Spruance had done the right thing in the opinion of those whose opinions counted, and they included Admirals King and Nimitz. In fact, many believed that Ray Spruance was to be commended for his ability to make a decision and—believing it correct on the basis of known facts—to stick to it. The judgment of history seems to be that the conquest of the Marianas was the decisive turning point in the Pacific war; the Fifth Fleet commander emerges with distinction.

One thing is certain: The troops on Saipan did not care what was right or wrong. They were pleased to have the fliers back to provide air support; glad, too, to have all the ships back to apply their firepower when occasion demanded, which was frequent. As for Admiral Clark, TG 1 ran into heavy weather and rough treatment off Iwo Jima. Here again, that ability of the Japanese to restore seemingly wrecked flying facilities in no time had been at work. Unaware that they had been sighted, the carriers sent out 51 Hellcats with as many 500-pound bombs to comb Iwo Jima's airfield. Only four got that far. The remaining F6s had to drop their bombs and warm their machine guns when a swarm of Zekes flew forth to block them. At the same time, two separate waves of Zekes, Jills, and Bettys attacked the carriers—or tried to. The CAPs and AA batteries handled them very nicely. When losses were totaled for all three attacks, the enemy had lost 70 planes at a cost to TG 1 of 4 Hellcats.

Meanwhile, Admiral Hoover's and General Hale's land-based bombers and fighters continued their pressure against the Carolines while SoWesPac aircraft cracked at the Palaus and the western Carolines. One would think that these efforts would keep a tight lid on Admiral Kakuta's combat kettle, but not at all. Japanese torpedoplanes and bombers from Truk, the Palaus, and Yap, even from Iwo Jima and Guam, operated at night against the Fifth Fleet and with fair, though costly, results. The BB *Maryland* was disabled by a torpedo and had to head east for repairs. Transports and landing craft were also hit. However, after Army P-61 night-fighters joined the 101 Army P-47s already on Isely Field and gave the Navy night-fighters a helping hand, the night visitations decreased through sheer attrition. By mid-July, they had ceased.

On Saipan itself, the 100,000 or more amphibious troops that had successfully avoided casualty lists, had a difficult time putting an end to enemy resistance. Progress had been slow, sporadic, and costly in manpower. In the early days of the invasion this was, in part, owing to the inability of the Infantry to adjust to Marine tactical methods. The situation improved after Howling Mad Smith got so mad that he sent the Infantry commander packing. Early in July, with southern Saipan under control, General Smith moved northward and, like the driver of a bulldozer, pushed the defenders before him in steadily increasing numbers. Seeing the island slip away from him, and his troops being corralled like cattle, General Saito ordered a desperate last charge—and committed suicide. Following this example, Admiral Nagumu also joined his ancestors.

Pursuant to the last command of their dead general, some 3,000 Japanese soldiers rolled against American positions at 0400 on 8 July and poured irresistibly through them. But reinforcements drove them back. It was a long and tiring battle; when it was over, the field was covered with dead. Although pockets of resistance still survived in jungle foxholes and mountain caves, Saipan was declared secure at 1615 on 9 July. To show just how insecure that declaration was, on 10 July a Marine regiment killed 711 enemy troops. American casualties from D-Day on amounted to 3,400 dead and some 13,000 wounded. Even as the combat troops fought bravely, so SeaBees and Army engineers labored boldly to expand and rebuild Isely Field for the use of General Arnold's B-29 bombers. One night they met and rolled back a banzai charge of some 500 Japanese troops. Five months later, 100 B-29s took off from Saipan on the first of thousands of sorties to Japan.

During the mopping-up stage on Saipan, carriers and gun-support vessels of the Fifth Fleet found time to deliver frequent and precise gunnery attacks and air strikes on Guam—next on the invasion list —and Tinian.

All things considered, the assault on Guam was by far a better show for American troops than that on Saipan had been. The difference was time and preparation. By H-hour on W-Day—0830, July 21—practically all enemy artillery had been silenced. Before the 3rd Marines, the 77th Infantry, and the 1st Provisional Marine Brigade went ashore, heavy naval gunfire and 312 bombing and strafing aircraft paved the way. During and after the landing, some 100 Hellcats strafed and bombed the areas adjacent to the beachheads. These were north and south of Apra Harbor, which faces the Philippine Sea almost midway on the west coast of the island. All the Marines and many of the Infantry, having spent weeks and weeks aboard transports in Admiral Conolly's Southern Attack Force and a short breather in the Marshalls, were probably glad to come to grips at long last with the enemy. The assault troops were under the over-all command of Major General Roy S. Geiger, USMC. The invaders, according to Operation Forager's original schedule, were a month late in landing, but they made up for that delay on the double. With blitz action, the troops moved north and south to consolidate their lines, and inland to expand their beachhead. These lightning moves gave Roy Geiger control of Apra Harbor, as well as all of Orote Peninsula and its valuable airfield, by 29 July. Next, his troops moved across the southern end of the island to the east coast and then on to its northern tip. In these operations, the ground fighters received extensive and precise air and gun support.

Two factors were obvious from the start on Guam. One, that the protracted air and naval assaults had smashed all the enemy's prepared defense positions as well as his artillery; two, that the spirit of resistance was as strong on Guam as it had been on Saipan. The emperor's soldiers surrendered only to death. On 10 August Guam was declared secure. The count of enemy dead was just under 11,000; American losses were 1,400 killed. But although organized fighting may have ended, thousands more of the enemy's do-or-die soldiers remained hidden in the mountain and jungle terrain. These were eventually wiped out by systematic sweeps of the Marines. The cleanup was slow but greatly aided by the Marine air group that landed on Orote field on 4 August, less than a week after the Marines had seized it. U.S. SeaBees and Army engineers were as good as the Japanese when it came to restoring cratered airfields to active status in a miraculously short time.

Even before Guam was declared secure, Commodore Carter and advance units of ServRon 10 arrived from the Marshalls to put Apra Harbor in shape and to provide repair, service, and supply facilities. In a very short time, Admiral Nimitz was to move his headquarters to Guam; but before his arrival ComSubPac received permission from him, despite vigorous objections from his staffers, who always seemed to regard submarines as too humble for real naval status, to move subs and their tenders into Apra Harbor. This move cut a cool 2,000 miles from the round-trip distance from the Majuro base and patrol areas in the Western Pacific, China Sea, and other waters vital to Japanese shipping. By the early fall of 1944, submarines had sunk more than 4,000,000 tons of Japanese shipping, two-thirds of all she had, and American sub crews were eager to have a crack at the remaining third.

If the occupation of Guam was a change for the better, that of Tinian was even more so. Begun three days (24 July) after the invasion of Guam was launched, it ended nine days (1 August) before Guam was declared secure. Here again, prolonged, well-planned, and well-executed air and gunnery support paid dividends. In addition, Army and Marine artillery, standing hub to hub on the southern coast of Saipan, sent their shells across the water between the two islands and covered the beaches where the 2nd and 4th Marines would land. To further isolate the expanding beachhead area from enemy attack, aircraft bombs virtually tore the highways and rail tracks to the south to shreds, thus preventing enemy troop reinforcements from that direction. In this assault, napalm fire bombs were used for the first time. They did not, at first, prove as incendiary as had been expected, but before Tinian was taken, the men had found ways to improve their effectiveness.

The Tinian beachhead expanded so rapidly that by 27 July Ushi Point Airfield and its nearby satellite field were taken; next day, American fliers made use of them. The end of Japanese rule came when the caves—in cliffs at the southern end of the island, where the enemy made his last stand—were stormed and left full of Japanese dead. As for Rota, severely bombed, it was left to wither on the vine.

And that was journey's end for Operation Forager. Some 60,000 Japanese who had tried to stop this mighty juggernaut were dead, along with about 5,000 Americans. Spectacular though it was, Forager was but one act in the great drama to be staged on the Philippine Sea.

In Japan the loss of the Marianas was a matter of gravest concern. Because General Tojo had given his personal assurance that Saipan would be invulnerable, the burden of the fiasco was placed squarely on his shoulders. The result was that the saber-rattling soldier-politician was requested to resign, which, after a vain attempt to remain in power, he finally did. His successor, General Kuniaki Koiso, was asked by the emperor to explore avenues to peace negotiations.

This request, though Imperial, was ignored because the project seemed doomed from the start by the Roosevelt-Churchill prior agreement to accept only Japan's unconditional surrender. This demanded more loss of face than the Japanese leaders felt they could afford, although the future looked very bleak for Japanese arms. The air fleet, of which she had been so proud and on which she depended so much, had not only lost important ships but also, for all practical purposes, all its air personnel. When Admiral Ozawa retreated from the Philippine Sea he had only 35 pilots left and hardly enough planes to send them aloft.

Among Americans who had fought the battles of the Marianas and had observed the fanatical and suicidal manner in which the Japanese sacrificed their lives, the belief grew that Japan's surrender would never come until every foot of soil on the homeland had been soaked in blood. This fanaticism had much to do with the later decision by the United States to use the atomic bomb.

But that was in the future. As of August 1944, Tojo's wall had been pierced and could not be rebuilt. The lifeline to the south had been ruptured beyond restoration; in short, Japan's "absolute line of national defense" was threatened at many points on the island perimeter along the rim of the Philippine Sea as well as north and south of it. Biak had been taken by General MacArthur on 21 June, when gallant Colonel Kuzume died by his own hand as the last surviving defenders were flushed out of their caves. Operation Kon had gone on permanent inactive status. Within weeks, all of New Guinea would be under General MacArthur's control.

Now the admiral at Pearl Harbor and the general at Hollandia were ready to move westward and northward respectively. But the differences of opinion as to what should be done about the Philippines had not been ironed out despite an ultra high level meeting held in Hawaii toward the end of July.

On 26 July the CA *Baltimore,* with President Roosevelt aboard, berthed along a pier in Pearl Harbor. FDR's main reason for making the journey from San Diego was to unravel the knot of contention between General MacArthur and the Navy on the subject of bypassing or liberating the Philippines. Before *Baltimore* arrived, General MacArthur had reached Oahu by plane and gone to Fort Shafter. Among the generals and admirals on hand to greet the President were Admirals King and Nimitz. In the presidential party was Admiral William D. Leahy, C of S to the President. General MacArthur soon arrived on invitation from the President. After the welcoming ceremonies, Mr. Roosevelt went ashore to occupy the palatial Holmes residence at Waikiki, where conferences were to be held on 27–28 June on the place of the Philippines in future war plans.

At these meetings, the only person to speak for General MacArthur's views was the general himself. He had brought along no staff members of his own, and none had come from Washington to speak for General Marshall, C of S of the Army. For two days the discussions went on. At the start, Admiral Nimitz expressed the belief that the best and quickest way to win and end the war was to bypass Luzon, the heart of the Philippines, and attack Formosa. General MacArthur maintained that Luzon should be secured not only for military reasons but also because the long-suffering Filipinos deserved the liberation that would follow such action. When the discussions ended, the President indicated that he favored General MacArthur's plan. Of course, his acceptance was not an official order. Actual directives had to come from JCS, where Admiral King still opposed the inclusion of Luzon and General Marshall now accepted General MacArthur's proposition. In early September the JCS planners finally had a program on paper. It was to be presented at the Octagon conference to start in Quebec on 11 September, when Prime Minister Churchill and President Roosevelt would meet with the Allied Combined Chiefs of Staff. This proposal gave, in the guise of a program of operations to 1 March 1945, way stops and timetables—agreed on and pending—for Admiral Nimitz' Central Pacific Force and General MacArthur's Southwest Pacific Force. It provided:

Angaur and Peleliu, in the Palaus, to be occupied by CenPacFor on 15 September. On the same day, SoWesPacFor would invade Morotai Island in the Moluccas.

Yap and Ulithi, in the western Carolines, would be occupied on 5 October by CenPacFor; Salebaboe Island, in the Talauds, to be invaded by SoWesPacFor on 15 October.

On 15 November SoWesPacFor would land on Mindanao in the Philippines and move on Leyte Gulf on 20 December, as would CenPacFor. From there, the united forces would do one of two things: either attack Luzon by 20 February 1945, or make the longer haul to Amoy, China, by way of Formosa, by 1 March. There was that old bugaboo again—failure to come to grips with reality in the Philippines.

Long before this, Admiral Halsey and his C of S, Rear Admiral

Robert B. "Mick" Carney, had started shaping up plans at Hawaii for the Third Fleet, which he would take over as soon as Admiral Spruance finished with it as the Fifth Fleet. Admiral Turner and General Smith would go ashore with Admiral Spruance to work with him on future Fifth Fleet operations. Their places, in the Third, would be filled by Rear Admiral Theodore S. "Ping" Wilkinson and Marine Major General Roy S. Geiger, as over-all commander of amphibious troops.

Admiral Wilkinson's amphibious forces were to be split into two groups. One would embark the 1st Marine Division to invade Angaur and Peleliu under the command of Major General Julian C. Smith; the other, with the 24th Infantry, under Major General John R. Hodge, would tackle Yap and Ulithi. Later, the roles of Generals Geiger and Smith would be reversed, because General Geiger had to remain in Guam longer than planned under Operation Forager. Task Force 58 would become TF 38; and although there would be new faces among task group commands, the wrinkled visage of Pete Mitscher would continue to look down on the flight deck from CV *Lexington,* the Force flagship. An effort to nudge him out of command and put Vice Admiral J. S. "Slew" McCain in his place had fallen flat. Instead, McCain was given Jocko Clark's command of Task Group 1. Admiral Mitscher's immediate task—after a pre-invasion softening up of the Palaus, Yap, and Ulithi—would be to keep Japanese heads and planes down in the central and southern Philippines during the early beachhead stages, some 500 miles across the Philippine Sea, by making hit-and-run attacks on enemy air installations along the coasts of those areas.

Bill Halsey had a well-earned reputation for being resourceful, impulsive, and explosive. In those and many other respects he was totally unlike Admiral Spruance. Instead of being wrapped in a cloak of remote and unruffled calm, Admiral Halsey was equally ready to laugh lustily or to bellow angrily. He could outroar even Jocko Clark. Because of his hefty bellow, Bill Halsey had been called "Bull" in some quarters, but never to his face and seldom by his friends.

A carrier man at heart, Halsey had wanted to hoist his flag on a flattop. But because he feared that their vulnerability might endanger command communications under critical combat conditions, he settled for the new BB *New Jersey* instead. The Fifth Fleet became the Third Fleet officially on 26 August, when all the loose ends of Forager had been gathered. But the occasion was not marked by the ceremonies that usually take place on changes of high commands. On 26 August Halsey simply set to sea in BB *New Jersey,* accompanied by three destroyers. At that time the newly named Task Force 38 was winding up a series of strikes in the Jimas under the tactical command of Admiral Mitscher in the absence of Admiral Spruance, who was steaming east, and in the absence of Admiral Halsey, who was steaming west. By the time BB *New Jersey* reached the Marianas, TF 38 had ventured south, to strike invasion targets, and west, to hit the Philippines. It was here, near Mindanao, that Admirals Halsey and Mitscher met on 11 September. Old friends of long standing, it was a happy meeting for both aboard the CV *Lexington.* Here the new fleet commander received a firsthand report from Pete Mitscher, who was deeply disappointed. He had bombed and strafed Mindanao on 9–10 September only to discover that Army fliers from southwest bases had pancaked enemy air installation so completely that there were few Zekes, Bettys, or Jills left to fly and few structures left to flatten.

With three of his four carrier groups—one had been left to hammer Peleliu—Pete Mitscher and his fliers had gone to Mindanao full of purpose to spend six days neutralizing important airfields, knock out aircraft and military installations, sink ships, and take pre-invasion pictures. This, on the theory that the island, about the size of Indiana, would be defended by some 200 planes from nine major bases and numerous satellite fields. Instead, the air defenses were weak. Only 6 planes were sighted aloft and shot down. On the ground, 58 were destroyed. A convoy of 32 loaded coastal cargo ships and 20 sampans was destroyed.

Realizing that Mindanao was not a threat to the Palau or Morotai invasions, commander TF 38 suggested to Admiral Halsey that instead of wasting time pounding Mindanao, the central Philippines be given a good going-over since air bases north of that were too remote to menace Palau landings. The admiral fell in line with that plan. During the next two days, 300 enemy planes were either shot down or demolished on the ground in the Visayas. Sorties were also made with profit against installations and shipping. Thirteen large merchant ships and 55 lesser craft were sunk at the cost of 8 carrier planes. The resistance was so feeble that Admiral Halsey characterized Philippine defenses as a "hollow shell."

Never having favored the Palau, Yap, and Ulithi landings, and certain that General MacArthur's over-all progress could be stepped up, Admiral Halsey sent identical messages to Admiral Nimitz and General MacArthur suggesting that landings on Peleliu, Angaur, Yap, Ulithi, Salebaboe, Morotai, and Mindanao be canceled and that CenPacFor concentrate with SoWesPacFor on landing at Leyte Gulf. The proposal, somewhat amended, reached Quebec from CincPac in Hawaii the night before the Octagon conference broke up. In less than two hours, the JCS had cleared new proposals with Admiral Nimitz and General MacArthur. CenPacFor invasions, on recommendation of Admiral Nimitz, were reduced to Peleliu, Angaur, and Ulithi. As for General MacArthur, his main forces would, at the proper time, proceed straight from Hollandia and Manus to Leyte with no stopovers. A smaller amphibious group would occupy Morotai on 15 September. Target date at Leyte was 20 October instead of 20 December, a saving of two months.

The troops, ships, and equipment intended for Yap and Ulithi were assigned to "General MacArthur's Navy," meaning the Seventh Fleet commanded by Admiral Kinkaid. Also, all transport and supply ships in the Palau landings would be transferred to Seventh Fleet when unloaded; lastly, fire-support and escort carrier groups in Admiral Wilkinson's force would join the Seventh Fleet when no longer needed at the beachheads. Thus, virtually overnight, Operation King II, a term derived from a daring and aggressive chess move, came into being. But no disposition had as yet been made with respect to liberation of the Filipinos.

When the final orders on Leyte came through from Quebec, the scheduled 15 September and 5 October operations on the southeastern rim of the Philippine Sea were in advanced stages of activation. The Yap attack force, with its entire panoply of jeep carriers, combat screens, packed troop transports, and what not, was actually at sea. By radio, the Force was directed to shape course at once for Manus to join the Seventh Fleet. Ready to depart from Hawaii was the Palaus–Ulithi attack force. It was ordered to proceed as planned, but to detach all vessels that could be spared as soon as possible after the landing operations and send them to Admiral Kinkaid.

All of this may sound simple, but the bodily transfer of one fleet command to another under such conditions was difficult. It took miraculous top-level skills and cooperation; both Admiral Nimitz and General MacArthur had them. The delicate meshings in shifting command gears was performed without the stripping of a single cog.

After he detached Oldendorf's bombardment and fire-support units for service with the Seventh Fleet, Admiral Halsey's Third Fleet was reduced to the elements of Mitscher's task force. The group screens of TF 38, of which Admiral Halsey had tactical command, were bolstered with the fast and heavy fighting ships of Admiral Lee's battle line and its fire-support vessels.

Meanwhile the time had come for TF 38 to provide air support for the 15 September landings on Morotai and Peleliu. TG 1, under Vice Admiral McCain, was sent to Morotai; another steamed to Peleliu to give a hand to the TG already there; the fourth remained in Philippine waters to pound air concentrations that might come to the assistance of the invasion islands. Admiral Halsey went along with the group destined for Peleliu.

Morotai offered the least resistance. The 500 Japanese troops on the island ran for the hills when the amphibious force hove into sight, and thereby saved Rear Admiral Daniel E. Barbey a lot of time and fire support. However, nearby well-garrisoned islands were gunned by cruisers to prevent reinforcements from reaching Morotai by barge convoys. The only opposition to the landings was provided by nature. Obstacles in the water endangered navigation, and when the troops waded ashore they were hindered by mud and chest-deep water. But the combat troops, 28,000 infantry men from the 11th Corps, commanded by Major General C. P. Hall, got ashore intact and in good order. There were also 12,000 service troops who had to make an airfield out of an unfinished airstrip that had been abandoned by the enemy because the soil was too soggy. That airfield, completed after backbreaking work, was to become a vital refueling point for short-range aircraft bound from SoWesPac bases to the Leyte area.

If the Morotai landings were rather a milk run, Peleliu proved to be something else again. As part of the invasion plan, Admiral Halsey had requested a reconnaissance line of nine submarines across the Philippine Sea and about 400 miles northwest of Palau to detect and discourage naval visitors from Tokyo. Although the United States, at that time, did not know how seriously the First Mobile Fleet had been mangled off Saipan, she did know that it had been hurt; U.S. forces also knew that the Japanese backed up against a wall in a fight were doubly resourceful and aggressive adversaries. So the precaution was well taken. But when Admiral Mick Carney wanted to incorporate this patrol line into the Third Fleet and use it as a permanent picket line in fleet operations, ComSubPac put his foot down. Although Uncle Bill supported his chief of staff, Uncle Charlie, as Vice Admiral Lockwood was known to his SubPac force, did not want to immobilize so many submarines in a picket line. The results of such a line used earlier in the isolating of Palau had been zero. Therefore, with Admiral Nimitz' approval, submarines were stationed off the exits from Japanese ports and the Inland Sea. They were also stationed singly or in wolf packs all the way down to the north end of Luzon, in the China Sea, and across the Philippine Sea to Saipan. This was to produce excellent results. Likewise, ComSubSoWesPac covered the approaches to the Philippines from the directions of Tawitawi and Singapore.

Operations against Peleliu began on 6 September with carrier sweeps that lasted until the 9th. Then Admiral Oldendorf's battle-wagons took over, bombarding villages and beaches for five days. They accomplished a great deal of military destruction but not where it really counted. In camouflaged coral caves, where they were immune from the naval shelling, thousands of well-armed Japanese soldiers waited for the invasion.

The initial wave of Marines landed at 0830 on 15 September just south of the airport, and quickly established a wide beachhead. In spite of fairly heavy artillery and mortar fire, the early landing waves suffered only about 200 casualties. All appeared to be going according to plan.

Since Peleliu is surrounded by a reef, the 1st Marines arrived on the beaches in tracked landing craft, which had few difficulties with off-shore obstacles such as coral heads and boulders. Unfortunately, the reefs were too shallow for smaller, nontracked craft to negotiate; moreover, the coral heads were too deep for causeways to be built to the edge of the offshore reef, although UDT units labored manfully to provide them. This meant cargo had to be transferred from ships to small boats and then to amtracs—putting a serious crimp in the vital flow of supplies to the beachhead. Suddenly, the operation began to look tougher.

Then the wind rose, and swells from the southwest made it impossible to beach even amtracs. The only type of vessel that could labor through the rolling seas and pounding surf between reef and beach was the LST—and only six of these were available. Then, during a sudden blow, three fully loaded LSTs went aground. The wildly boiling surf broached them, slammed them up against the jagged edge of the reef, and tore out their bottoms.

Night fell, and the work of supply went on with the three remaining LSTs. At sea, transports and cargo vessels were ablaze with work

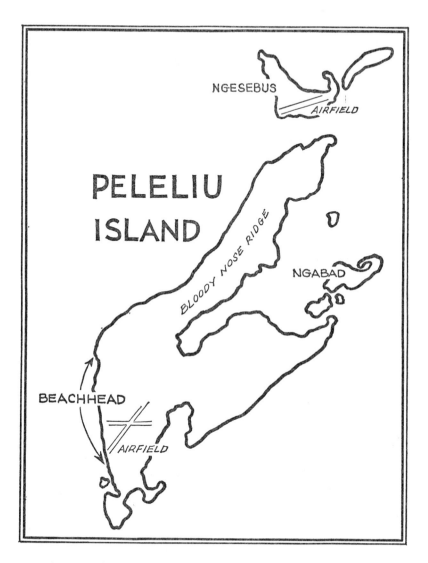

*Umurbrogol Ridge, commonly called "Bloody Nose
Ridge," is a long, squat hump of coral, honeycombed
with caves on the island of Peleliu in the western
Carolines. In the fall of 1944 it was a Japanese fortress
that could not be reached by bullets, rockets, bombs,
shells, or bazookas. It was finally conquered by long-range
flamethrowers mounted on tanks.*

lights despite danger from enemy planes and submarines. Ashore, weary and bleary-eyed truckers hauled their cargoes to supply dumps, unloaded them, and turned about for more as snipers' bullets whined past their vehicles. While the blow lasted, it was touch and go whether the flow of vital supplies would be kept moving. The success or failure of the entire Peleliu operation depended during those hours on just three LSTs.

Once established on the beaches, the Marines advanced rapidly despite several counterattacks. Within two days, they gained possession of the southern part of the island, including the airport. The invasion appeared to be going so well that the 81st Infantry was relieved from standby reserve status and ordered to take Angaur. Landings on that island were made on 17 September. Four days later it was declared secure, although numerous pockets of resistance remained to be wiped out.

On Peleliu, meanwhile, the airfield was restored for use by "grasshopper" spotting aircraft on 18 September; within two weeks, all of Marine Air Group 2 was in residence. The infantry offensive nearly ground to a halt, however, as the Marines began to encounter the defenders in the caves of Umurbrogol Ridge—soon to earn the name "Bloody Nose Ridge."

Umurbrogol Ridge stretches for a distance of about a mile along a slim finger of land halfway between the northern and southern ends of 4-mile-long Peleliu. Beneath the thick coral hide of the ridge was a labyrinth of interconnecting caves where Japanese soldiers, well stocked with weapons, ammunition, and other supplies, were prepared to fight to the last man. Gun positions in these caves were hidden behind sliding steel doors, or by natural or artificial camouflage. Shells and bullets could not destroy the cave fortresses. This was a new type of defense in depth, and, as the Marines were to learn, the Japanese defenders could inflict much more punishment than they received. But no matter what the cost, the cave system had to be destroyed and the ridge taken in order to command the island and to prevent the 25,000-man garrison at by-passed Babelthuap from sending reinforcements to Peleliu.

The Marines initially thrust northward through rough territory and heavy jungle growth, almost constantly under fire from caves that were difficult to locate and impossible to capture. The strain of this nightmare offensive was so great that a regiment of the 81st Infantry was called back from Angaur to support the 1st Marines. Days, weeks, months, went by as the invaders hacked their way to a show-down on Bloody Nose Ridge.

Marine fliers and naval vessels, meanwhile, kept alert for convoys or barges that the Japanese might try to send from Babelthuap, some 30 miles away. An element of the 81st was deployed from Angaur to Ulithi, which, abandoned by the enemy, was taken without opposition. Other outlying islands of defensive value were invaded and occupied.

On Peleliu, however, the Japanese fought on from their underground redoubts in Umurbrogol Ridge. There was no way of defeating them until flamethrowers, with extra long range, arrived. Installed on tanks, they did what other weapons had failed to do. Gradually, caves were cleaned out and sealed up. Toward the end of November, termination of organized resistance was signified by the suicide of Colonel Nakagawa, the island commander. But the mopping-up went on until February 1945.

From a military standpoint, this protracted resistance had no value. Long before it ended, American operations were well under way on Peleliu. Babelthuap posed no problem. Unable to move by air or sea, unable to receive substantial support from Japan, and continuously bombed by Marine aviators, the 25,000 soldiers on the island neither died in large numbers nor faded away; they just sat and waited for better days that never came.

Allied losses amounted to 1,950 killed and 8,500 wounded. Japanese casualties reached 13,600. While the price paid was large, the benefits were proportionate. In Japanese hands, Peleliu, with its excellent air facilities, would have been a dangerous dagger at Yankee backs during the Philippine operations. Moreover, without taking Peleliu the Americans could never have occupied Ulithi and turned it into a large, well-equipped anchorage right in the Empire's front yard—an essential factor in operations that were to come. As to by-passed Yap, it never became a threat. It was enclosed in a set of pincers by U.S. occupation of some nearby islands, from which planes could sortie against Yap if and when occasion demanded.

Chapter Nine

AIR WAR OVER THE PHILIPPINES

FAST TASK FORCE 38, ending covering operations in mid-September at Peleliu and Morotai, reunited its full strength of 17 heavy and light carriers, an increase of two over TF 58. There were also more planes: 596 fighters, 358 bombers, and 224 torpedo-planes—a total of 1,178 Hellcats, Wildcats, Helldivers, and Avengers. As always, a strong array of screening vessels was on hand. Admiral Willis A. Lee, in BB *Washington,* commanded, as a separate unit, BBs *Massachusetts, South Dakota,* and *Alabama,* a division of four CLs headed by Rear Admiral Laurance T. DuBose, and a destroyer screen of 14 DDs. The battleships *Iowa* and *New Jersey*—Admiral Halsey's flagship—were in TG 2's screen. As usual, Admiral Mitscher flew his flag on CV *Lexington* in TG 3, and Arleigh Burke, now a commodore, was still his chief of staff. It is no secret that Pete Mitscher looked askance at Arleigh Burke when he reported aboard early in 1944 as his right-hand man. Pete had wanted an aviator and Burke was a destroyer sailor. But Captain Burke was a quick learner. His reputation, gained in DDs as "31 Knot Burke," left no doubt as to his courage and aggressiveness. Pete Mitscher was soon not only mollified but also pleased. After the many changes in the fast carrier force, the task groups shaped up in the following manner:

TG 38.1: Vice Admiral John S. McCain commanding.
>   CV *Hornet,* Capt. A. K. Doyle commanding; Air Group 11, Cdr. F. R. Schrader.
>   CV *Wasp,* Capt. O. A. Weller commanding; Air Group 14, Cdr. W. C. Wingard.
>   CVL *Cowpens,* Capt. H. W. Taylor commanding; Air Group 22, Lt. Cdr. T. H. Jenkins.

CVL *Monterey,* Capt. S. H. Ingersoll commanding; Air Group 28, Lt. Cdr. R. W. Mehle.

TG 38.2: Rear Admiral Gerald F. Bogan commanding.

CV *Bunker Hill,* Capt. M. R. Greer commanding; Air Group 8, Cdr. R. L. Shifley.

CV *Hancock,* Capt. F. C. Dickey commanding; Air Group 7, Cdr. J. D. Lamade.

CV *Intrepid,* Capt. J. F. Bolger commanding; Air Group 18, Cdr. W. E. Ellis.

CVL *Cabot,* Capt. S. J. Michael commanding; Air Group 29, Lt. Cdr. W. E. Eder.

CVL *Independence,* Capt. E. C. Ewen commanding; Air Group 41, Cdr. T. F. Caldwell.

TG 38.3: Rear Admiral Frederick C. Sherman commanding.

CV *Essex,* Capt. C. W. Weiber commanding; Air Group 15, Cdr. David McCampbell.

CV *Lexington,* Capt. E. W. Litch commanding; Air Group 19, Cdr. T. H. Winters.

CVL *Langley,* Capt. J. F. Wegforth commanding; Air Group 44, Cdr. M. T. Wordell.

CVL *Princeton,* Capt. W. H. Buracker commanding; Air Group 27, Lt. Cdr. F. A. Bardshar.

TG 38.4: Rear Admiral Ralph E. Davison commanding.

CV *Enterprise,* Capt. Cato D. Glover commanding; Air Group 20, Cdr. Dan F. Smith.

CV *Franklin,* Capt. J. M. Shoemaker commanding; Air Group 13, Cdr. R. L. Kibbe.

CVL *Belleau Wood,* Capt. John Perry commanding; Air Group 21, Lt. Cdr. V. F. Casey.

CVL *San Jacinto,* Capt. M. H. Kernodle commanding; Air Group 51, Cdr. C. L. Moore.

Something else had been added to TF 38: a logistic group commanded by Captain J. A. Acuff, whose trying, often thankless, job was to provide fuel, ammunition, replacement planes, and towing services for the Halsey–Mitscher team in mid-ocean. So valuable were the treasures Captain Acuff dispensed that he had a strong destroyer and flattop screen for his numerous oilers and escort carriers. The latter made air deliveries in mid-ocean to replace lost planes and air personnel. Half a dozen ammunition carriers stocked supplies for all guns on ships and planes, plus bombs and fish for VB and VT planes. Finally, there were ten or so fleet tugs to haul crippled vessels to Ulithi where complete port facilities were being constructed.

Fast Carrier Task Force 38 set out at flank speed on 20 September. Destination: Luzon. After protracted waiting, Americans were returning to Manila. The return was staged in the early morning hours of 21 September and caught the local Japanese defenders unawares. Out of the morning sun and from a clear blue sky, American fliers swooped upon the prime target of the Philippines with jabbering machine guns and screaming bombs.

This was familiar terrain to Americans, unlike Saipan and Peleliu. Carefully briefed, various plane divisions flew straight to their targets—airfields, harbor areas, Cavite naval base, oil-storage tanks, railroad yards, barracks and other military installations, warehouses, and so forth. One moment all was serene; the next, as if a switch had been turned on, buildings blew up, ships sank, oil storages blazed. So great was the surprise, so pinpointed were the attacks, that the enemy had to struggle to send planes aloft before they were wrecked on the ground. The strikes had been slated to continue through 22 September, but unfavorable weather made Admiral Mitscher call it quits. Leaving the skies over Luzon black with smoke, TF 38 stood to sea to refuel. As it was, 169 enemy planes had been shot down in combat, and 188 were destroyed and 45 damaged on the ground. A sizable amount of shipping, including 3 destroyers and 3 tankers, had been sunk and a large number of ships damaged, including 2 floating dry docks. American losses were 11 planes, 10 pilots, and 5 crewmen.

Without losing any time, TF 38 descended upon the Visayas again, this time to hunt for shipping that had taken refuge in the central Philippines after escaping from Luzon. A big share of this was found at Coron Bay in the Calamian Group; two large tankers and other vessels were sunk for a total of 31,000 tons. Air opposition was light but flak was heavy. Seven enemy planes were shot down and 29 were destroyed on the ground. Although 10 U.S. planes were lost, all but 5 pilots and 3 crewmen were rescued by Filipino guerillas and given places of hiding.

After this last attack, it was time for TF 38 to take a breather at Ulithi. And there it was when, on 3 October, the JCS at long last announced that General MacArthur's way—the road to Luzon—had been adopted. Now all the lights were green for General MacArthur

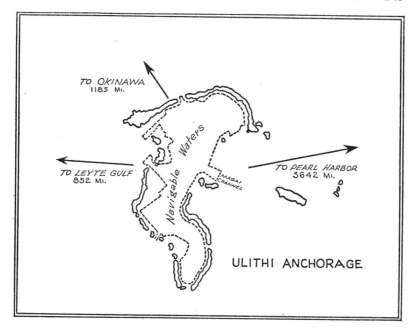

*Ulithi Atoll in the western Carolines. Admiral Nimitz
planned to take this anchorage and make it the principal
jumping-off point for naval operations against the
Philippines, Formosa, Iwo Jima, Okinawa, and Japan. In
time it became an important pillar in the American structure of victory, mainly because of its highly efficient
service facilities.*

and Admiral Nimitz. They knew where they were going and how.
First step was to send the Halsey–Mitscher wrecking crew on the
road again as part of a program to further confuse the Japanese, who
already were off balance from the blitz strikes on the Philippines. To
that end, a series of strikes, all deeply disturbing to Japan, was
planned to start on 9 October.

When Operation A-GO became a useless scrap of paper after the
First Battle of the Philippine Sea in June, Admiral Toyoda had to
take new measures. Toward the end of July they were ready under
the general name of Operation SHO, meaning *victory*. The plans were
written to meet four different situations. SHO 1, whose activation the
admiral considered most likely, covered the defense of the Philippines; SHO 2 would meet invasion threats on Formosa or Okinawa

or both; SHO 3 would deal with an assault on Honshu, the heart of Japan; and SHO 4 was aimed at the defense of Hokkaido, northernmost island of Japan.

Because Admiral Toyoda's hunch, with respect to SHO 1 being the important number, was correct, we need not be concerned about the other three. Briefly, it was based on the belief that the Japanese Army, even assisted by maximum land-based Japanese air power, could not repel an American invasion of the Philippines without total naval support. It was therefore decided that, in the event of SHO 1 being activated, the whole fleet would be sent into battle—a great gamble. In doing that, the fleet would have to depend upon its gunpower in cooperation with land-based air because the fleet's own air arm had only a handful of pilots and few planes. In July, when the plan was being formulated, there were hopes that Admiral Spruance's Fifth Fleet had suffered heavy ship, plane, and personnel losses that would slow down Admiral Nimitz' combat pace. This would give Japan time to train pilots and build planes. But now, with September gone, there had been no signs of slow-down. On the contrary, the metronome was ticking faster than ever and the plight of the Imperial Navy was desperate. Parts of it were in Asiatic waters, where there was plenty of fuel but no ammunition; the rest was in Japanese waters, where there was plenty of ammunition but no fuel. Toward mid-October the distribution of the Japanese Fleet was:

At Lingga Roads near Singapore: the First Force, Vice Admiral Takeo Kurita commanding. This force was divided into three sections —two night combat units, one headed by Admiral Kurita, the other by Vice Admiral Yoshio Suzuki, comprised the Main Force. A third group was commanded by Vice Admiral Shoji Nishimura. The strength of the entire organization was 7 battleships, including the super-BBs *Yamato* and *Musashi,* 13 cruisers, and 19 destroyers.

In Japan: The main body of the Mobile Fleet—still commanded by Admiral Ozawa, to whom Admiral Kurita was responsible—was anchored in the Inland Sea. Attached to the main body was the Second Striking Force, commanded by Vice Admiral Kiyohide Shima. Also present was the advance expeditionary force of 17 submarines, commanded by Vice Admiral Shigeyoshi Miwa, and a troop transport group, commanded by Vice Admiral Naomasa Sakonju. Admiral Ozawa's Mobile Fleet was reduced to four carriers with a total air arm of 80 fighters, seven dive-bombers, and 29 torpedo-bombers.

There were no battleships except the hybrids *Ise* and *Hyuga,* two overage BBs whose stern turrets had been removed to make room for landing aprons. But the two ancient battlewagons carried nary a plane. There were 8 cruisers and 16 destroyers.

The day of 9 October was a day of shock, surprise, and uncertainty in Tokyo. First came the news that Marcus Island in the Central Pacific was being attacked by a surface fleet that was knocking out all installations rebuilt since the May raid. In May, Operation TO had been secretly alerted to repel possibly impending air strikes on Japan. As consideration was given to the re-alerting of Operation TO, alarming news came from islands much closer to home.

While naval guns were pounding Marcus, TF 38 had launched planes far to sea off the Ryukyu Islands of which Okinawa, the largest and most important, lies about 300 miles south of Japan. Strong formations of TF 38 combat planes had delivered tons of destructive hardware before Tokyo adjusted to what was going on. Some of the unwelcome visitors devoted themselves to naval and merchant shipping; others tackled planes, airborne or on the ground; still others concentrated on buildings, barracks, and defense installations. When the job was done, great fires raged and bleak ruins lay in heaps on Okinawa and other islands in the chain. Many vessels were sunk, including 1 destroyer escort, 4 small submarines, and a submarine tender. The number of ships probably sunk or damaged was also highly satisfactory. Installations destroyed or damaged included 1 ammo and 4 fuel dumps, 3 hangars, and many barracks and warehouses; several harbors were devastated.

The air combat action was not heavy, as revealed by the rather small number of planes shot down—23. On the ground, 59 aircraft were smashed and 37 damaged. American losses amounted to 8 planes, 5 pilots, and 3 crewmen.

In Toyko the attack was regarded as a harbinger of invasion, and Operation SHO 2 was alerted. To everyone's surprise, the task force recovered planes in the early afternoon and departed. Admiral Halsey had a great deal of hard, tough work to do and no time to linger, as much damage had to be inflicted upon the enemy over the widest possible area that guarded the Philippines. Beyond that, by hitting the Japanese hard, again and again, the enemy was to be confused and kept confused as to the ultimate objective of American forces.

Two days later, while the emperor's High Command was still trying to figure out what hit them, one carrier group swept over northern Luzon while the rest refueled. Score: 10 to 15 planes; opposition: negligible.

On 12 October came a real rouser when Admiral Mitscher's warbirds spread ruin and wreckage over Formosa's 25 to 30 airfields, shipping, and military installations. During these operations, the submarine *Trigger* was on lifeguard duty. Up to that morning the submarine service was rather confident—largely because of a long string of successes—about its ability to rescue aviators downed at sea. That confidence was not destroyed, but it was considerably shaken about 1100 hours on that windswept morning when a burning fighter plane made a crash landing some 300 yards from the *Trigger,* disintegrated, and sank. The pilot had worked himself free from the wreckage; but, buffeted by a strong wind and manhandled by high combers, his strength was ebbing. Realizing that the pilot stood no chance of reaching the sub under his own power, Lieutenant (jg) C. J. Roberts dived into the water and swam to the rescue, disregarding the rough sea and ignoring the stern fact that an approaching enemy plane could force the sub to dive at any moment and leave him behind. Roberts brought the Hellcatter safely aboard, and he was returned to his carrier, CV *Bunker Hill.* But that incident was important in the Submarine Rescue League because it initiated the creation of volunteer teams of strong swimmers aboard rescue subs, a group of unsung heroes who stood ready to take chances as grave as those faced by Lieutenant Roberts.

Other spectacular rescues, which did not include subs, were to be performed in TF 38 while off Formosa. Perhaps Friday the 13th had something to do with it. During a sunset attack against TG 1, CA *Canberra,* a recently commissioned heavy cruiser, was critically damaged by a torpedo. Some commanders would have scuttled her, but not Bill Halsey. After inquiry, he decided that the ship could be salvaged and ordered the cruiser *Wichita* to take the wounded vessel out of the combat area under tow. The next morning Captain Acuff's fleet tug *Munsee* took over for the long haul to Ulithi. Air action over Formosa was relatively light on the following day, although a strike by B-29 bombers out of China gave much weight to the occasion. Late in the afternoon another Japanese sortie against TG 1 was staged. A good baker's dozen of new twin-engine torpedo-bombers (Frances) bored in against Slew McCain's carriers again, hit none, but socked a torpedo into CL *Houston.* At first it was believed that she had been too severely hurt to survive, but her skipper, Captain W. W. Behrens, and crew fought so manfully that she remained afloat. Again, Bill Halsey had a tough decision to make. He ordered the cruiser *Boston* to take her lighter sister in tow, which she did until fleet tug *Pawnee* took over. Meanwhile Admiral Halsey had assigned Rear Admiral DuBose to head a protective unit of two light carriers, CVLs *Cabot* and *Cowpens,* cruisers *Birmingham, Mobile,* and *Santa Fe,* and eight destroyers. Thus escorted, the cripples steamed at 3½ knots toward the atoll, about 1,300 miles away.

For all practical purposes, TF 38s strikes against Formosa ended on the 14th with satisfactory results. Some 390 planes had been downed or wrecked, and extensive damage had been done to airfields and military installations. A lot of marus and other ships had been sent to the bottom and a number had been damaged. Toward the end of day Japanese airdromes became extremely busy. Soon strong units of bombers and torpedo-planes roared down from Japan to stage running attacks on TF 38 far out at sea on 15–16 October. They were supported by attack waves sent out from Luzon. None of these sorties were successful, but they were made expensive by interception, CAP activity, and antiaircraft guns, all of which scored very heavily. A thin reward for the meatball pilots was a torpedo in the stern of the crippled *Houston.* In one of these encounters, a semihero of Japan was created. The story is that Rear Admiral Masafumi Arima took off from Clark Field near Manila with the avowed intention of making a deliberate suicide attack on an American vessel. He belonged to the school of thought, endorsed by Vice Admiral Takijiro Onishi, that argued that Japan could fight its way to victory through the self-sacrifice of Kamikaze pilots who aimed to destroy enemy ships by crash-landing upon them with a 500-pound bomb. Alas, Admiral Arima misjudged the factors involved and crashed harmlessly, except for himself, into the water. Even so, he was loudly acclaimed in Japan as the premier Kamikaze pilot, and a rumor that he had actually been shot down was ignored.

That night Japanese fliers reported an amazing victory. Tokyo maintained—for the fifth or sixth time—that the naval strength of the enemy had been rendered insignificant. TF 38 listeners to Tokyo Rose's radio program that night heard that their force had been reduced by 11 carriers sunk and 6 damaged, 2 battleships sunk and 1 damaged, 3 cruisers sunk, and so on. There was a strong probability that the Japanese would send out ships and planes to mop up the

cripples and finish off what remained. Admiral Halsey decided to run
a bluff against the opposition by changing Admiral DuBose's protective unit into bait. During the fighting, the two units had come quite
close together. Now the admiral took TF 38 below the horizon and
let the salvage unit and its protectors float on the sea, lone and lost as
winged ducks. If Japanese warships sortied out, Bill Halsey would rush
up over the horizon. True enough, believing their own propaganda
fabrications, Vice Admiral Shima steamed out of Bungo Strait with
his Second Striking Force of 2 heavy and 1 light cruiser and 8 destroyers, with a protective escort of land-based airplanes. All seemed
fine until a far-ranging snooper sighted TF 38 and gave the alarm.
Admiral Shima ran for the nearest port, which happened to be
Amami-O-Shima in the Ryukyus.

In his report to CincPac that night, Admiral Halsey ironically observed that all ships reported sunk by Tokyo Radio had been salvaged and that he was "retiring at high speed *toward* the Japanese
fleet."

Admiral Toyoda's acceptance of overoptimistic battle reports was
a costly error. In the first place he committed about 50 percent of the
half-trained fliers of Admiral Ozawa's CarDivs 3 and 4 to Formosa,
where half were destroyed and the other half remained. This weakened the scant air strength in Admiral Ozawa's command. Also, in
not ordering Admiral Shima to return to Japan he created a situation
that robbed Admiral Ozawa's main body of badly needed gun support.

Japanese losses in the air battle off and over Formosa were 650
planes, including both those shot down and those hit while on the
ground. On the American side, 76 planes were lost in combat or op-
erationally. In damaging the *Canberra* and the *Houston,* the Japanese
won a temporary victory. Both reached port, underwent repairs, and
returned to the fleet.

On 17–18 October TF 38, to Toyoda's profound surprise, hit
Manila and northern Luzon, sank shipping, smashed airfields, and
wrecked planes.

Because he feared a sudden emergence by elements of the Japanese
Navy from Empire waters, Admiral Halsey believed it best to remain
on guard in the Luzon area. For that reason, he notified General Mac-
Arthur that he would not be able to deliver strikes on the central
Philippines prior to and during the landings on October 20, as

planned. Because of this, the strikes were undertaken by jeep carriers in Admiral Kinkaid's fleet, with excellent results.

While the Halsey–Mitscher team ranged up and down the islands in the Far Pacific, General MacArthur collected and loaded the impressive force of 738 vessels, of which 157 were large, medium, and small combat ships. There were also 420 landing craft of various types for ferrying some 133,000 invasion troops and mountains of supplies to the beachheads south of Tacloban and north of Dulag on the eastern shores of Leyte Gulf.

The commanders of this vast organization of ships and men were experienced beachhoppers. In over-all command of the Seventh Fleet and attack forces was Admiral Kinkaid, with Admiral Wilkinson, on loan from the Third Fleet, as his deputy. General Walter Krueger, of Hollandia fame, was in over-all command of troops. The Northern Attack Force for the Tacloban end of the gulf was headed by Rear Admiral Daniel E. Barbey. Its two attack groups, commanded by Admiral Barbey and Rear Admiral W. M. Fechteler, respectively, embarked the 24th Infantry (Major General F. A. Irving) and the 1st Cavalry Division (Major General Verne D. Mudge). Rear Admiral A. D. Struble commanded Panaon Attack Group, with the 24th Division's 21st RCT (Lieutenant Colonel F. R. Weber), as well as the Dinagat Attack Group, with the 6th Ranger Battalion and Co. B, 21st Infantry (Lieutenant Colonel H. A. Mucci). There were three fire-support units—one of three battleships and destroyers, another of two cruisers and destroyers, and a third of five Elsie gun and rocket ships. These would provide covering fire for the groups in the order given. Reinforcement groups, escorted by destroyers, would arrive with additional troops two days, four days, and nine days after A-day.

The Southern Attack Force, to land near Dulag on Leyte Gulf, was commanded by Vice Admiral Wilkinson. Attack Group *Able,* commanded by Rear Admiral R. L. Conolly, carried the 7th Infantry (Major General A. V. Arnold). Attack Group *Baker,* commanded by Rear Admiral F. B. Royal, embarked the 96th Infantry (Major General J. L. Bradley). These infantry divisions were part of the 24th Army Corps, commanded by Major General J. R. Hodge.

The guns of Admiral Olie Oldendorf's battleship and cruiser divisions, plus destroyer squadrons, were there to protect the landings, as were Rear Admiral Thomas L. Sprague's three CVE escort carrier groups, each with six baby flattops and their destroyer and destroyer escorts. These CVE groups were commanded by Admiral T. L. Sprague (Taffy 1); Rear Admiral Felix B. Stump (Taffy 2), and Rear Admiral Clifton A. Sprague (Taffy 3). Their close covering group of cruisers and destroyers was commanded by Rear Admiral R. S. Berkey. To survey the beaches and to clear the gulf of mines, Seventh Fleet brought along several units of UDT swimmers commanded by Lieutenant Commander C. C. Morgan; Commander W. R. Loud commanded a flock of minesweepers.

Anticipating that trouble might enter Leyte Gulf from the west and through Surigao Strait in the shape of Japanese men-o'-war, 33 PT boats, commanded by Commander S. S. Bowling, patrolled the waters beyond the southern entrance into the strait. To take care of this long procession of ships in "MacArthur's Navy," was Rear Admiral R. O. Glover's service force of oilers, provision ships, ammo providers, water tankers, repair and salvage ships. The services performed by this sterling unit had much to do with keeping the fleet, its men and planes on the move.

In contrast to the battle of the Philippine Sea, all submarines, Pacific, were withdrawn from the Philippine Sea as battle flags began to flutter, while those of SoWesPac maintained scout patrols. This was to give Seventh Fleet ships full freedom to fire on any sub sighted. The only exception was a safety lane which ran east-west from Saipan to Luzon Strait. When, eventually, the battle areas became well defined, ComSubPac stationed a line of subs from Formosa to Luzon to cut off escapees. They included two wolf packs—Roach's Raiders and Clarey's Crushers.

Chapter Ten

RETURN TO LEYTE

LEYTE GULF, THE PHILIPPINE SEA, and the straits of San Bernardino and Surigao—as well as the air space above them—provide the background for battles that ran simultaneously in four closely grouped areas.

Leyte Gulf runs north-south, is about 40 miles wide and 55 long, and lies south of Samar in the central Philippines. On the islands that frame the gulf, forbidding jungle-clad mountains rise from the water lines. The only hospitable beaches on Leyte run some 20 miles south from Tacloban, the capital, to Dulag, a small village. On these, north and south beachheads were to be established. The gulf has two entrances, facing east and south. The first runs westward from the Philippine Sea, where several small islands and Desolation Point on Dinagat, a larger island, stand guard; the second runs northward through Surigao Strait from the Mindanao Sea. The latter, shaped like an hourglass, is about 15 miles wide at its center and about 30 miles wide at top and bottom; it runs nearly 75 miles, framed by mountainous islands blanketed with dense jungle vegetation. At its southern end lies Panaon Island. The Mindanao Sea, a large spread of inland water, connects the strait with the Sulu Sea.

Above Leyte Gulf, and about 100 miles as the rocket flies, lies San Bernardino Strait, which gives passage to eastward from the Sulu and China Seas by way of the Sibuyan Sea and which opens into the Philippine Sea just north of Samar Island. Although there is plenty of room and deep water in the Sibuyan Sea, navigation under war conditions becomes quite difficult once an eastbound fleet has passed between Burias and Ticao islands. But the navigator's leeway is even less when he enters the narrow channels, rocks, tide rips, and strong currents of San Bernardino Strait. To pass through this at night without beacon guides, as Admiral Kurita proposed to do, took courage and seamanship—and a fair measure of desperation.

Among the central Philippine coastal islands lies a bewildering pattern of waterways that run through a helter-skelter archipelago of large and small mountainous islands. Some of these are spaced well apart; most of them are bunched closely together. This may be a sailor's paradise but it is not an airman's. There are few places to land in emergencies, and the deep shadows cast on narrow waters by fairly high island elevations makes surface surveillance from above extremely difficult. The airline distances between the Philippine Sea and the Sulu Sea by way of either passage is about 200 miles. Of the two, Surigao is the less winding. As for the Philippine Sea itself, the area of action stretched 500 miles from Desolation Point on Dinagat Island to Cape Deception (Engaño) at the northern tip of Luzon.

First of the invasion forces to reach Leyte Gulf were the 500 fighting men of Lieutenant Colonel Mucci's 6th Rangers in the Dinagat Attack Group. After a brief cannonading by ships in the group's screen, the Rangers disembarked from the fast destroyer-transports into landing craft and went ashore on tiny Suluan, the outermost of the two islands in the mouth of the gulf. That morning the Rangers were riding the tail end of a near typhoon; the wind was high, the sea was rough, and visibility was zero. Even so, they made a quick job of running down the few Japanese on the island while the natives cheered. After Suluan, they were supposed to capture the northern tip of Dinagat Island; but the high-rolling surf had wrecked their landing boats. Unable to land on Dinagat, there they were on Suluan, warmed by the joy shown by the natives over their coming and proud of being the first American liberators to step on Philippine soil at Leyte.

But they were mistaken in thinking they were the first. Seven nights earlier, after a daring flight from the SoWesPac area in a Black Cat (night Catalina flying boat) that skimmed the wave tops to avoid enemy radar, a plane had dashed into the gulf, where it had landed for just the time it took two men to toss out a raft and jump after it. One man, clad only in shirt, shorts, and shoes, was Commander Charles "Chick" Parsons, hero of Filipino guerillas and General MacArthur's master spy. The other, Colonel Frank Rowall of 6th Army Intelligence, wore jungle garb and was loaded with combat gear. Chick carried no weapons, not even a knife. His job was to avoid the enemy and gather information.

As a long-time prewar resident and businessman of Manila, Chick Parsons spoke Spanish and Filipino dialects like a native; in fact, having the stature of one, with coal-black hair and deeply bronzed skin, he could and did pass for a Filipino. These assets, plus courage and perception, had made Commander Parsons head and organizer of General MacArthur's Philippine Spy Squadron, known as Spyron. Starting in January 1943, when Spyron began operations, SoWesPac submarines made runs at four- to five-week intervals to the Philippines with coast watchers and other personnel. They also carried clothing, weapons, and supplies for the quickly growing, well-armed, and highly disciplined Philippine Guerilla Army, which had the United States' official blessing. Commander Parsons was a regular commuter on those runs. For his expanding radio network, Commander Parsons invariably brought along a dozen or more small radio sending and receiving sets. He also distributed Japanese invasion money by the bundle to help finance the guerillas. On return trips the submarines carried evacuees and intelligence too bulky for radio transmission.

The result was that King II, when its hour came, had better and later information on enemy movements and targets than invasion commanders usually possess. This data reached its peak of importance during the Philippine campaign about to begin.

Commander Parsons, after he had provided sources for Colonel Rowall, contacted Colonel Roberto Ruperto K. Kangeleon, commander of the Central Section of the Philippine Army, whose radio network stepped up its flow of information. Natives in the Leyte area were warned to seek safety in the hills and not to return until allowed to do so. Guerilla units were placed in ambush positions along trails, paths, and roads used by Japanese troops in retreating from the Leyte Gulf region to stronger inland positions. The landing beaches had to be searched for mines, barbed wire, and other obstacles. But Chick's largest contributions were, first, the arrangements he made for full and frequent radio reports on enemy activities; and second, paving the way for integrating the Filipinio Army into General MacArthur's operations.

One thing disturbed Commander Parsons: because the forthcoming invasion was supersecret he could give no explanations. Therefore, arrangements were not easy to make. Still, thanks largely to Colonel Kangeleon's unstinted and unquestioning cooperation, it was done.

Chick Parsons' earliest contact with the occupation forces of King II occurred on the morning of 20 October, near the Tacloban beachhead, as the GIs stormed ashore. He was under orders to bring

Colonel Kangeleon and his signal officer aboard Admiral Kinkaid's flagship *Wasatch* for conference with General Krueger, commander invasion forces. Chick was to report to Commodore Valentine S. Schaeffer, C of S to Admiral Kinkaid.

In Tokyo, Admiral Toyoda's spirits could hardly have risen when he received word from the Philippines about the Rangers having landed. The message arrived at 0809 on 17 October. Instantly, he rang the bells that alerted SHO 1. While the invasion was expected, Admiral Toyoda would have blessed every hour of the time lag he had hoped for. The canny commander must have been fully aware of his fleet's unsound disposition and that it would have to be committed piecemeal in four salients. Three of these would have to accept passages through restricted waters because there was no time to steam around the islands into the Philippine Sea. Having no air arm, these ships must look to land-based air, which was hampered by lack of planning and training, as well as by equipment shortages and poor communications.

To fully appreciate this suicidal program, one must realize that the enemy, in risking the loss of his fleet, had little choice in the matter. With the Philippines gone, the Japanese Navy could engage in no really serious combat, because men-of-war in home waters would be short on fuel and those in Asiatic waters would be short on ammunition.

The fourth group, an elaborate decoy of lightly screened carriers with few planes aboard, would sail south from Japan through open waters on a desperate gamble that its mere presence would be a threat that TF 38 could not ignore. With TF 38 lured from the invasion area, it was hoped that at least one of the three salients, steaming east through the Surigao and San Bernardino straits, could reach the Leyte beachheads and break up the invasion. The gamble was desperate, but it almost succeeded.

According to plans, the Japanese forces would move as follows:

> At Lingga: Admiral Kurita's First Striking Force of two groups, comprising 4 battleships, 7 heavy and 1 light cruiser, plus 11 destroyers, would make for Brunei Bay, Borneo, to await activation orders. So would a third group, under Admiral Nishimura, consisting of 2 battleships, 1 heavy cruiser, and 4 destroyers.

> At Amami-O-Shima: Admiral Shima, instead of providing fire support for Admiral Ozawa's carriers, would take his 3

cruisers and 4 destroyers to the Pescadores, in the Strait of Formosa, and await further orders.

In Japan: At the proper time, Admiral Ozawa would sortie from the Inland Sea with 1 heavy and 3 light carriers, 2 BBs converted into semicarriers, plus a screen of 4 light cruisers, 5 destroyers, and 6 destroyer escorts. His few pilots were so inexperienced that most of them had orders, if they became airborne, not to return to their flattops but to land on Luzon. Admiral Miwa would send his submarines to the Leyte area. Hardly had Admiral Toyoda started the SHO 1 alert when the commanding general of the Japanese Army in the Philippines asked for 900 plane reinforcements, an order that was greeted by a hollow laugh in the homeland.

Dawn of 18 October over Leyte Gulf brought improvement in the weather. The Rangers ferried to Dinagat and found no Japanese. Then they rushed to Homonhon Island, 15 miles north and to the west of Suluan, deeper into the entrance of the gulf. There, too, they found no Japanese.

Admiral Oldendorf, with his battlewagons, escort carriers, minesweepers, and UDT men, as well as the Rangers, began bombarding the green wilderness on the mountains that surrounded the landing areas. There was no opposition as Commander Loud and his minesweepers began paravaning the gulf, where they found no mines. However, in the channel just below Homonhon Island they discovered a large area planted with mines. They also found some of those meanest of killers—floating mines.

Next, UDT men were put over the side of their destroyer-transports to check on Chick Parsons' beach report; they found it to be absolutely correct. As if the sight of the UDT men provoked them, Japanese gunners in the hills opened fire and thus enabled the big guns to demolish a few positions. That night, Admiral Oldendorf prepared for a day-long bombardment at sunrise.

At dawn 19 October the battle line and the fire-support vessels subjected the landing areas and adjacent territory to a thorough going-over. At the same time, Admiral T. L. Sprague's jeep carriers launched air combat patrols to protect against air and submarine action and to stage neutralizing strikes on Leyte and other islands. While they met some opposition, it was not in great strength. A tougher job fell to fliers who served as spotters for Admiral Oldendorf's gunners. Enemy batteries, well hidden beneath the dense jungle growth, were difficult to spot, especially since the artillery used smokeless powder. To the north, the Halsey-Mitscher team was on the alert—westward and northward—for Japanese warships as well as for the familiar outlines of Zekes and Judys.

The actual landings on A-day operated with precision. Veterans, through experience, and novices, through countless drills, had learned how to scramble down the nets draped over the sides of tall transports from rails to the landing vessels below. With their eyes on the feet of the man above, they slid into the landing boats so jammed there was hardly breathing room. Then they headed shoreward to expand the beachheads.

Just off the landing beaches south of Tacloban, as the first wave came ashore, were a relaxed group of Filipinos, some of whom were armed with rifles; among them sat Chick Parsons and Colonel Kangeleon. Barefooted, clad in worn, stained shorts and shirt, his head covered by a floppy-brimmed native hat, there was nothing to identify Chick as an American and certainly not as a commander in the U.S. Navy. He and the colonel were waiting for transportation to Admiral Kinkaid's flagship, which was lying quite a distance offshore. But all boats were too busy to give them a lift. The two men were hard put not to display impatience. About noon, after two hours of waiting, Chick caught the attention of the OOD on a nearby destroyer. He signaled a message for the flagship. The signal was relayed by blinker to the *Wasatch,* and the destroyer was ordered to bring the party aboard. Having seen the party of roughly clad armed men, someone aboard the DD concluded that there was something fishy about them. Japanese in disguise, maybe. The DD skipper evidently decided to play it safe and put over a boat full of steel-helmeted, fully armed sailors.

Seeing the approaching boatload of bluejackets ready to shoot, the Filipinos began to feel for their triggers. The situation was getting tense. If Americans killed Filipinos or vice versa, much trouble could result. Fortunately, an unharmed fishing boat was beached nearby. With the help of a couple of Filipinos, Chick had it launched and set out to meet the DD's boat, now circling guardedly offshore. Only helmets and gun muzzles were showing. Chick, not easily worried, shouted at the boat officer and stated his business. Luckily, the ensign in charge believed him. The boat picked up the three passengers and delivered them aboard the flagship. After seeing Colonel Kangeleon warmly welcomed by General Krueger, Chick reported to Commodore Schaeffer. During a long conference he made the mistake of suggesting ways to clean up a Japanese radio station and an observation post on southern Leyte, and despite his objections, drew the job of disposing of them. There being no way out, he did it.

H-hour was 1000, and on the dot waves of landing craft, led by waves of amtracs, approached the smoke and din that hung over Leyte. Battleships, cruisers, and destroyers were pumping shells into the island's hidden defenses. After the Elsie gunboats and amtracs came seemingly endless waves of LVTs, carrying assault troops, and LCMs with still more troops.

Greeting the eyes of the GIs as they hit the beach and its piles of debris was the U.S. flag flying from the top of a tall coconut tree, the first to be raised in the liberation of the Philippines. In the first assault wave an LST skipper had given his ship's flag to a young Army lieutenant, who promised to run it up as soon as he got ashore.

Thus the Stars and Stripes were already flying when General Mac-Arthur, accompanied by Sergio Osmeña, president of the Philippines, set foot on Leyte. A Signal Corps microphone, placed on the beach, had been hooked up with the underground Voice of Freedom radio network. General MacArthur stepped up to the microphone. Wind-driven rain coming down in sheets did not deter him. After a brief pause he said: "People of the Philippines, I have returned."

Following these words, the liberator of the Philippines delivered an eloquent and stirring message in which he asked the Filipinos to fight their oppressors at every turn.

General MacArthur had walked ashore from the CL *Nashville's* motor whaler and thereby hangs a story. One of his aides, on learning that the beach shelved so slowly that the whaler could never reach dry land, telephoned the beach for a small landing craft to which the general could transfer. At that moment the beach was hectic with activity. LSTs, their bows well up on the sand, were unloading cargo. Hundreds of small landing craft were squeezed onto the beach, ramps down, and bulldozers were unloading them. Everywhere was bustle and confusion. Bullets fired by snipers hidden on the thickly wooded slope whizzed by like angry bees. It was no time to disturb an over-burdened beachmaster. Angrily, he told the lieutenant to "let 'em walk." That was why the general and his party were wet to their knees.

Later in the day, after snipers had been killed or driven out, Fili-pinos, hundreds of them—ragged, haggard, and undernourished, but smiling and laughing—drifted down to the beach from the hills. GIs and sailors fed them all they had. K-rations were never so popular. Doctors gave first aid to those in need of help. Young men and boys, on meeting men of our forces, jumped to stiff attention, saluted smartly, then broke into wide grins.

A-day on Leyte produced a surprising lack of resistance. Perhaps Lieutenant Colonel F. R. Weber, commander of the 21st RCT, 24th Infantry Division, and his men had the greatest surprise of all. Panaon Island at the southern end of Surigao Strait occupied a strategic position and had to be taken at all cost. It was said to be heavily garrisoned.

Protected by its screen, the Panaon Attack Group, commanded by Rear Admiral A. D. Struble, approached the island. Colonel Weber was miffed when the silence that hung over the island was not broken by the roar of the screen's guns. In short order, the colonel and his troops were put over the side and set ashore. The combat team followed their commander up the empty beach and stopped short when a stream of Filipino women, children, and old men poured out of the woods, waving American flags and singing "God Bless America." Colonel Weber later learned that Chick Parsons, knowing that Panaon and Tacloban had been evacuated by the enemy, had asked that the two localities be taken off the bombing list.

Naval aviation played a strong but not a lone hand in air-support operations during the Philippine campaign. It was joined by several of the Army's air forces: The 5th (assault) Air Force operated from the Celebes Sea to Leyte; the 13th (support) Air Force neutralized enemy air on eastern Borneo and supported 5th AF operations when needed. The 7th Air Force operated in Southern Luzon under Third Fleet orders; from far off Chica, the 14th and 20th air forces attacked China coast and Formosa installations.

Opposition at Leyte was deceptively light and sporadic. The enemy, in line with the new, and smart, tactical policy, no longer wasted men and ammunition on the beaches. Instead of yielding foot by foot and staging suicidal banzai charges, they withdrew—as on Peleliu—to the hills and mountains and waited for the Americans to come to them. Therefore, a landing opposed by only light artillery and small-caliber automatic fire of fairly short duration, did not mean an unopposed invasion, as General MacArthur's troops were to learn the hard way when they extended their operations. By nightfall on A-day, 60,000 men occupied greatly expanded beachheads and the Tacloban airstrip. A swarm of PT boats patrolled beyond the Panaon area, guarding the southern entrance to Surigao Strait. In addition to thousands of troops, General MacArthur's amphibious force carried 1,500,000 tons of supplies and 500,000 tons of combat hardware from tanks to artillery, from automatic weapons to flamethrowers. This is an awful lot of military muscle.

If Admiral Toyoda had hoped to sneak up on the American forces at Leyte, he had been blind to the alertness of American subs. As early as 18 October, Pacific subs sighted Admiral Shima pushing toward the Pescadores. Several days later Admiral Ozawa was sighted by another Saipan-based submarine as he emerged from Bungo Strait. Under "observe and report" orders, these subs had to refrain from taking torpedo action.

Similarly, alert SoWesPac subs were on the prowl off the western side of the Philippines. Near midnight on 21 October the SS *Dace* (commander B. D. Claggett) made radio contact with three large, fast-moving ships near Palawan. He reported his sighting to Admiral Christie, gave chase, but could not match knots with his targets. From Australia, the news was flashed to all concerned. The Mac-Arthur–Kinkaid forces set themselves for attacks that might come at night through either the San Bernardino Strait or the Surigao Strait, or both, as did the Halsey–Mitscher team in TF 38. TG 1 (Admiral McCain) and TG 4 (Admiral Davison) were en route to Ulithi for badly needed fuel and supplies. Admiral Davison was recalled and ordered to refuel at sea. Admiral McCain, whose resources had been worn rather threadbare off Formosa, was ordered to proceed but to make a quick turnaround. This left Pete Mitscher with three task groups.

Admiral Kurita and his First Striking Force, in three groups, arrived at Brunei, Borneo, at noon on 20 October, having received orders to activate SHO 1 at 1808 on 18 October while at sea. The subsequent operational orders received by him set 25 October as X-day and 24 October as Y-day. Specifically, these orders provided for the first two groups in the main force (Admiral Kurita) and the third group (Admiral Nishimura) to proceed as follows:

> 1. Main Force to sortie from Brunei at 0800, 22d. Speed of advance, 16 knots; north Palawan course; south of Mindoro on 24th and thereafter, speed 20 to 24 knots. Arrive east entrance to San Bernardino at sundown of same day and at 0400, X-day, arrive vicinity of

Suluan Island, from whence break through to
anchorage.

2. 3d Group will depart Brunei during afternoon of 22d. It will arrive east entrance to
Surigao Straits in the Mindanao Sea at about
sundown on X-day minus one after crossing the
Sulu Sea. In coordination with Main Force of
1-YB, will break through to anchorage at dawn
on X day.

Admiral Ozawa was shorn of all commands save that of his
phantom carrier fleet. Admiral Kurita was taken out of his jurisdiction and placed under the direct command of Admiral Toyoda;
Admiral Shima and his gun-support unit were assigned to the commander, Southwest Area Force, with orders to proceed to Manila.
These instructions were later canceled and Admiral Shima was directed to follow Admiral Nishimura into Surigao Strait. He was not,
however, placed under Admiral Nishimura's command; nor was
Nishimura placed under Admiral Shima. Admiral Ozawa's orders
were to coordinate his actions with those of Admiral Kurita and that
"the Mobile Fleet will maneuver in the seas to the east of Luzon for
the purpose of luring the enemy to the north and at the same time
utilizing any opportunity to attack and destroy him."

Admiral Toyoda further directed that the "main strength of the 6th
Base Air Force (Luzon) be deployed to make an all-out attack
against the Task Force on Y-day (24 October). For this purpose the
6th Base Air Force was placed under the tactical command of C in C
Southwest Area Fleet, who was also given command of all naval air
forces concentrated in the Philippines so as to carry out destructive
attacks against the enemy's carrier and landing forces. Also, in
cooperation with the Army, counterattacks would be staged against
the enemy's land forces.

Indicating the jittery state of mind in Admiral Kurita's main force
as it steamed toward the Philippines were the numerous false sightings, between 1431 and 1735 on 22 October, of submarines and
mines. Three cruisers, *Noshiro, Takao,* and *Atago,* the admiral's flagship, reported submarines, and the two superbattleships, *Yamato* and
Musashi, reported sighting mines. Incidentally, the mines could have
been authentic. Our submarines sighted large numbers of mines that
had broken loose from their anchors and they exploded them with
machine-gun fire. Night fell and almost passed while the Main Force

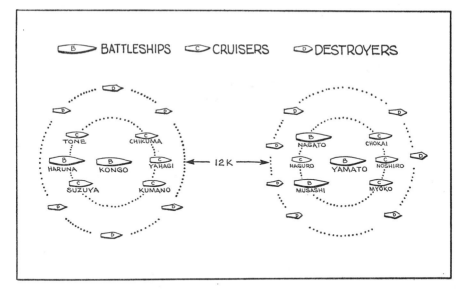

BATTLESHIPS   CRUISERS   DESTROYERS

TONE CHIKUMA HARUNA KONGO YAHAGI SUZUYA KUMANO

← 12K →

NAGATO CHOKAI HAGURO YAMATO NOSHIRO MUSASHI MYOKO

On 24 October 1944, without air cover and depending solely on the firepower of his guns, Vice Admiral Kurita steamed in antiaircraft formation across the Sibuyan Sea toward San Bernardino Strait in bold defiance of TF 38 aviators, who sank one battleship and put a cruiser to flight. But their combat reports so grossly overestimated their victories that Admiral Halsey no longer considered Admiral Kurita's force a threat, which was far from the case.

rolled out 18 knots on a zigzag course. Then, at 0532 on 23 October, the jitters were justified. Four torpedoes, launched from SS *Darter* (Commander D. A. McClintock), blasted into the mighty *Atago* with such force that the cruiser sank. A few minutes later, *Darter's* packmate *Dace* (Commander B. D. Claggett) sent a spread of six torpedoes toward *Maya,* another heavy cruiser, sinking her almost immediately. During this short time Commander McClintock sent another string of torpedoes into a third heavy cruiser, *Takao.* She did not sink but was so badly disabled that she fell out of column and retreated. A fourth cruiser, *Aoba,* was crippled by another SoWesPac sub, SS *Bream* (Commander W. G. Chapple). *Takao* and *Aoba* returned to Brunei under escort.

Within a few minutes the guns on about 50,000 tons of cruisers had been silenced, ample testimony to Admiral Kurita's phrase that "to be sighted is to be sunk." But *Darter* was lost that night when she ran aground on Bombay Shoal on the edge of Palawan Passage. After all hands were taken aboard *Dace*, *Darter* was shelled to prevent her from being salvaged by the enemy. Before that, Admiral Kurita had performed the unpleasant duty of reporting his losses.

At 2034 on 23 October, as Admiral Kurita steamed toward Mindoro, he received an estimate of the situation from Admiral Toyoda as of noon that day. The message began: "It is very probable that the enemy is aware of the fact that we have concentrated our forces."

That was one of the major Japanese understatements issued during the war.

Chapter Eleven

CROSSING THE "T"

FROM THE TIME OF THE LANDING on 20 October and throughout the next three days, beachhead expansions and air operations were slowed by foul weather. By 24 October it was again fair flying weather. Search planes were sent aloft from TF 38 with the result that a pilot from the CV *Intrepid* sighted Admiral Kurita's main force as it entered the Sibuyan Sea through Tablas Strait shortly after daylight. From there it was an open-water run of some 80 miles to the pass between Burias, Masbate, and Ticao islands, which lead to San Bernardino Strait. The absence of carriers was noted.

As soon as he received word of the sighting, Admiral Halsey characteristically took the bit in his teeth. At that time TG 3 (Admiral Sherman) was off Luzon's east coast opposite Manila. About 150 miles to the south of this position, opposite San Bernardino Strait, was Admiral Bogan's TG 2; and some 120 miles to the south of him, off Samar and near Leyte, was TG 4 (Admiral Davison).

Hardly had the orders been issued for TGs 3 and 4 to join TG 2 at San Bernardino when a large flock of bogeys turned up on Admiral Sherman's radar screens. From his carriers, Hellcats roared out to meet the bandits, who proved to be about 200 land-based aircraft of all varieties. Meeting the Hellcats head-on, they were turned back with 50 percent losses. During the encounter, some 40 Zekes formed the nose-to-tail circle known as a Lufberry Ring, a protective aerial buzzsaw that is dangerous to tackle. From higher altitudes 8 *Essex* Hellcats regarded the show with the patience of cats watching mice at play. Finally the ring broke up and the Hellcats pounced on their victims. Commander David McCampbell, boss of *Essex* Air Group 15, added nine scalps to his already large collection.

The *Princeton* pilots were coming in when, suddenly, one lone Judy dived out of the cloud cover over their carrier. Disdaining the burst of antiaircraft fire, the Japanese pilot landed a 550-pound bomb that penetrated both flight and hangar decks before it exploded and started a fire that triggered the warheads of six torpedoes. Their violent explosions added to the intensity of the blaze. Under the courageous leadership of Captain W. H. Buracker, her skipper, all hands fell to the seemingly impossible task of quelling the blaze.

Aboard his flagship, the *Essex,* Admiral Sherman was watching the battle against the flames when he received orders to stand south to San Bernardino. Instead, the admiral assigned the CLs *Birmingham* (Captain Thomas B. Inglis) and *Reno* (Captain R. C. Alexander), along with three destroyers, to assist in the fire-fighting and rescue operations while TG 3 stood by to provide air cover. The cruisers concentrated mainly on overcoming the fire; the destroyers devoted themselves to saving the lives of men still aboard the carrier and those who had jumped into the sea. As senior officer present, Captain Tom Inglis was in charge of the operation.

In the midst of their heroic undertakings, and when success seemed near, another air alarm came in and a submarine was reported sighted. Preparing for action, the cruisers cast off lines and fire hoses as they withdrew to find maneuvering space. The submarine alarm proved false, but 76 planes from Ozawa's carrier force hurled themselves against TG 3. Fortunately, there was just time to scramble fighters. Result: About 50 enemy planes were flamed or splashed. At 1523 the missiles in *Princeton's* ready bomb storage exploded. Her flight deck rose and disintegrated into tons of debris. This flaming pile was flung with tremendous force on the deck of *Birmingham,* killing 229 men and injuring 440. While doctors and corpsmen took care of the wounded, Captain Inglis, himself wounded, stood by until *Princeton* was finally abandoned and torpedoed. Of the CVL's complement, 7 were dead, 99 missing, and 190 injured. Only then did the proud *Birmingham* stand eastward for Ulithi, and under her own power at that.

In the Mindanao Sea, meanwhile, Admiral Nishimura's 3rd Group was sighted by TF 38 long-range search fighter-bomber units as it began its 140-mile run to Surigao Strait on the morning of 24 October. After reporting their discovery, the TF 38 pilots attacked, giving the enemy formation a good going-over that ended abruptly when the planes were recalled to base to prepare for bigger game. The results of their call included bomb hits on the BB *Fuso* that wrecked the airplane catapult system and started aviation gas fires that destroyed the battleship's observation planes.

In the flag-plots of Admirals Halsey and Kinkaid—when the reports from the Sibuyan and Mindanao Seas were unified—it was clear that the enemy planned to enclose Leyte Gulf in a pair of pincers designed to strangle the landing forces after disposing of air and sea defenses. There was nothing new in this finding to either admiral. It only confirmed moves that had been anticipated by both commanders, and each, in his way, was fully prepared to deal with the two-pronged attack of the Japanese fleet. The only factor that was conspicuously lacking in the picture was Japanese carrier support. Neither Kurita nor Nishimura had flattops in their forces. This absence was disturbing because it left unanswered a vital question: "Where were the carriers?" At that time American naval intelligence had only fragmentary information about the disastrous effect of the downing of Japanese pilots and planes on 19 June, as well as of the punishment inflicted by submarines on carriers that day and by aircraft at sunset on 20 June. No one on the American side had positive knowledge that Admiral Ozawa's air arm had virtually lost all its strength.

If Admiral Kurita had been less taciturn and more prone to express his thoughts in writing, he might have given military history a valuable chapter on how it feels to run a sitting-duck fleet during a day-long downpour of aircraft hardware without the shelter of an air umbrella. Earlier in the year he had been caught in a similar position at Rabaul and had run for shelter at Truk as quickly as he could get away. This time the situation was different. Under orders to proceed and attack, he had to keep going and make the best of it. To be sure, a handful of land-based Japanese planes made contact at daylight. But they were like sparrows against hawks compared with what Pete Mitscher could throw against them. On the other hand, Admiral Kurita's array of battleships and cruisers, not to mention destroyers, could provide a very hot time for enemy aviators who ventured too close. It has been reported that one of his battleships mounted 150 antiaircraft guns while the rest, and his cruisers, had some 100 apiece. In addition, the Japanese had learned to elevate the barrels of large- and small-caliber guns so that they could be directed at aircraft, either approaching or overhead. Even the gargantuan 18-inchers were depressed and fired into the sea against low-flying torpedo-planes in the hope that the enormous geysers formed by their splashes would rise in the paths of planes and knock them down.

According to Admiral Kurita's action reports, the first contact with enemy carrier planes was established at 0810 on 24 October. All hands in the main force were called to general quarters and gun crews stood at their weapons as Kurita's force separated into two groups and formed battle circles with BB *Yamato* (the admiral's flagship) in the center of one and BB *Kongo* in the center of the other. Each circle was about 5 miles in diameter and they steamed about 8 miles apart. There were two circles in each ring: an inner one of other capital ships and cruisers and an outer one of destroyers. In line with orders, the admiral increased his speed to 24 knots but later dropped back to 20 knots. The next action entry reads:

> 1055 Main Force (1-YB) reports being engaged by 30 carrier-based planes which were beaten off.
>
> 1135 I-YB spot report. *Myoko* received one torpedo hit. Can make only 15 knots. She is ordered to retire alone to Brunei.
>
> 1220 1-YB spot report No. 2 announced that *Musashi* also hit by one torpedo.

That first attack paid off handsomely. Hellcats, Avengers, and Helldivers from *Intrepid* and *Cabot* reached the enemy force by penetrating an unprecedented storm of flak. The Avengers, dropping through it to torpedo-release altitude, sent their fish and escaped at deck-level heights. Hellcats raised the mortality rate among gun crews with devastating machine-gun fire while Helldivers did a lot of damage by dropping their semi-armor-piercing bombs on steel decks. The smoke from guns, bombs, and fires wrapped the force in a thick, black blanket that reduced visibility to almost nil. There was no air opposition to speak of; the few Japanese planes that stuck around to give fight were soon splashed.

When the fliers broke off, Admiral Kurita resumed course, which he had been forced to leave in order to take evasive action. A few minutes before he heard that *Musashi* had taken a torpedo, a signal from Admiral Nishimura informed him that Group 3 had been sighted and BB *Fuso* hit.

As 1-YB steamed eastward over the placid surface of Sibuyan Sea, fire-control parties fought flames and damage-control units made repairs while gun crews remained ready for the next attack.

> 1225 1-YB reports being attacked by second wave of planes, consisting of about 30 carrier-based aircraft.

This time there was a preponderance of torpedo-carrying Avengers in the attack formations. They made run after run on the mighty

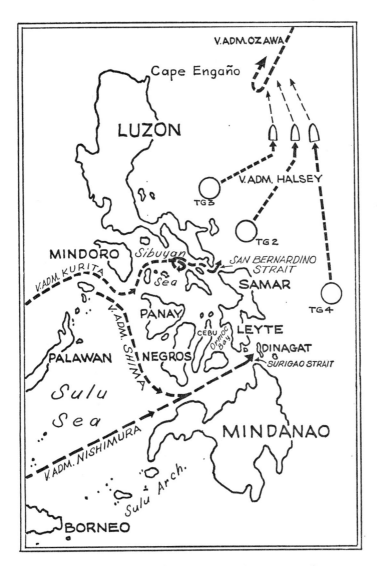

On 24–25 October, Admiral Kurita entered San Bernardino Strait. The entrance to the strait had been left unguarded when Admiral Ozawa, with a phantom carrier fleet, had decoyed Admiral Halsey's Third Fleet away from the area. Admirals Shima and Nishimura approached, but failed to enter, Leyte Gulf. At Surigao Strait, Nishimura's fleet was badly mauled by U.S. forces under Admiral Oldendorf.

Musashi, delivering their fish, then pulling away. Overhead, fighters and bombers sprayed the decks. Their rattle and bang, combined with that of the guns of the ships, set up an ear-piercing din wrapped in a welter of heavy smoke. The attack was of short duration. One moment the air was filled with planes; the next, they were gone. Unemotionally, Admiral Kurita made the following entry:

> 1250 1-YB action spot report No. 3. *Musashi* receives three (making a total of four) torpedo hits and many near misses. Maximum speed 22 knots.

That the absence of promised air support was in the forefront of Admiral Kurita's mind is revealed by the following all-points message:

> 1315 1-YB to Main Body, Mobile Fleet, and Southwest Area Fleet; information Combined Fleet, 1st Air Fleet, and 2nd Air Fleet: We are being subjected to repeated enemy carrier-based air attacks. Advise immediately of contacts and attacks made by you on the enemy.

In other words, he was asking Admiral Ozawa what he had accomplished in contacting TF 38 and luring it north from San Bernardino Strait. He was also asking the commander, Southwest Area (in Manila), who controlled all land-based aviation, what had caused the program of cooperation to go out the window. If a seasoned battlewagon mariner ever needed help from the sky, this was the time.

A few hours passed before the next wave attacked the main force.

> 1342 1-YB action spot report No. 4. Third wave consisting of about 80 carrier-based planes attacked us.

This period of agony lasted less than half an hour, but the attack was of great, almost fearsome, intensity. *Musashi* was again the principal target for bombers and torpedo planes, and they struck at her unmercifully. When Pete Mitscher's boys left, the formidable *Musashi* was no longer a threat. Admiral Kurita reported with great restraint:

> 1452 1-YB action spot report No. 5. *Musashi* receives one (totaling five) torpedo hit; *Yamato* receives one bomb hit; *Musashi*'s operational capacity has been impaired. *Kiyoshimo* (DD) is guarding her and she will proceed to Baco via Coron, if necessary, under her own power.

Soon another wave of American planes attacked with bold indifference to the antiaircraft barrage, emptied their cartridge belts, bomb bays, rocket and torpedo racks, and vanished whence they had come. Wrote Admiral Kurita:

> 1510 1-YB spot action report No. 6: Fourth wave, consisting of 25 planes, attacked. *Yamato* received bomb-hit forward.
> 1530 1-YB action report No. 7. Being engaged by 5th wave consisting of over 100 planes.

With these few words, Admiral Kurita disposes of an attack that swept 1-YB with the force of a Kansas cyclone. Air, ships, and sea shook as bombs, rockets, and torpedoes exploded, as fire from machine guns swept decks, gun positions, turrets, and command bridges probing for soft spots. To hold them off, large and small guns—hundreds of them—on all ships sent up a continuous fire through which it seemed impossible for men to fly—but they did. The smoke from the continuous cannonading was so dense that it appeared to turn the scene into a black volcanic island in fiery and fierce eruption. When the battle was over, Admiral Kurita noted:

> 1602 1-YB action report No. 8. During the attack of the 5th wave, additional damage has apparently been inflicted on *Musashi*. Details are as yet undetermined. (CA) *Nagato's* maximum speed, after being bombed, is 21 knots. *Yamato* has received further bomb hits but her fighting power is unimpaired . . . . (DD) *Kiyoshimo* bombed, maximum speed 20 knots. (CL) *Yahagi* suffers from near misses; maximum speed 22 knots.

During the 5th wave, *Musashi's* fate was sealed when she was hit by many bombs and torpedoes. She slowed from 6 to 2 knots and sat deep in the water. Despite every effort to keep her afloat and moving long enough to run her aground, she sank with her captain and some 1,000 men who remained aboard.

Despite the many delays caused by air attacks, the main force was nearing the channel between Masbate and Burias islands, which marks the end of the open sea and the beginning of island-cluttered waterways. Believing that there was enough daylight left for TF 38 to deliver two more attacks, and not relishing the idea of being pinned down in highly restricted waters, Admiral Kurita decided to reverse course so as to have room in case of attack and to learn, if he could, what support he might expect from land-based air operations against the American carrier task force.

As his fleet made the westward turn, Admiral Kurita sent a signal to Admiral Toyoda informing him of the reversal of course to maintain maneuverability in case of air attack and adding a request for cooperation by land-based air against TF 38. A rather pessimistic note was injected with the observation that continuation of the present course would have little chance of succeeding.

Having done this, Admiral Kurita wrote plainly and forcibly an estimate of the situation as he saw it at that hour (1600).

> Originally the main strength of 1-YB (Admiral Kurita's main force) had intended to force its way through San Bernardino Strait about one hour after sundown, coordinating its moves with air action. However, the enemy made more than 250 sorties against 1-YB between 0830 and 1530, the number of their planes involved and their fierceness mounting with every wave. Our air forces, on the other hand, were not able to obtain even expected results, causing our losses to mount steadily.
>
> Under these circumstances it was deemed that were we to force our way through, we would merely make of ourselves, meat for the enemy, with very little chance of success to us. It was therefore concluded that the best course open to us was to temporarily retire beyond the range of enemy planes and reform our plans. At 1600 we were in the Sibuyan Sea (13° 00′N. 122° 40′E.) on course 290°, speed 18 knots.
>
> Summing up the situation, whereas the enemy air attacks became more intensified with each wave, our air forces failed to obtain satisfactory results against the enemy task forces located in the Lamon and Legaspi areas. Moreover, apparently the main body of our Mobile Force was not succeeding in diverting or attacking the enemy. Our various forces were not successfully coordinating their actions and because of this, 1-YB, placed in a position of fighting the entire battle alone, was being whittled down with nothing to show for its sacrifices.
>
> If 1-YB were to continue eastward in the face of these circumstances, it seemed very likely that it would be subjected to terrific pounding from enemy aircraft in the narrows to the east of Sibuyan Sea. In view of this danger, the wider and more maneuverable central Sibuyan Sea was selected to carry out our antiair engagements. This was the situation which prompted the CinC of 1-YB to submit his opinions.

An hour passed without the reappearance of TF 58 carrier planes. This respite from battle was devoted in 1-YB to putting ships in the best shape possible for the next one. The sun was westering heavily and still no answer to his questions. Admiral Kurita was now many hours behind schedule and the entire program for taking Leyte Gulf was in jeopardy. Suddenly, at 1715, he ordered a reversal of course. The ships, now in column formation, headed for the strait. The only combat information Admiral Kurita had received that day was a signal from Admiral Nishimura, based on an early morning report by a 3rd Group reconnaissance pilot. He reported sighting, in and near Leyte Gulf, 4 battleships, 2 cruisers, 12 carriers, 80 transports, 18 destroyers, and a dozen small boats.

The long line of ships, straight as a string, was steaming between Masbate and Burias toward San Miguel Island and Ticao Pass when this signal arrived from Admiral Toyoda:

"1815—Combined Fleet DesOpOr 372. With confidence in heavenly guidance, the entire force will attack!"

Held to 20 knots by his slowdowns, Admiral Kurita informed his chief that he planned to pass through the strait at about 0100 on 25 October; that he would proceed southward down the east coast of Samar and break into Leyte Gulf at about 1100. Fed up with the lack of information from organizations over which he had no control, he radioed, at 1939, the commander of his reconnaissance unit of catapult float-planes. They had been landed that morning on Mindoro and had passed into the command of Southwest Fleet Air. But since he had the right to re-assume command, Admiral Kurita ordered:

"1-YB is advancing. Report enemy situation in areas to east of Legaspi, east of Samar and Leyte, immediately."

At 2020, Admiral Nishimura radioed: "We plan to break through to Dulag at 0400." But the reconnaissance unit was never heard from.

About three hours later, a dispatch from Admiral Shima, who was now in the Mindanao Sea some 40–60 miles behind Admiral Nishimura, announced that he would "pass through the south entrance to Surigao Strait at 0300. Plan to break through with speed of 26 knots."

Although that would be crowding Group 3 considerably, Admiral Kurita took no steps, so far as is known, to change the program. Oddly enough he instructed Admiral Nishimura to join him 10 miles to the northeast of Suluan Island at 0900 next morning, though the main force could not expect to arrive there until much later. Perhaps the best indication of the admiral's frame of mind was that—despite his belief that he would be met at the strait by everything within Bill Halsey's and Tom Kinkaid's reach, from battleships to submarines —he radioed orders to have the navigation lights on Capul Island, Calantas Rock, and San Bernardino Island turned on. He suspected that he had been sighted—and he was right. Two black chickens off CV *Independence* had spotted him at 1935 and again at 2120.

October 25—a day that was to witness important events in the Pacific—was just 35 minutes old when Admiral Kurita broke out of San Bernardino Strait. He sought and was ready for a fight. Surface action, that was what he wanted; that was what he loved and understood.

Unfortunately, because of a failure in American communications there was no one there to oblige him. Kurita could find not the slightest trace of surface craft. Nor were any submarines on hand. The fact was that the exit from the strait into the Philippine Sea was as unguarded as the skies and waters of Pearl Harbor had been on that December Sunday in 1941.

The first inkling that Third Fleet commander Halsey had of Admiral Ozawa's whereabouts was the attack on TG 3 by carrier planes that afternoon. Although he had been attacked by carrier planes without carriers in the battle off Formosa earlier in the month, Bill Halsey had a hunch that TG 3's attackers had been launched from carriers to the north of his own position. He therefore took immediate steps to get further information by sending long-range search planes out to find them.

While the hunt was on, Admiral Halsey weighed his next step. What he wanted to do was to go north and give battle as soon as the carrier fleet was located. But were the circumstances such—with respect to the Japanese main force in San Bernardino Strait—that he could do it with impunity?

Based upon reports by pilots who had been lambasting Admiral Kurita's ships, it would seem that at least 4, probably 5, battleships had been torpedoed and bombed, 1 probably sunk; a minimum of 3 heavy cruisers torpedoed and others bombed; 1 light cruiser sunk; 1 destroyer probably sunk and 4 damaged. After incorporating these observations in his Action Report, the admiral added that the enemy had "beyond doubt been badly mauled with all of its battleships and most of its heavy cruisers tremendously reduced in fighting power and life." He also commented that our losses amounted to only 18 planes.

The reports of his pilots—which, to say the least, were overoptimistic—were Bill Halsey's main sources of information in arriv-ing at his estimate of the situation. He also considered Admiral Kurita's reversal of course at 1600 as a sign of weakness. Later, on learning that the Japanese were heading for San Bernardino Strait again, the admiral was neither surprised nor disturbed. He had fore-seen that contingency, as proved by his outlining of a stand-by battle plan, which he might execute when and if Admiral Kurita's force should attempt to enter the Philippine Sea. This plan, purely tenta-tive, would draw 4 battleships, 5 cruisers, and 14 destroyers from the carrier screens to constitute Task Force 34 commanded by Admiral Lee. To prepare them for this eventuality, he transmitted the plan to his commanders at 1512 that afternoon.

By chance, a Seventh Fleet communicator intercepted the message and passed it on to Admiral Kinkaid, to whom the dispatch was not addressed and who was not a party to the information. Unfortu-nately, Kinkaid misinterpreted it as an order for the actual forming of TF 34.

At 1730, TG 3 search pilots reported sighting an enemy carrier force 300 miles north of San Bernardino and 200 miles east of Cape Engaño on the northern tip of Luzon. The force consisted of 3 flat-tops, 2 light cruisers, and 3 destroyers steaming southwest at 15 knots. By that time, Admiral Kurita was again standing east for the strait, but the Third Fleet commander was not as yet aware of that. As for the enemy carrier force, it was too late in the day to attempt an immediate attack. Besides, in view of the factors involved, such action required thorough consideration. Admiral Halsey had a diffi-cult decision to make and it was not made easier when he learned that nightsnoopers had discovered Kurita's main force steaming in column toward San Bernardino Strait. Halsey discussed the situation with members of his staff, then went into executive session with him-self to reach his command decision.

The basic situation was that four hostile forces—three from the west, through San Bernardino and Surigao Straits, and one from the north—were converging on Leyte Gulf. The forces of Admirals Nishimura and Shima could be dismissed as being of no immediate concern to TF 38 because they were completely outclassed in num-bers and in gunpower by Admiral Oldendorf's ships. With respect to Ozawa's carrier force and Kurita's main force, Admiral Halsey could either remain at the strait and let them come to him, or he could pull away to engage Ozawa. If he remained, he would have three sources of opposition: Admiral Ozawa's carrier planes, Admiral Kurita's guns, and Admiral Mikawa's land-based aircraft. Such a situation could be dangerous. And what about Task Force 34 if it were created? If he ventured north to fight the carriers and left TF 34 to guard the strait, TF 34 would have no protection against land-based planes; at the same time, the fire-support screens of TF 38 would be greatly weakened if their gunpower were reduced.

The orders issued by Admiral Nimitz gave the Third Fleet commander a wide radius of action. Even as Admiral Kinkaid was responsible only to General MacArthur, so Bill Halsey had to answer only to Admiral Nimitz. Therefore, though his orders provided that the Third Fleet should "cover and support the forces of the Southwest Pacific in order to assist in the seizure and occupation of objectives in the central Philippines," they also stated that "in case opportunity for destruction of a major portion of the enemy fleet offers or can be created, such destruction becomes the primary task."

Bill Halsey fully realized the danger of Admiral Ozawa's carrier fleet. If it were not destroyed or seriously crippled, and thus prevented from making contact with other enemy forces, General MacArthur's position at Leyte Gulf could become extremely insecure.

Some 300 miles to the north a few hours earlier, Admiral Ozawa had watched the TF 38 search planes as they made their observations and had seen them disappear to the south. The admiral drew a breath of profound relief. He had, at long last, been discovered by the enemy. Throughout the day, by various means, such as making smoke and sending radio messages, the admiral had hoped to draw American attention to his presence. His purpose was to lure TF 38 north to engage in battle, thus leaving San Bernardino Strait unguarded. The 76 fliers he had sent against TG 3 had been a move of sheer desperation, but it had worked when nobody had sighted his smoke or intercepted his radio communications. Now it was just a matter of hoping that the Halsey–Mitscher team would appear so that he could flash Admiral Kurita the important news that the carriers were out of his way.

The decision to do just that was made by Admiral Halsey aboard the *New Jersey,* shortly before 2000, when he walked into flag-plot and looked at the operation chart. In his characteristically decisive manner, the admiral jabbed his right index finger at the charted position of the enemy carriers, turned to Admiral Carney, and said: "Here's where we're going, Mick! Start them north!"

Mick Carney expedited orders to increase force speed to 25 knots and change course to due north. A radio message to Admiral McCain directed him to refuel at sea and join up at best possible speed.

To Admiral Kinkaid, Bill Halsey sent word that the Japanese main force was, according to strike reports, too heavily damaged to be a serious threat, and concluded: "Am proceeding north with three groups to attack carrier force at dawn."

To make certain that the fleets would not pass each other in the night, Admiral Mitscher was instructed to send—starting at midnight —night-fighters to distances of 350 miles to search for the enemy from north by east to northwest. He was also given tactical command.

When Admiral Kinkaid read the dispatch informing him that Admiral Halsey was pulling out with three task groups, he assumed that Admiral Lee and his TF 34 would remain to guard the strait and made no further inquiry. As a result, he did not send any forces to the area vacated by Halsey. Some believe it unfortunate that Mick Carney did not frame a more specific message. But it must be remembered that TF 34 had never been more than a tentative plan in Bill Halsey's mind and that whatever knowledge about TF 34 reached Admiral Kinkaid, it had not been intended for him. As a matter of fact, in flag-plot of Third Fleet no one was aware that Tom Kinkaid had such information.

The pros and cons of this situation can be argued from here to Doomsday without the confusion ever lifting. However, a divided command seldom produces satisfactory communications and understandings between the commanders involved. If the Third and Seventh fleets had been under a single instead of a split command, it is doubtful if the lack of understanding and sluggish flow of information between the two fleet commanders would have resulted.

In his autobiography, *Reminiscences,* General MacArthur states that responsibility for the situation, which could have changed the trend of the war, rested with the joint chiefs of staff. In opposition to that conclusion, many felt that closer communication between the naval forces involved was a necessity, and that Bill Halsey was chiefly to blame for the lack of it from his end.

As Halsey sped northward, Admiral Nishimura and his group made steady and undisturbed progress through the Mindanao Sea under quiet conditions. After that first morning strike, he had met no interference from Pete Mitscher's carriers or even those commanded by Admiral Tom Sprague at Leyte Gulf. The former were busy mounting attack waves against Admiral Kurita, what with TG 1 absent and TG 3 providing cover for the burning *Princeton* as well as beating off the fliers launched by Admiral Ozawa. Admiral Sprague's fliers were involved with delivering strikes against enemy ground positions and providing beachhead protection against land-based raiders. These preoccupations allowed Group 3 to make slow but steady knots toward Surigao Strait. Admiral Nishimura's force consisted of the elderly battleships *Yamashiro* and *Fuso,* the heavy modern cruiser *Mogami,* and four destroyers. Trailing this force by some 40–50 miles, was Admiral Shima with one light and two heavy cruisers plus four destroyers.

As separate entities, these two units did not pack a great deal of heavy metal; united, they could become a fairly potent force. But that was not to happen. First, because the authorities in Tokyo had not so ordained; second, because the two admirals were barely on speaking terms. It was unfortunate for Japan that these mutually antagonistic commanders should be brought together under conditions that called for cooperation. Admiral Nishimura, an able but cantankerous officer, had spent most of his Navy years on sea-duty while Admiral Shima navigated staff desks most of the time. At the outset, Kiyohide Shima had been junior to Shoji Nishimura, but when the former reached his captaincy ahead of the other, the situation grew more tense. Now, as vice admirals, Shima was the senior, a situation that did not lessen the strain between them. Had Admiral Shima decided to exercise his seniority on that October day, he could have taken command of both forces by merely informing the other of his presence. But that he did not do. Nor did Admiral Nishimura communicate with his long-time rival. After the war, when asked why he had not contacted Admiral Nishimura, Admiral Shima replied that he did not want to break radio silence.

When in midafternoon, 24 October, Admiral Oldendorf received orders from Tom Kinkaid to prepare for night action, he was ready. Since his arrival at Leyte, he had spent every spare moment in familiarizing himself with Surigao Strait and knew exactly what he proposed to do—namely, catch the enemy in the restricted waters of the strait and knock him out with the massed power of his 6 battleships, 8 cruisers, including *Shropshire* (*RAN*), and 26 destroyers, not forgetting a gaggle of PT boats. According to plan, the little PTs would be the first to establish contact with the enemy. Though they would try to launch torpedoes at the invaders, their primary function was to observe and report. Behind the PT boats would be a picket line of destroyers, which, with other destroyer squadrons, would deliver hit-run torpedo attacks, after which Olie would crush the enemy with fire from the 16-inch and smaller guns of his ships.

Admiral Oldendorf, one of the most popular admirals in the Navy, was a cheerful, considerate fellow; and life in his force, particularly around the bridges, was pleasant because of it. He well knew the spit and polish of the peacetime big ships, but he accepted without griping what was available under war conditions. As a campaigner, Olie never took anything for granted. Rear Admiral Samuel H. Hurt (USN-Ret.), captain of the CA *Louisville,* Oldendorf's flagship, testified to this in the following observation:

> Target practices were, of course, carefully gone over; shore bombardment of many simulated landings were also carefully rehearsed in rear areas prior to departure on an operation. But I know of no battle, save that of Surigao Strait, of which it can be said that *it was rehearsed* in advance (on the actual scene of combat).
>
> In anticipating a probable approach of an enemy force via Surigao Strait, Admiral Oldendorf cruised in advance at the Strait with most of the heavy ships in nearly the same tactical organizations and maneuvers they were to use during the battle.

The Sunday cruise atmosphere for Nishimura's Group 3 ended about 2300 when it found itself confronted by a cluster of PT boats. As if he disdained such small fry, Admiral Nishimura ordered a hard turn to starboard and kicked on searchlights while the destroyer *Shigure,* in the van, slammed shells among the approaching boats and hit one of them. After valiant efforts to come within torpedo range, the best the PTers could do was to run for it in order to make contact reports. The first of these reached Admiral Oldendorf at 0030 on 25 October. A few minutes later, he received reports on Admiral Shima's approach. Now Olie knew where he stood, and he stood good and ready.

After the PT-boat encounter, Admiral Nishimura spent much time arranging his forces but did not wait for Admiral Shima to join him. The BB *Yamashiro,* flagship, with BB *Fuso* and CA *Mogami,* flanked by destroyers, steamed up the strait prepared for trouble and were not disappointed. Out of the darkness came DesRon 54 (Captain J. C.

Coward) at 30 knots. In order not to give their positions away by gun flashes, only torpedoes were used. As the squadron, separated into two well-spaced divisions, came within torpedo range, the first division let go torpedoes. Under strong but inaccurate enemy fire, they reversed course without being hit. Not so the enemy. The BB *Fuso* had taken a torpedo that slowed her down and made her swing out of line. The DDs of the second division bore down on the enemy at high speed and fired their spreads, which hit three destroyers and lamed the *Mogami*. That done, they too reversed course and escaped unhurt. Other servings of destroyer torpedoes followed in short order when DesRons 24 and 56, of the battle line's right and left flanks, added to the decrepitude of BB *Fuso*, torpedoed BB *Yamashiro* with good effect, and gave *coups de grâce* to a couple of wounded destroyers. It has been said, and truthfully, that the destroyers (which included the Australian *Arunta*) that night covered themselves with so much glory that the action stands out as one of the best destroyer performances in the war. But those wonderful destroyer-men also paid for their success. Caught in a crossfire between friendly and enemy guns, DD *Albert W. Grant* (Commander T. A. Nisewaner) was knocked out of the running, as were 34 officers and men killed and 94 wounded. But, on being lashed to another destroyer and hauled away, the ship was saved from destruction and taken to Ulithi, from which she later emerged fit for battle once again.

During this period, Admiral Oldendorf's battle line had been standing on short east-west courses at slow speeds near the Surigao Strait outlet into Leyte Gulf. The six battleships were flanked by eight cruisers, which were flanked by two destroyer squadrons. Admiral Hurt, then a captain and skipper of the flagship *Louisville,* had full opportunity to watch Olie Oldendorf approach the event that marks the peak of a battlewagon sailor's career, a peak that is reached but once in two-score years or more: the Crossing of the T. Admiral Hurt wrote:

> From the first contact report, received on board at 0026 25 October to 0351, the time we commenced firing seemed an interminable suspense of half understood, half mystifying reports that—because of garbles, arrival out of sequence, hurry and excitement of the senders—failed to fit in with sporadic flashes on the horizon. Most of this time Admiral Oldendorf stood on his bridge 10 feet below me receiving reports from his flag-plot and watching to the south.

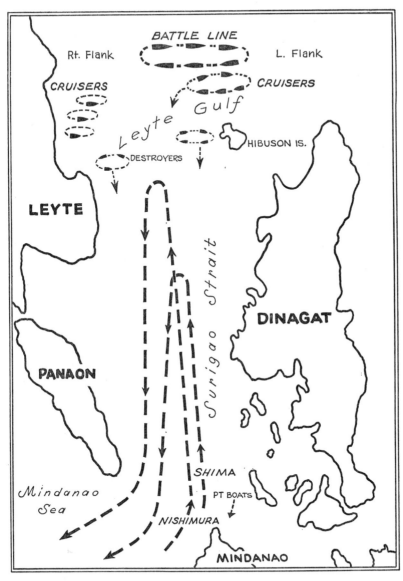

Admiral Oldendorf's "T" in Surigao Strait, 24–25 October 1944. This classic tactical position was attained when he turned his battleships at right angles to Admiral Nishimura's approaching ships, thus delivering devastating broadsides to which the Japanese commander could only reply with his forward guns. Added to this hail of shells were cruiser projectiles and destroyer torpedoes. One Japanese vessel, a destroyer, survived.

There was coolness and deliberation, little noise or activity. Reports from our battle line, west flank cruisers and destroyers—now released to attack—as well as the continual flow of evaluation of radar pips and ranges, always closing. I think he showed great restraint in not ordering the big ships to commence fire earlier or to be drawn into a pell-mell chase after his cease fire. He had a plan, a classical situation, and he stuck to it.

There have been all too few fleet battles in history that did not degenerate into melees with all plans forgotten, or thought up afterwards, to show adversity or prescience.

Coolheaded Admiral Oldendorf pressed the firing button when the range was down to 23,000 yards, and BB *West Virginia* fired the first eight-gun salvo of armor-piercing projectiles. A brief description of the battle, which lasted 18 minutes, was given by the admiral in his war diary. He wrote:

A methodical, deliberate and destructive fire of all calibers was poured into the enemy forces by the battleships, cruisers and destroyers. The sky was blanketed with red-hot steel sailing toward His Imperial Majesty's Navy, which seemed bewildered and confused. One after another, the enemy ships exploded, illuminating the entire area. The enemy (toward the end) appeared to have turned to the southward, desiring to break off the uneven engagement and save the remainder of his ships.

In hammering Admiral Nishimura's force into junk with scant opposition, Admiral Oldendorf enjoyed the advantages that fall to the sailor who crosses the T. This happens when one force can deliver broadsides, as Olie Oldendorf did, into an enemy when the latter, approaching bow-on, can only bring forward or bow guns to bear, as Nishimura did. Admiral Nelson crossed the T at Trafalgar in 1805, and Admiral Togo performed the feat against the Russians in 1905. And now, in 1944, Admiral Oldendorf joined the small, distinguished group of T-crossers when his six elderly battleships crowned their sunset years by doing it—probably for the last time in naval history.

In his last dispatch to Admiral Kurita, sent at 0150 on 25 October, Admiral Shima had stated:

2-YB [his task force], two cruisers, one light cruiser, and four destroyers expect to break through from south entrance to Surigao Strait at 0300. Plan to make a clockwise sweep of

Leyte Gulf after passing the Dulag area and head for the
south entrance to Surigao Strait (0900) destroying the enemy
wherever he may be found. At 0900 2-YB will have enough
fuel left to last for two days and nights at a speed of 18 knots.

At the time the dispatch was written, Shoji Nishimura was well
ahead of Admiral Shima and still in possession of his life, two battleships, one cruiser, and four destroyers, never dreaming that he and
thousands of men aboard his ships were facing their last hours of life
and that of Group 3, only one tiny survivor, DD *Shigure,* would limp
out of Surigao Strait. All the rest would either go down or become
flaming derelicts.

The PT boats, still churning water south of the strait, had better
luck with Admiral Shima's force than they had with Group 3. One
planted a torpedo in CL *Abukuma* that cut her speed to 10 knots.
Having heard the far-off thunder of battle and seen, in the distance,
the exploding shells and streaking tracers, Admiral Shima began to
doubt the wisdom of romping around Leyte Gulf destroying every
enemy in sight. This doubt increased when the burning bulk of BB
Fuso drifted past in two sections. In the darkness, he took them to be
the wreckage of *Yamashiro* as well as *Fuso.* Next he saw *Mogami*
glide by out of control and raked by fires, which her men fought to
extinguish. Last came *Shigure* whose skipper, too punchdrunk to report what had happened, only shouted that he had steering trouble as
his shadowy craft glided by on the current. But Shima was not ready
to retreat—yet. He called for 28 knots and sent the destroyers ahead.
Radarmen presently reported sighting two enemy ships at 13,000
yards. The two cruisers rushed toward their targets. *Ashigara* picked
one; *Nachi* took the other. Bearing down on their victims at full speed
and watching them get big on the radar screens, they fired full spreads
of torpedoes at extreme range and heard them explode. But nothing
else happened; the targets did not sink. Being islands, not ships, they
were unsinkable.

Admiral Shima now recalled his destroyers, turned about, and
shaped course for the Mindanao Sea. But he had to reduce speed
after the *Nachi* collided with the *Mogami,* whose crew had won their
fight against the fire. Shima was slowed to 18 knots because of the
cruiser's injury. This was a stroke of fortune for *Mogami,* whose battered power plant was just able to grind out 18 knots and would not
be able to maintain even that for a great length of time.

As they retreated down the strait, the enemy vessels were attacked by PT boats and destroyers. Even Oldendorf's cruisers entered the hunt. The badly crippled *Mogami* was soon aflame again; however, she got away. The third of Admiral Nishimura's damaged destroyers was sunk by gunfire. A few minutes after she sank, Admiral Oldendorf learned that Admiral Kurita was on the loose in the Philippine Sea off Samar and that Rear Admiral Ziggy Sprague's jeep carriers were doing all within their power to hold him back.

This, decided Olie Oldendorf, was no time to chase Shima's escapees or Nishimura's cripples; the aviators could tend to that when time allowed. His job was in Leyte Gulf. Issuing a recall order, he reversed course up the Strait.

Chapter Twelve

THE ORDEAL OF TAFFY 3

JUST ABOUT THE TIME Admiral Oldendorf was cooling his big guns, having hurled 300 rounds of 14-inch and 16-inch battlewagon ammunition and some 4,000 rounds of cruiser ammo at Admiral Nishimura, Tom Kinkaid tried to communicate with Admiral Lee at San Bernardino Strait but received no reply. Deeply worried, he asked—at 0412 on 25 October—Bill Halsey if TF 34 was guarding the Strait. Again there was no reply. Evidently the inquiry did not reach Admiral Halsey until 0645, by which time Admiral Kurita's presence in the Philippine Sea was no longer a secret. Bracing himself against all eventualities, Admiral Kinkaid recalled the men, cruisers, and destroyers that were pursuing stragglers in Surigao Strait. Admiral Tom Sprague's planes, launched from their respective units to perform tactical missions, were recalled and ordered to attack Kurita.

Tom Kinkaid did the best he could with what he had; but he had less to do it with in a hurry than appears at first blush. For the time being he had to write Admiral Oldendorf's battleships and destroyers off the books. Most were so low on ammunition and fuel that they had to be serviced before they could go into combat. Thus, at his immediate disposal, the Seventh Fleet commander had only the plane complements aboard Admiral T. L. Sprague's 18 jeep carriers, their 24 destroyers and destroyer escorts. But these three units were stationed up and down the coast at wide intervals. Jeep planes already airborne were ordered to concentrate over Leyte Gulf; strikes against Leyte defenders were canceled and directed northward to repel attacks on Taffy 3 (Adm. Clifton A. Sprague), which being nearest the enemy had come under Japanese fire at 0658.

Loud and frequent calls—in code, even in voice—for assistance zipped from Seventh Fleet to Third Fleet. But Admiral Halsey shrugged them off in the belief that Admiral Kurita's force was so weak that Seventh Fleet's battle line and fire-support vessels, along with the planes of 18 jeep carriers, could handle the situation. Admiral Halsey just could not imagine that his opponent could continue to remain powerful after strike on strike delivered by Admiral Mitscher's airmen. Moreover, he firmly believed that victory would depend on his ability to destroy Admiral Ozawa's carriers. In view of this, Admiral Halsey's only concession to Admiral Kinkaid was to order Admiral McCain to make for Leyte at best possible speed with TG 1, which would put that group at the strait in the afternoon. During the night, anticipating surface action with heavily gunned Japanese screening vessels, Admiral Halsey formed Admiral Lee's Task Force 34. This sped ahead of Admiral Mitscher's three carrier groups to engage Ozawa's forces. In the early hours of 25 October, TF 38's early birds located the enemy carriers again. Deckloads of Hellcats, Helldivers, and Avengers were immediately airborne.

Firmly resolved to beat Admiral Ozawa to the draw, Pete Mitscher, after launching search planes just before daylight, waited only an hour or so to send strike formations in the direction of the enemy. This foresight paid off so well that when the contact report was flashed at 0710 the strike force was less than an hour's flying time from Admiral Ozawa's force and ready to pounce. The blow came at 0800 when fighters, dive-bombers and torpedo-planes swarmed upon the carriers. The ack-ack fire was intense, but the air opposition was pitifully feeble. There were enough American planes to give each of the four carriers competent attention. As in the first battle of the Philippine Sea, Admiral Ozawa had bad luck with his flagship: the *Zuikaku,* his only remaining heavy carrier, was torpedoed and he had to move his flag to *Oyodo,* a heavy cruiser and former flagship of Admiral Toyoda. Of the three light carriers still afloat, *Chitose* was clobbered by bombs and *Zuiho* suffered one bomb hit. A screening destroyer was sunk.

With bombs and torpedoes gone, the first wave of attack retreated and the second came roaring in to continue the onslaught. The *Chiyoda* was set afire and given a heavy list by bombs. Having no power, she drifted off, dead in the water. The third strike, containing more than 200 planes, entered on a major clean-up job. *Zuikaku* took several torpedoes and eventually sank. *Zuiho* was set ablaze, but the fire was put out and she tried to get away. Although she took a terrible licking, she did not sink. Attack followed attack and after the sixth wave had gone home, Admiral Ozawa's four carriers were sent to the bottom. The cruiser *Tama* caught a slowing torpedo.

While the aviators were busy sinking inadequately defended ships,

Admiral DuBose disposed of cripples and engaged surface vessels. He sank the dying *Chiyoda* and, after a memorable stern chase, disposed of the destroyer *Hatsuzuki*.

Admiral Ozawa and his remaining screening ships shaped course for the South China Sea in time to steam out of range of Admiral Du-Bose's guns. He did not know that his sacrifice had been in vain. True, Ozawa had lured TF 38 away from San Bernardino Strait. But Japan did not have a single carrier to its name, excepting the two re-built carrier-battleship hybrids, *Ise* and *Hyuga*. Ozawa had sent a message informing Admiral Kurita that the mission to lure TF 38 from the strait had been accomplished, but he had not learned that Kurita had never received it.

The swift vessels in Admiral Ozawa's force met no trouble in mak-ing for safer waters. But two stragglers encountered unexpected opposition from Roach's Raiders and Clarey's Crushers, who had been stopped in the Philippine Sea en route from Saipan to the South China Sea. The personnel of these two submarine wolf packs had spent a hellish day listening to bellowing guns and blasting bombs. Their fixed stations were so near the battle area that it hurt not to be allowed to take a hand in the game. Orders were orders, but they asked ComSubPac if they could not be changed. With the sanction of Admiral Nimitz, ComSubPac sent a message to Admiral Mitscher asking if his submarines could join the party. The admiral's reply, "Come on in," was unfortunately so delayed that it was not received until the battle was over.

However, nearing midnight the sonar on *Jallao* (Commander J. B. Icenhower), one of the "crushers," picked up heavy screws. A fast and daring periscope run brought the sub close enough to the vessel for the skipper to recognize the light cruiser *Tama*. Three bow tor-pedoes ran straight toward target; but in the last minute, the cruiser made a radical zigzag toward the *Jallao* so that the three torpedoes missed. Quickly, Commander Icenhower swung around, and at 700 yards sent four fish from his stern tubes. Three of them hit and *Tama*'s days were done.

Commander I. J. Galantin of *Halibut* (one of Roach's Raiders) picked up a battleship of the *Ise* class, screened by a cruiser and a destroyer. At 4,000 yards, he shot the works from his six bow tubes. The sub's log recorded five hits at the intervals expected—and also that the sub went deep to avoid a counterattack by the battlewagon's escorts. Unfortunately, *Halibut*'s claim for this sinking did not stand up after the war because the Japanese made no record of it. This was nothing new. Perhaps the Recorder of Sunken Ships just never caught up with his work.

The reason Ching Lee's guns had not been heard from was because Task Force 34 and Admiral Halsey had headed for San Bernardino that forenoon. The precursor for that reversal of plan was a message from CincPac at Pearl Harbor. At his headquarters, Admiral Nimitz kept in touch with the situation through interception of radio dispatches. He, too, failed to understand the situation with respect to Admiral Lee's task force and therefore sent this inquiry: "Where, repeat, where is Task Force 34?" For security reasons padding was added at random by the communications officer who handled the message. But for no particular reason, after the double letters that indicated where a message ended and padding began, he inserted: "The world wonders." In decoding the signal aboard the *New Jersey,* those three words were not removed but left as part of the text, which now read: "Where, repeat, where is Task Force 34—the world wonders." The effect was that Admiral Nimitz and the rest of the world were wondering where TF 34 was hiding.

Admiral Halsey read the message in midforenoon, doubly embarrassed when he discovered that copies were addressed to Admirals King and Kinkaid. Explosively, he ordered TF 34, to which *New Jersey* had been attached, to reverse course and head for Leyte at 1115. To the north, only 40 miles away, lay the enemy. As the southbound TF 34 passed the northbound TF 38, Admiral Halsey exchanged signals with Admiral Mitscher, which resulted in Admiral Bogan's task group joining TF 34 to provide air cover. In return, Admiral Halsey detached Rear Admiral Laurance T. DuBose with four cruisers and ten destroyers to strengthen Admiral Mitscher's firepower.

In going south on what became known as the Battle of Bull's Run, Bill Halsey not only forfeited his chances to make a complete wreck of Admiral Ozawa's force, but also found himself in a position where he could not expect to make enough knots to reach Leyte beachhead until that night. By the time TF 34 reached San Bernardino, Admiral Kurita had been gone many hours.

On debouching from San Bernardino Strait shortly after midnight on 25 October, undaunted by his lack of information as to the enemy's whereabouts, Admiral Kurita formed night search disposition to guard against being surprised by the enemy. To the south, about 100 miles away, lay Leyte Gulf, Admiral Kinkaid's Seventh Fleet, and General MacArthur's beachhead. Instead of making straight south for those tempting targets, he ran eastward for several hours before he reversed course and turned south for Leyte. Unfortunately for him, Admiral Kurita had not considered the Seventh Fleet's escort carrier group. Fortunately for the Allies, Admiral Kurita did not receive Admiral Ozawa's message that he was in contact with TF 38. Thus he remained ignorant of its whereabouts, a very serious handicap to him.

When *Yamato* lookouts spotted masts on the horizon, the admiral concluded that TF 38 lay in wait for him. Because of a thick, low overcast, there was no sun; a stiffening trade wind swept in from northwest and whipped the sea into choppy waves. Through the rain and a heavy haze, it was difficult to get a good picture of what lay ahead or to identify the carriers as heavy or light. To add to the confusion, destroyers dimly seen were taken to be cruisers. At the time of the sighting, the Japanese force was shaping into wheel formations to produce the strongest possible concentration of antiaircraft fire for mutual protection. In the midst of that difficult maneuver, the admiral signaled "general attack." The result was that the various units leaped ahead at top speed, fast ships in the lead and the rest trailing.

"It was subsequently definitely established," reported Admiral Kurita, "that the masts belonged to a gigantic enemy task force, including six or seven carriers accompanied by many cruisers and destroyers. Some carrier-based planes were in the air."

There are several quite contradictory stories about how the enemy force was first discovered by Taffy 3. Certainly the most colorful of these is that of the *Kitkun Bay*. According to Captain J. P. Whitney, the first evidence of the presence of the Japanese fleet, as detected by the communications department, came from two sources. The first was the signal gang in their high perch on the carrier's island. "The ships," said Captain Whitney, "were observed through a long glass several minutes before they began firing and their presence reported, though it was not known whether they were friendly or enemy vessels. They were too far away to be challenged.

"The second indication of their presence was the transmission of Japanese on 37.6 megacycles. This was noted prior to the announcement of the presence of the fleet, but it was thought that the transmissions were only attempts at jamming, as had been done on other occasions.

"It was later learned that the Japanese used this circuit—the same as our Inter-Fighter Net—as we use the TBM for communication between ships."

The "gigantic enemy task force of carriers, cruisers, and destroyers" noted by Admiral Kurita actually consisted of six baby flattops whose flight decks were about 500 feet long—ships that could do 19 knots, carried up to 28 aircraft, and whose armament consisted of one 5-inch gun and eight twin 40mm machine guns. There were no cruisers, only three screening destroyers—*Hoel, Heerman,* and *Johnston,* with five 5-inch gun batteries—and four destroyer escorts with two 5-inch guns. Total gunpower for Taffy 3: twenty-nine small guns.

Taffy 3, as this unit of escort carriers was called, was commanded by Rear Admiral C. A. F. Sprague, better known throughout the Navy as Ziggy, and not related to Tom Sprague. His was one of three similar units under the over-all command of Rear Admiral Thomas L. Sprague, whose flagship was in Taffy 1. During the night of 24–25 October, the three units were spaced well to seaward along the coast above, off, and below Leyte Gulf.

At 0530 and at 0607, twelve Air Patrol Hellcats, four antisubmarine patrol torpedo-planes, as well as the local antisubmarine patrol and the local combat air patrols, had been launched off *Fanshaw Bay,* the flagship. The five other carriers—*St. Lo, Kitkun Bay, Gambier Bay, White Plains,* and *Kalinin Bay*—were making similar launchings. Among the men aloft was Ensign Brooks, one of the pilots off *St. Lo,* flying a torpedo-plane with a rack of depth bombs intended for submarines.

He sighted no subs, but 18 minutes after launch he was flabbergasted to see a huge armada of warships ahead. The sky was heavily overcast and visibility was bad. As he swung closer to identify the force, he was greeted by heavy bursts of ack-ack. Retreating from AA range, he sent a contact report to the flagship, from which the antiaircraft barrage had been observed. In his message, Ensign Brooks said that he had been fired upon by a group of unidentified battleships and cruisers bearing 340 degrees, distance 20 miles from Taffy 3.

Admiral Sprague, by TBS, immediately ordered course changed to 90 degrees, which he deemed close enough to the wind to permit launching planes and still avoid shortening the gap between him and the enemy. Launching of planes and flank speed were ordered. After that would come a general retirement to the southwest in the hope that surface support might be obtained from Seventh Fleet forces in

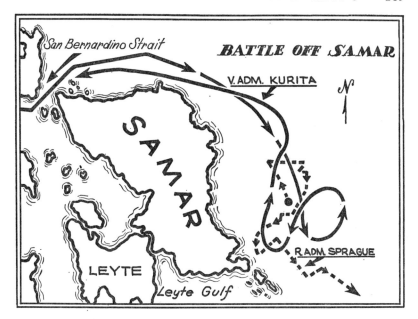

*Admiral Kurita entered the Philippine Sea just after
midnight on 25 October 1944. Finding the strait unguarded
and fearing a trap, he cruised until daylight when he came
upon Admiral Clifton Sprague's baby flattops. The
surprise was mutual. After 2½ hours, during which the
Japanese were badly mauled by CVE aircraft, destroyers,
and destroyer escorts, Admiral Kurita broke off the
battle and re-entered the strait. Kurita had sunk 1 carrier,
2 destroyers, and 1 destroyer escort. In return he had lost
3 heavy cruisers and was slowed down by several
cripples.*

Leyte Gulf. Soon all available aircraft were aloft, with orders to attack. All ships were directed to do likewise, and at 0701 the admiral
broadcast an urgent contact report, requesting assistance. This report,
given in plain language, was also heard by the Japanese.

But at that time no assistance was available except from Taffy 2
and 3. Surface men-o'-war had to receive fresh loads of ammunition
and to refuel, a rather slow process under beachhead conditions. Admiral Oldendorf's battleships and destroyers were not ready to function as a battle force until later in the morning, and by then it was too
late.

"At 0706, the enemy was closing with disconcerting rapidity and the volume and accuracy of fire was increasing," wrote Ziggy Sprague in his action report, and continued:

> At this point it did not appear that any of our ships could survive another five minutes and some counteraction was urgently and immediately required. The task unit was beset by the ultimate of desperate circumstances.
>
> All escorts were ordered to attack the Japanese with torpedoes. At this time, direct view of the enemy was obscured by smoke and the results of the attacks could not be ascertained. But it is believed that, regardless of hits, they succeeded in turning the battleships away at least momentarily, and created a diversion of great value.
>
> Shortly after that, two heavy cruisers came almost abeam of the unit, and from ranges as low as 10,000 yards delivered numerous 8- and 5-inch salvos. All available aircraft were diverted to this threat and several bomb hits were obtained. Hits were also being scored by the 5-inch gun on the fantail of every carrier. But, notwithstanding our desperate efforts, the cruiser fire was practically continuous and so effective that eventual destruction of all our ships seemed inevitable.

At 0750–58 *Fanshaw Bay* was hit twice. At 0824 DD *Johnston* vanished from sight, and at the same instant CVE *Gambier Bay,* hard hit, dropped astern to sink. A pilot reported DE *Roberts* hard hit and sinking. The last report from DD *Hoel* was that she had an 8-foot hole at the waterline. Large-caliber armor-piercing shells occasionally tore into the thin port sides of the jeeps, only to emerge unexploded through the starboard plating. The hard noses of the AP shells could not be detonated by the soft skins of the carriers. Mainly for that reason Taffy 3 lost only one baby flattop, the *Gambier Bay.*

"We are being pursued by a large portion of the Japanese fleet," said a voice over the ship-to-ship radio phone to Commander E. E. Evans, skipper of destroyer *Johnston* in Taffy 3's screen, at the start of the battle. The range was given as 34,000 yards; speed of enemy: 23 to 25 knots; bearing: northwest. As the carriers turned east into the wind to launch planes, Commander Evans ordered engine rooms to prepare to make maximum speed. As he swung out of his screen position and reversed course to interpose the destroyer between the carriers and the enemy, the vessel, now under full steam, shot forward as if propelled from a catapult.

A destroyer, small as it is, has three means to oppose an enemy—make smoke, fire her ten torpedoes, and use her five 5-inch guns. At this moment smoke, which would hide the jeep carriers from the enemy, was called for. Ordering black funnel smoke from the engine room and white PS chemical smoke from the smoke generator detail, Captain Evans began to zigzag back and forth in corkscrew turns between the oncoming enemy and the flattops.

Hardly had this operation begun before shell splashes rose and fell like huge fountain displays all about him. To enable gunnery officers and spotters to see where their shots fell the splashes were of many colors—green, pink, yellow, purple. At 0700 the carriers had launched planes and gone on a southwestern course. The DD changed her smoke pattern accordingly. On occasion, the deck crew caught glimpses of CVE planes attacking the enemy but were unable to see the results. At any rate, the enemy kept coming, and presently the range between them and *Johnston* had narrowed to 18,000 yards.

Now the five 5-inchers began barking. Several enemy cruiser units took her under fire so close that shells often straddled the ship. Ernie Evans knew that the popguns of one lone destroyer could not stop the onrushing big bruisers. Calmly he ordered to prepare for torpedo attack and headed toward the nearest cruiser till he had closed to 10,000 yards, extreme torpedo range. Setting the fish at slow speed to lengthen their runs, Captain Evans gave the enemy the works, a full ten-torpedo salvo fired at 3-second intervals. To draw attention from the trails of his submerged messengers, he had the 5-inchers slam 200 rounds at the cruiser. Under the circumstances, the torps were making their runs too slowly to allow *Johnston* to stick around to await results. Big shells were rumbling toward her as Commander Evans dived into a smoke screen. At the proper time, two or three underwater explosions were heard. When the destroyer emerged from the smoke a minute later, the leading cruiser was seen astern and burning furiously. It was 0730.

At that instant, the ship was hit by three 14-inch projectiles. Before she stopped rocking from the impact, three 6-inchers tore into the badly wounded vessel. The enemy had the range and the end could come at any moment. But a rain squall suddenly swept upon the *Johnston,* hiding her from enemy gunners who believed they had a sure kill. The low visibility within the squall's area not only protected *Johnston* but also allowed those aboard her to make temporary repairs.

Lost were the after fire and engine rooms. All power to the steering engine and to the after three 5-inch guns was gone; the gyro compass was useless. When the destroyer was finally able to be under way again, her speed had been cut from 35 knots to 17 and steering had to be done manually from the emergency wheel on the fantail. The gun crews of the three powerless guns were able to fire manually with make-do sightings, settings, and handling.

After providing fire support by acting as tail-end Charlie in a torpedo attack by other destroyers, *Johnston* found herself in a world of shifting walls and swirling streams of black and white smoke. She emerged from that world to find herself almost bow to bow with a Japanese battleship of the majestic *Kongo* class. Without hesitation, the BB was taken under fire. Forty rounds were flung at the giant, whereupon Ernie Evans retreated back into the smoke to avoid the tall splashes that were skipping toward him from the larger ship. At this period *Johnston* was several miles astern of Taffy 3, and as she tried to head southwest to join the carriers she found the enemy battle force and cruisers to port and its destroyers to starboard.

Suddenly the CVE *Gambier Bay,* under fire from a heavy cruiser and listing, hove into view to port. Coming gallantly to the rescue of the flattop, the destroyer steamed toward the cruiser at her best speed and pumped projectiles at her in order to arouse the enemy's wrath and attention. But the cruiser was interested in bigger game and paid no attention to the DD. Just then a shout from a lookout revealed that six enemy DDs, headed by a destroyer-leader, were sweeping toward the carrier formation to starboard. Turning on a dime, *Johnston* made for the destroyers at her full 17 knots while her guns fired at the leader, getting twelve hits; all the enemy DDs fired back, and the destroyer was hit several times but not really hurt. Despite lack of speed and other handicaps, her undaunted captain decided that here was a made-to-order setup to cross the T. Then, to quote *Johnston*'s action report:

> . . . a most amazing thing happened. The leader turned 90° to the right and broke off the action. Fire was immediately shifted to the second destroyer and hits were observed at initial range of about 8,000 yards. During firing on this second destroyer, the Captain attempted to Cross the T on the Jap column. However, before this was accomplished, amazingly enough, all remaining six Jap destroyers turned 90° to the right and range began to open rapidly.

As the enemy DDs disappeared, a TBS call from flag requested destroyers to interpose between the carriers and enemy cruisers which again were pressing close to port. Trying to be in two places at once, *Johnston,* for the next half hour, engaged cruisers and destroyers alternately in a somewhat desperate attempt to keep the enemy from closing on the carrier force. Continues the report:

> The ship was being hit with disconcerting frequency during this period. Finally, about 0930 we found ourselves with two cruisers dead ahead of us; several Jap destroyers on our starboard quarter and two cruisers on our port quarter. The battleships were still well astern of us. At this fateful time, numerous Japanese units had us under fire, all of those ships being within 6,000 to 8,000 feet of us. An avalanche of shells knocked out our lone remaining engine and fire room. Director and plot lost power. All communications were lost throughout the ship. All guns—except #4, which was in local control and still shooting—were out. As the ship went dead in the water, and its fate long since inevitable, the Captain gave the order to abandon ship.

The destroyer was under constant fire up to the time she rolled over and sank. For a final thrust, a Japanese destroyer closed the range to 1,000 yards to insure the *Johnston*'s destruction.

Although they were zoomed by three different friendly planes within two hours after the ship sank, *Johnston*'s 141 survivors clung to the rafts and float-nets for two days and two nights before being rescued. Before rescue, 45 survivors died of shock, wounds, or exposure. Among those lost were Commander Ernest E. Evans, a most daring and heroic destroyerman.

One aviator who had had a front seat at the entire show on the surface and in the air was Commander R. L. Fowler, commander of Carrier Air Group 26 and commanding officer of *Kitkun Bay's* Composite Squadron 5. With only breaks to refuel, he remained airborne for eight hours from the time he winged off the *Kitkun Bay* at 0700. Rendezvousing the group on that squally morning was difficult and required 30 minutes. When the planes had gained altitude for attack (8,000 feet) the weather was so dirty that all were on instruments. That the enemy had instruments too was revealed when the planes were taken under very accurate antiaircraft fire.

"Large groups of 5-inch flak burst very close," said Commander Fowler's action report. "Many small tracers passed among the planes.

The overcast we were flying in was so black that tracers were exceptionally clear. One torpedo plane went down, probably hit by AA. It was impossible to see enemy surface vessels. The enemy fire was no doubt radar controlled. We were tracked along and fired on for four to five minutes with the ack-ack uncomfortably close throughout."

Seeing no chance to attack from that point, Commander Fowler led his flock to 1,500 feet for a low-level attack. From there he had a full view of the surface situation. To port he saw battleships in two columns. Ahead of them a string of cruisers was about to penetrate the smoke curtain that hid Taffy 3 from view. To starboard, a number of enemy destroyers headed for the smoke screen at flank speed. It was an impressive scene, enhanced by the columns of varicolored water that leaped from the surface and the equally colorful ack-ack that burst all around his group.

But Commander Fowler and his fliers were not there to look at scenery. Realizing the immediate threat the cruisers were to the carriers, they grabbed altitude to attack. As they climbed, another group of fighters and torpedo-planes made a pass on the cruisers. After climbing into a cirrus cloud for cover, Fowler and his men attacked from out of the sun and caught a *Mogami*-class cruiser so completely by surprise that the group met no ack-ack fire at all.

"At this time," commented Commander Fowler, "we had only four torpedo-planes as the 12 fighters and other torpedo-planes had fallen out of formation in the thick weather. We completed the dives in about 35 seconds, scoring five hits amidships on the cruiser's stack, three on the stern, and two on the bow. After pulling out of the dive, I observed the cruiser to go about 500 yards, blow up, and sink within five minutes."

Before that, Commander Fowler had regretted the fact that the torpedo bombers, preloaded for antisubmarine patrol, did not carry torpedoes instead of bombs. But loading torpedoes into planes is a long, slow job and there had been no time before launching to remove bombs and depth charges. Even so, his 500-pound semi-armor-piercing bombs had not performed badly. The depth charges, which were hastily armed with detonators in their blunt noses to make them explode on contact, also were effective.

Because of the distances between Taffy 3 and the enemy ships, the ranges were always too wide for the men at the 40mm and 20mm guns to go into action. There was much griping about this. Finally, when cruisers were closing to 12,000 yards, a battery officer passed the word: "Just wait a little longer, boys. We'll soon pull them into 40mm range!"

The Japanese, meanwhile, tried a new device to improve their long-range marksmanship. Captain D. J. Sullivan had swung CVE *White Plains* into the wind to launch the planes stacked on the after part of the flight deck. Some 31,300 yards to westward the enemy was approaching at full steam. Two shells burst a mile or so from the ship. Captain McKenna made note of them because of their singular appearance; later he learned that they were the only two of their kind sighted in the action. During the 19 June battle, the Japanese had employed a certain type of aluminumlike metal cut into strips and pieces. Released from aloft, they floated slowly toward the sea and created radar interference. On this 25 November they tried a new wrinkle in the form of what appeared to be radar beacons exploded from shells.

Though opinions vary, the shells probably burst from 200 to 500 feet above the surface and sent out silvery showers of small particles, which fluttered into the sea. There was practically no smoke and very little combustion from the bursts, all of which led to the conclusion that the shells were to assist radar spotting, a type of electronic range marker. A minute or so after the bursts, splashes were observed at 4,000 yards, followed instantly by a salvo of large-caliber shells that fell uncomfortably close—300 yards on the starboard bow.

Exactly at 0700 the ship was straddled by a three-gun salvo of 14-inch caliber or larger. Two minutes later, as Captain Sullivan commenced to launch fighters, came another straddle. The next events he summed up in *White Plains'* action report:

> 0704—Straddled again! This salvo measured the carrier as calipers, diagonally from the port quarter to the starboard bow; four shells dropping microscopically close forward and two aft. One of the latter two exploded below the surface under the port side of the stern. Splash water from forward whipped across the bridge.
>
> The vessel was shaken and twisted violently, throwing personnel in some parts of the ship off their feet. Steering control was lost, gyro [compass] and radar failed, damage was received in the starboard engine room and all lights were extinguished throughout the ship. All electrical power was lost until it was discovered that the generator circuit breakers had been opened by the shock.
>
> The black gang found themselves in darkness, fragments of

lagging were falling about, soot and dust filled the engine spaces, loose floor plates were up-ended, one engine commenced heavy vibration, blower air ducts blew out and many thought the ship was hit and might be ruptured; yet, all stuck by their jobs. Necessary repairs were done in short order.

As the result of the flight deck undulations one of the Hellcats, awaiting the opportunity to launch, parted its winglines, jumped its chocks, and rolled into the fighter ahead, where its whirling prop chewed about three feet off the other Hellcat's port wing.

The moment the ship was straddled, the captain issued orders to the engineer officer to make smoke and to set the stacks so as to belch smoke from one stack to port and from another to starboard. This order was followed by one to the helmsman that called for erratic steering and another for launching the remaining fighters. Those takeoffs—on a stubby, rainswept, gusty deck while the ship was making violent zigzags—will be remembered by every pilot in that launching.

Meanwhile electrical power was being restored, the radar and gyro were returned to full operation. Captain Sullivan steadied on course long enough to send two torpedo-planes away, whereupon he took cover in a heavy rain squall.

The captain had concluded that the perfect straddle, followed instantly by erratic steering, a peculiar manner of making smoke, and the hasty launching of aircraft had convinced the enemy gunners that they had scored a kill. For that reason they either ceased firing or moved to another target. At any rate, there were no more straddles or large-caliber near misses. Still, many salvos of intermediate caliber splashed close aboard during the remaining time Taffy 3 was under bombardment.

Less fortunate was the DD *Hoel*. Driving at flank speed toward a narrow alley formed by a column of battleships on the left and one of cruisers on the right, the *Hoel* was ringed by green blotches produced by enemy shells with dye markers. This was torpedo action against two approaching columns of enemy ships, so Commander L. S. Kintberger, captain of the destroyer, planned to expend his ten torpedoes by delivering five against the leading vessel of each column. At 18,000 yards he began firing at the lead battleship. As the gap closed, the BB scored a hit on *Hoel*'s bridge that destroyed all voice-radio communication. A few minutes later, at 9,000 yards, Commander Kintberger sent five torpedoes toward the battlewagon; then, without awaiting results, he swung starboard toward the cruisers. Again *Hoel* was hit. Three of the vessel's five 5-inch guns were put out of action; worse yet, the main engine room was wrecked and the steering control smashed.

Despite these handicaps, Captain Kintberger, on one engine and by hand steering, reached torpedo position on the lead cruiser and let fly five fish at 6,000 yards. Shortly after he scored a hit and a large column of water was seen to rise from the cruiser.

But in a sea battle the situation is never static. Where, a few minutes earlier, *Hoel* had been heading down an alley, she now was in a box. As Commander Kintberger explained in his action report:

> Retirement was attempted to the southwest, but was impossible as the ship was boxed in by capital ships. By fish-tailing and dodging salvos this vessel was able to remain afloat in this precarious position, with enemy battleships 8,000 yards on the port beam and enemy cruisers 7,000 yards on our starboard quarter. During this period, guns #1 and #2 fired continuously, each gun expending more than 250 rounds of ammunition. It is estimated that more than 300 two- and three-gun salvos were fired at our ship many of which were of major caliber. Practically all major caliber ammunition was armor piercing and penetrated both sides of the ship without exploding.

At about 0830 power was lost on the remaining engine and all the engine spaces were flooding. Gun #1 magazine was on fire and it was apparent that the *Hoel* was about to go down. As enemy shells continued to score hits or near misses the destroyer was abandoned, and a few minutes later she rolled wearily upon her side and sank stern first.

"The success attained by a small number of light forces in an unsupported, uncoordinated attack against capital ships of a major Japanese task force," observed Commander Kintberger, "is far and beyond the wildest expectations. It hardly seems possible that, during daylight, a destroyer could close to ranges of 6,000 to 10,000 yards of a battleship or a cruiser, launch torpedo attacks, and then remain afloat for more than an hour while surrounded by them."

Meanwhile, the six baby carriers in Taffy 3 steamed southwest at every ounce of pressure their boilers could bear. From all their stacks, black funnel smoke was billowing in long, lazy plumes to hide the flattops from enemy eyes. But, being on the windward flank of the circular carrier disposition, neither *Gambier Bay* nor *Kalinin Bay* benefitted much by the smoke curtain, since the east wind carried the smoke westward as rapidly as they produced it. Both vessels were, in truth, riding the coffin corner that morning, easy targets for the enemy. In addition, no screening destroyers steamed on their port flanks. The destroyers were astern, laying down smoke screens or staging torpedo attacks. This left two Japanese cruisers to close at will on *Gambier Bay* and pay slight attention to the nearby *Kalinin Bay*.

"They maintained a heavy and disastrous fire," wrote Captain W. V. R. Vieweg in his *Gambier Bay* action report, "with eight-inch guns and salvos from the enemy's main body astern falling dangerously close to the carrier. Notwithstanding this concentrated fire, *Gambier Bay* kept out of harm's way by chasing salvos."

Chasing salvos is a technique men-o'-war use to avoid being hit by steering toward shell splashes as they occur, on the theory that the gunners will shift their sights before firing the next salvo. From 0750 to 0815, twenty very long minutes, the *Gambier Bay* avoided projectiles. Then the enemy gunners really got her number and began to whittle her down. First the forward engine room was put out of action by a hit below the water line. When it became uncontrollably flooded, the engine room was secured. Now the ship slowed to 11 knots and dropped astern. Shells continued to fall on her without causing serious damage, but at 0837 one hit the bridge, and steering control forward was lost. Although steering control was quickly shifted to after steering, it did no good. The shift had barely been made when a shell exploded with deadly damage in the #3 boiler. At 0845 *Gambier Bay* was dead in the water.

Now the cruisers closed to a point-blank range and the enemy gunners slammed shells into the carrier. Fires raged within the sinking ship, and Captain Vieweg gave that saddest of orders a skipper can give: "Abandon ship." As men scrambled over the side into rafts and float-nets, the Japanese fired into the *Gambier Bay* at ranges of less than 2,000 yards, until she capsized and went under.

Her station in the formation had indeed been coffin corner.

Upstairs, under the low ceiling, Admiral Sprague's fliers and those of Taffy 2 (Rear Admiral Felix B. Stump) shuttled back and forth between pitching flight decks and enemy targets. No one counted strikes or costs; all hands worked on the double; pilots landed wherever they could on jeeps or Tacloban airstrip; when fuel could not be hosed in, tanks were filled from buckets; when bombs and torpedoes were gone, the fliers turned to rockets, contact bombs, even depth charges; fighters out of ammo made faked strafings on enemy deck personnel just to keep them off center. One *Teratsuki* class DD was so heavily strafed that all her small-caliber guns were silenced through the expenditure of 5,000 rounds of .50 ammo, some 60 percent of which were hits. In fact, almost continuous strafing runs kept many of the enemy destroyers from attacking the CVEs.

It was later estimated that in 435 strikes, 83 torpedoes and 190 tons of bombs were dropped. The volume of air activity is best demonstrated by the nine torpedoes, thirty 500-pound bombs, and 20,000 rounds of ammunition expended by Composite Squadron 5 alone during the melee. Taffy planes suffered 128 operational and combat casualties. Up to that day, the term *flyboy* in the jeeps had carried a slight tinge of disrespect among men in "MacArthur's Navy"; from then on, it expressed the same deep and friendly respect Navy men had for the older Tailhook Navy.

Unique among gun encounters that morning was the fight put up by CVE *Kalinin Bay* against six destroyers attacking her in echelon. Each of the DDs, being of the *Teratsuki* class, had two gun mounts forward and could therefore bring twelve 5-inch guns to bear on the carrier against the flattop's one and only 5-inch "pea-shooter" as her skipper, Captain T. W. Williamson, called it.

At first, as the destroyers were spotted a long way off, they were thought to be Seventh Fleet friends coming to the rescue. But when the high-bowed ships opened fire at 14,500 yards and closed the range while shooting, their true identity was apparent. Japanese shells fell short into the sea or whined across the carrier, but none hit it. On the other hand, the *Kalinin Bay*'s gun hit one of the enemy destroyers, which immediately was enveloped in white smoke. Cheers went up on the carrier's deck, then stopped cold as all hands, popeyed with wonder and relief, saw the enemy DDs make radical maneuvers and withdraw; but the Japanese tin cans continued shooting. Just then, providentially, a friendly destroyer crossed the *Kalinin Bay* astern at 500 yards and made smoke as she drummed off at flank speed to engage the enemy destroyers.

Attention was drawn from the vanishing enemy destroyers by the rising smoke curtain and a radio call from Lieutenant L. E. Waldrop of *St. Lo*'s Composite (Air) Squadron 65. He reported torpedo attack astern. At the same time his plane, which had been circling *Ka-*

linin Bay 100 yards astern, went into a steep glide, machine guns rattling and bullets ripping into the sea. Then, according to Captain Williamson's action report, two explosions were heard as two torpedoes fired by the retreating enemy were destroyed.

"This," he continued, "was the first warning of a torpedo attack launched against this ship. Immediately after these torpedoes were exploded another was sighted directly astern. It appeared to be porpoising. Our 5-inch gun on the fan tail opened fire and a shell exploded about ten feet ahead of the approaching torpedo; it was next observed veering to port." At least twelve other torpedo wakes were sighted on parallel courses on both sides of the ship, but by smart handling, all were avoided.

At 0910, after 140 minutes of unremitting combat, destroyer escort *Samuel B. Roberts* was lying dead on the sea with a heavy list to starboard, down about four feet in the water by the stern, her slim hull riddled with shell holes. Her forward 5-inch gun was useless; her other 5-incher, on the after deck, could still fire manually and was manned by a gun crew that refused to call it quits. Of the 650 rounds of ammo in her lockers that morning, only 42 remained.

For all practical purposes, she was out of action. Most of her complement of 6 officers and 180 men were either dead or wounded. Those who were able, prepared to abandon ship, according to captain's orders, or tended the wounded. Earlier, when the enemy was sighted, Lieutenant Commander R. W. Copeland, the skipper, told his men—most of them newly inducted, married, unaccustomed to Navy ways—that this was a fight against overwhelming odds from which survival could not be expected. They would have but little time, but he urged them to use that time to do what damage to the enemy they could. A ringing cheer greeted his remarks.

The torrent of steel that was to be *Roberts'* undoing first struck at 0851; she almost bounced out of the sea on being hit below the waterline by a salvo that put the main fireroom out of commission. Next, as the lamed DE became a target for merciless gunning, the main engine room was knocked out. After that, a direct hit blew the after 40mm gun, gun mount, director, and shield to fragments; other shells made other hits, none of which prevented *Roberts* from sticking to her appointed task: to stand as a shield between Taffy 3 and Japanese cruisers and to maintain the heaviest, fastest, and most accurate fire of which her two 5-inch guns, with their limited fire-control equipment, were capable.

It had been a busy morning for the DE, what with laying smoke screens, making a torpedo run within 4,000 yards of an enemy cruiser, firing her three fish and scoring one hit. After that, for a fiery 50 minutes she had exchanged shots in a running fight with a heavy cruiser. Now she was helping prevent cruisers from crowding in on the flattops.

Suddenly a salvo of 14-inch high-capacity projectiles from two or three guns smashed into the ship's side and ripped enough of her steel hide away to form a hole 30 to 40 feet long and 8 to 10 feet high. This salvo also wiped out the #2 engine room, ruptured oil tanks, and started fires. All power was lost and the ship, aft of the stack, was a battered mass of inert metal.

The forward gun was out of whack, but the heroic crew of the after gun refused to call it quits. According to Captain Copeland in the action report:

> After all power, air, and communications had been lost, and before the word to abandon ship was passed, the crew of #2 gun loaded, rammed, and fired six charges entirely by hand and with the certain knowledge of the hazards involved due to the failure of (the gun's) gas ejection system. While attempting to get off the seventh charge, there was an internal explosion in the gun, killing all but three members of the gun crew, two of whom subsequently died on rafts.

The entire service life of DE *Samuel B. Roberts* was barely six months. With Lieutenant Commander Copeland as her first skipper, she had been commissioned 28 April 1944 at the Brown Yards at Houston, Texas.

The First Battle of the Philippine Sea was called the Marianas Turkey Shoot because of the ease with which our aviators downed their Japanese opponents. There are ample reasons why this, the Second Battle of the Philippine Sea, should be known as the Battle of the Peashooters. Never, in a major naval engagement, have so few small guns on so few small ships, opposed so many big guns on a large force of large ships.

The largest weapons on the Allied side were 5-inchers, throwing shells that weighed 55 pounds as against enemy metal that covered all major calibers and weighed up to 1½ tons. Taffy 3, counting all carriers and screening vessels, had only twenty-eight 5-inch guns. History will give but scant space to this battle but seldom has such heroism been displayed against such overwhelming odds. Every man deserved a Medal of Honor. Without the matchless valor in that pitifully small Taffy 3 Group, it is difficult to estimate what damage Admiral Kurita might have wrought in Leyte Gulf.

After two and a half hours of fighting, when victory seemed to be within his grasp, Admiral Kurita issued a retirement order at 0925. Admiral Sprague watched with unbelieving wonder when the cruisers to port countermarched at 0929. Much later, in a personal report to CincPac at Pearl Harbor, he said:

"Throughout the action, my Chief Quartermaster had kept close to me. When he saw the Japs do a 180 turn, he exclaimed: 'My God, Admiral—they're going to get away!' "

But that morning, as the range between the two forces opened, Cliff did not stop to ponder why the enemy turned tail. He quickly issued orders for aircraft to stage a fast pursuit. At that time he did not know where his planes were. Some had landed on carriers in Taffy 2, about 20 miles to the south; others had crowded in on Tacloban airstrip, which was barely usable. Some planes landed all in one piece; others cracked up, their pilots unhurt.

In summarizing the brisk but brief battle, Ziggy Sprague had this to say: "The failure of the enemy main body, and encircling light forces, to completely wipe out all vessels of this task unit can be attributed to our successful smoke screen, our torpedo counterattack, continuous harassment of enemy by bomb, torpedo and strafing air attacks, timely maneuvers and the definite partiality of Almighty God."

Too excited to be weary after the continuous morning runs to hit and harass the enemy, pilots waited impatiently while their torpedo-bombers and fighters were being re-armed—this time torpedoes were doled out—aboard the *Manila Bay* and other carriers in Taffy 2, commanded by Rear Admiral Felix B. Stump. Commander Fowler took charge of one group of about 32 fighters and torpedo-planes while Lieutenant Commander J. R. Dale headed a group of similar size. En route to their target, the fliers saw one battleship dead in the water and a cruiser with main deck awash. A destroyer was picking up survivors.

Following the trails of oil from bleeding bomb or torpedo wounds, the fliers found the Force shortly after noon, evidently heading for San Bernardino Strait. Four battleships were in a T formation, covered by five cruisers, inside a destroyer screen. Fowler lost no time in reporting the speed and location of the enemy. The plan was for Lieutenant Commander Dale's group to attack all ships on the starboard side of the formation; Commander Fowler's group would tackle those on the port side. Their strafing Hellcats were followed by coordinated attacks with glide-bomb and torpedo-planes. From starboard and port bullets, bombs, and fish struck the formation and scored hits on two battleships and two cruisers. One destroyer was seen to blow up.

The antiaircraft fire was strong but not deadly. Planes were hit by it but none went down. When the planes retired, the big ships fired their main batteries after them and tall splashes appeared ahead of the planes. But, as Commander Fowler observed, "These could be easily avoided."

As the groups withdrew, Commander Fowler noticed one of the battleships drop behind the other ships. And just before he hit the flight deck of a Taffy 2 carrier, he heard a pilot report from the scene that the enemy fleet consisted of three battleships, four cruisers, and eight destroyers.

Although Kurita was retreating, the ordeal of Taffy 3 was not yet over. Like other jeep carriers in Taffy 3, St. Lo had launched planes at 0718 while the enemy was closing the range and main battery salvos splashed among the CVEs in the unit. As the enemy drew closer, the six 5-inchers in the carrier units began to bark. Seeing a cruiser astern, closing and apparently not under fire from any of the other ships, Captain J. F. McKenna singled it out for action and scored three hits. Meanwhile, a heavy cruiser, accompanied by a large destroyer, had moved up on the port beam of the carrier formation and at 12,000 yards fired full broadsides at the ships in Taffy 3.

They were easy targets and many suffered severe hits. But not St. Lo. Splashes fell on every hand, some as close as 50 yards, but old St. Lo did not collect any hits. Nor was she touched by a flock of torpedoes that porpoised astern.

"The avoidance of the torpedo barrage closed the surface action," reads Captain McKenna's action report. "The enemy was retiring northwest. The St. Lo had suffered no structural damage. Only three men had received superficial wounds from shrapnel."

Then, at 1051, the picture of peace and quiet changed abruptly. Sharp bursts of antiaircraft fire were seen and heard forward, men ran to their stations as general quarters were sounded. Numerous planes, friend and enemy, were seen at 1,000 to 3,000 feet ahead on the starboard bow. They saw the planes swing aft to starboard and one of them went into a right turn toward St. Lo. The plane was a Zeke with a bomb under each wing. The after starboard 40mms and 20mms opened up on it but with no apparent effect. The Zeke's pilot continued his right turn smack into the groove over the CVE's wake just as if he intended to land. With engine on full power, the Japanese came over the ramp at an elevation of 50 feet and pushed over so that he hit the deck.

"There was a tremendous crash and flash of an explosion as one or both bombs exploded," commented Captain McKenna, who saw the drama from the bridge. "The plane continued up the deck leaving fragments strewn about and its remnants went over the bow."

No one aboard *St. Lo* had any way of knowing it, but they had just been attacked by Japan's newest secret weapon—the Kamikaze pilot who deliberately sacrificed himself by crashing his plane on an American ship in order to destroy it. On the *St. Lo* that day, they had no such fancy name as Kamikaze for the suicidal flier. They called him Devil Diver.

At first Captain McKenna believed that no serious damage had been inflicted. There was a hole in the flight deck with smoldering edges of flame. While this fire was being fought, he noticed that smoke was coming through the hole from below, and that smoke was appearing on both sides of the ship, evidently coming from the hangar. He tried to contact the hangar deck but could get no reply.

In less than a minute, an explosion on the hangar deck sent a column of smoke and flame through the hole in the flight deck. This eruption was followed in seconds by another and more violent explosion, which rolled back part of the flight deck. A third eruption tore out more of the flight deck and also blew the forward elevator out of its shaft. At this time, shortly before 1100, Captain McKenna decided that the ship could not be saved and passed the word to "stand by to abandon ship." During this time, some personnel had been blown overboard and some had been driven into the sea by flames. After four additional very heavy explosions, *St. Lo* sank. Many men were killed and many more were injured.

After surviving a furious battle without even scratching her paint, the *St. Lo* was on the bottom.

The *St. Lo* was not the first carrier to feel the fatal impact of the Devil Diver. The world premiere of this maniacal weapon was staged early that morning. At 0740, when Admiral Kurita's attack against Taffy 3 was nearing its peak, the air support the admiral had prayed for zoomed over the Philippine Sea in the guise of six very special

Japanese planes. But because they came up from the south, they sighted Taffy 1 first and directed their efforts at escort carriers in that, Admiral Tom Sprague's, unit some 125 miles south of Taffy 3.

The show began when radar operators in Taffy 1 picked up bogeys to southward—about half a dozen pips, 35 miles at 10,000 feet. When they got within visual range, they turned out to be six Zekes. Each fighter carried fragmentation bombs under its wings. The Zekes twisted and dodged to avoid flak and CAP planes as they plunged toward the jeeps. No bombs were released. It did not dawn on those below that these planes were manned bombs destined to be crashed in suicidal dives. This was the first appearance of the Japanese naval air arm's ultrasecret Special Attack Force—*the Corps of the Divine Wind*—Kamikaze fliers whose fanatic patriotism propelled them into self-destruction as a means of enemy destruction. Combat Air Patrols knocked down three Kamikazes short of their targets. The *Santee* was struck but not critically. However, the *Suwanne* took a Kamikaze on her forward elevator; a 500-pound bomb exploded on contact. Fires followed and spread, but luckily they were controlled.

The *Petrof Bay* was saved from death or damage by an alert Avenger pilot. Catching the lethal intruder in his gunsight in mid-dive, he sawed off the Zeke's tail with bullets. In a spin, the enemy plane tumbled toward the jeep's deck but was hosed away by the streams of bullets from the *Petrof Bay*'s heavy machine guns. Chunks of the craft splashed 50 feet from the jeep, but the bomb did not explode.

Admiral Halsey's decision not to leave TF 34 at the strait because he could not provide it with air cover may have brought unexpected good fortune. Had he left it there, chances are that the Kamikaze strike, which followed the early morning attack on Taffy 1 and hit Taffy 3, would have been aimed at the guardians of the strait with heaven only knows what results.

As it was, the second Kamikaze surprise was sprung when five suicide divers from Luzon attacked Taffy 3. One, as we know, attacked and sank *St. Lo*. Another damaged *Kitkun Bay* but not seriously; a third made a pass at *White Plains* that would have succeeded if good gunnery had not blasted it down inches away from the carrier's stern. The same fate was met by two Zekes trying to crash on *Fanshaw Bay*.

Naturally, the Kamikaze tactics aroused worldwide attention. Contrary to early belief, they were not spontaneous flights by individuals. The idea was the brainchild of the Imperial Staff's principal troubleshooter, Vice Admiral Takijiro Onishi. On 17 October he landed on Clark Field near Manila to take charge of the few land-based planes that were still operational, about 107. It did not take him long to realize that his new pilots could handle planes well enough, but their gunnery was too poor for air cover and their bombing-torpedoing unsatisfactory. Admiral Onishi had to provide air cover—but how? The suicide flights were his answer.

He called a meeting at Clark Field, spoke eloquently about the deathless fame that awaited Kamikaze fliers, and asked for volunteers. He found plenty. Thus, the suicide corps began. It was named after the Divine Wind, which, in the 13th century, wrecked Kublai Khan's Japan-bound fleet and thus prevented a Mongol invasion of the homeland.

As for Admiral Kurita, he should by now—having withdrawn from battle—have had a healthy respect for his enemy. To losses suffered before and during his passage through San Bernardino Strait, he could add some very painful new sinkings. To soften this blow, he reported three or four American carriers sunk, including one of the giant Enterprise class, also two heavy cruisers and some destroyers, plus heavy hits on one or two carriers.

His own bookkeeping is equally sketchy. In a report filed at 1000 while retiring, he lists as "friendly units heavily damaged" the cruisers Chikuma (torpedoed and sunk), Chokai (bombed and sunk), Kumano (minus her bow and making 5 knots). Suzuya (bombed and sunk) is not even mentioned.

But the day was not over for Takeo Kurita. In the early afternoon, he felt stings from the CVs Wasp and Hornet when Admiral McCain's TG 1 pushed within extreme striking distance and launched two attack waves. Bombs were used, but not with enough effect to cause any sinkings. Much has been written, from various viewpoints, on why Admiral Kurita fled from the battle he was winning. This was the way he looked at the situation as of 1230 on 25 October:

"Until about 1200, we were determined to carry out the plan to penetrate into Leyte Gulf in spite of repeated enemy (air) attacks." However, after intercepting Seventh Fleet plans to meet any fresh attack, the admiral decided that "preparations to intercept our forces apparently were complete, whereas we could not even determine the actual situation in Leyte Gulf. Moreover, in view of what happened to Admirals Nishimura and Shima's forces, it seems not unlikely that we would fall into an enemy trap . . . The wiser course was deemed to be to cross the enemy's anticipation by striking at his task force which had been reported in position bearing 5°, distance 113 miles, from Suluan light at 0945."

However, before that plan could be set into motion, Kurita's force was attacked by Slew McCain's fliers, and the Admiral evidently decided that it was wise to quit even if he was not ahead.

The hour was 2130 when Admiral Kurita's fleet passed through the strait "in view of the enemy situation and because of fuel considerations." If he gave thought to the whereabouts of the Third Fleet, he need not have troubled, because Admiral Halsey—in a slimmed-down edition of TF 34 that contained only the fastest ships—would not reach the Strait till several hours later. The only evidence that Kurita had been present was *Nowake,* a lame-duck destroyer, which was promptly sunk by gunfire by the vanguard of Halsey's ships.

The Second Battle of the Philippines had been fought and won by our naval forces. The sacred Japanese "they must not pass" line had been wiped out; numerous island stepping stones to Japan's shrinking colonial possessions had been freed from her domain—all in a series of amphibious operations on the perimeters of the Philippine Sea.

It would be grossly unfair to place responsibility for the destruction and damage inflicted on a major portion of the Japanese fleet, as well as for the failure of the accomplishments of their missions, on Admirals Kurita, Nishimura, and Shima. Admiral Ozawa's mission, to lure Bill Halsey north from San Bernardino Strait, was the only one that actually succeeded. The responsibility rests squarely on the planmakers in Tokyo.

Operation SHO 1 was a complete failure because the dice the High Command gambled with were heavily loaded with improbabilities. The greatest of these was the assumption that because stealth and surprise had worked in their favor at Pearl Harbor, they would continue to do so. Despite the Battle of Midway and other object lessons, the Japanese seemed to believe that, at sea, they were not only invincible but invisible. Witness Admiral Toyoda's orders to Admiral Ozawa in June to slip into the Philippine Sea "without leaving a trace." Also, it had been expected that three Japanese task forces could negotiate the inland waters of the Philippines without being seen.

Where did the wisdom lie in staging a do-or-die battle for the islands by sending vulnerable ships, without air protection, through inland waters? The enemy might have been in a better position to attack if he had waited until General MacArthur moved north and west to Mindoro and Lingayen Bay on Luzon. With more sea room the Japanese Navy might have been more effective and certainly less vulnerable.

And yet, perhaps it was ordained that on 24–25 October 1944, Japan was to suffer for the outrages she had committed on 7 December 1941.

Chapter Thirteen

END OF THE BATTLE

WHEN THE LAST of the Japanese stragglers and cripples had been hunted down and sunk after the 24–25 October debacle, it became obvious that the Third and Seventh fleets had won one of the greatest victories in naval warfare. More than 300,000 tons of combatant shipping had been sent to the bottom of the Philippine Sea and adjacent waters. This represented a complete battle force of 4 carriers, 3 battleships, 6 heavy and 4 light cruisers, and 11 destroyers. The loss of these ships within the span of a few days reduced Japan's Navy to a third-rate sea power. Although other Japanese carriers and fighting ships were under construction, they never reached the point of resurrecting Nipponese naval power; nor did they help restore the sea wall of steel and guns intended for the protection of the homeland.

The price the Allied forces paid for the victory was low enough, if one can ever consider human life expendable. Total personnel losses ran to less than 3,000; those of Japan were close to 10,000. Allied ship losses were 1 light carrier, 2 escort carriers, 2 destroyers and 1 destroyer escort; total tonnage: less than 40,000.

Whittling the Japanese Navy close to noncombatant size in the four major encounters in the Philippine Sea and two straits definitely closed the gap between war and peace. But they did not bring easy and early victory to General MacArthur and his troops; nor did they end carrier strikes against the islands, as had been expected. It had been anticipated that the Third Fleet would be on its own by 29 October, but the attacks begun against Taffy 1 and 3 on 24 October by the Green Hornets, as the Kamikaze fliers were also called, gained rapidly in frequency and intensity. This made life difficult and uncertain for Admiral Kinkaid because his escort carrier units had to return to Manus Island to recharge run-down human batteries, take aboard new planes, and make essential repairs. General Kenney had neither fliers nor fields enough to provide air cover.

At the same time, Japanese ground resistance became more determined, and efforts of the enemy to land fresh troops met with some success. Only three of eleven attempts succeeded. Land-based air operations on our side were hindered by lack of landing facilities. The airstrip at Tacloban was, due to the monsoon season, a hog wallow of mud. Conditions forced the postponement of landings on Mindoro to 20 December; those on Luzon, at Lingayen Gulf, were deferred to 9 January.

Group by group, units of TF 38 steamed to Ulithi for re-arming and essential repairs, with little time for rest or recreation for personnel. Admiral Mitscher turned his command over to Admiral McCain and took some well-deserved shore leave.

Slew McCain was to have his hands full in combating the suicide fliers. After the escort carriers left, they turned their attention to the task groups of TF 38. On 29 October, a Kamikaze hit *Intrepid,* doing only slight damage. The next day *Franklin* was so badly damaged that she had to return to Pearl for repairs. And on the following day *Belleau Wood* suffered such heavy damage that she, too, had to steam homeward.

For a change of pace, the suicide pilots returned to Leyte Gulf on 1 November, where they sank one destroyer and damaged three. A few days later, a Kamikaze plunged into *Lexington*'s signal bridge and inflicted 186 casualties. Needless to say, Admirals Halsey and McCain were deeply perturbed, not only by the freedom with which the Kamikaze attacked but also by the carrier attrition to TF 38. Two flattops had been put out of the running; in addition, two carriers were at Ulithi for the training of much needed night-fighter squadrons. The result was that TF 38 was reorganized from four to three groups and that steps were taken to increase the fighter contingents on each carrier at the expense of bombing and torpedo-plane contingents.

Measures were also taken to keep the Green Hornets at more than arm's length. The attackers had three means of approach: they came in high and bored right through the CAP, they came in so low that they flew under the radar net, or they tail-ended on American fliers returning from missions. To meet this situation the CAP was extended and expanded; a new CAP was established below radar range. To cut out the unwanted tail-end Charlies, picket destroyers were placed under the paths of returning planes, which had orders to pass over and circle the pickets in carefully prescribed patterns. If they failed to do that, they were enemies and were fired upon.

Even so, on 25 November four carriers—*Cabot, Essex, Hancock,* and *Intrepid*—were hit, the latter so seriously that she had to join the eastward procession. It has been estimated that the Kamikaze toll taken in the Third and Seventh fleets from 24 October to 29 November amounted to 5 vessels sunk, 23 severely hit, and 12 lightly hit.

The rain of blasting bombs, fragmenting planes, and Kamikaze pilots seemed far away to the men of the Third Fleet when they reached the Ulithi anchorage and its shelter of coral reefs. There they had a feeling of security, but not for long. Shortly after dawn on 20 November, a new kind of Japanese suicide pilot arrived—not borne aloft but carried beneath the sea. He and his fellows came in midget submarines that carried two torpedoes with enormous warheads and a man or two to operate the subs.

First alarm that Ulithi harbor contained such deadly fish came when the DD *Case* (Commander R. S. Willey) rammed one of them near the entrance to the harbor. Minutes later, fleet oiler *Mississinewa* (Commander P. G. Beck), riding at anchor, was torpedoed. Being ready to go, she carried 405,000 gallons of aviation gasoline, 85,000 barrels of fuel, and 9,000 of diesel oil—and go she did when a torpedo hit her magazine. In seconds she was wrapped in flames and smoke. The ship was lost, but lives were saved, thanks to quick action by rescue and other vessels as well as by the ingenuity and daring of Lieutenant B. C. Zamucen, a floatplane pilot of the *Santa Fe*. He taxied his plane in and out of the burning surface waters that surrounded the tug, trailing a line astern that survivors grabbed to be pulled to safety.

Meanwhile destroyers and destroyer escorts cut wide swaths with their sharp bows as they snaked at high speeds among the scores of craft in the harbor. In their eager hunt for midget subs, they dropped depth charges at intervals lest heavy salvos should damage the ships. When things settled down, there had been one sure kill in the harbor, another was blasted out to sea, and two were destroyed by hitting a reef. After the war it was learned that the midget subs had been transported to Ulithi mounted on regular submarines. These Kamikaze weapons, called *Kaiten,* were to do their share of damage as the war drew closer to the homeland.

Bill Halsey for a long time had admired Marine Corps aviation. He regarded the job done on Peleliu by the flying Marines in dive-bombers as magnificent. In fact, Admiral Halsey had obtained permission from CincPac to transfer Marine air units under his jurisdiction in the Palaus to General MacArthur, thus reinforcing General Kenney's Army Air Force fliers. These dive-bombardiers were soon called "The Flying Artillery" because of their smash-hit perform- ances. Carrier fighter pilots finally became so scarce that the dare- devil winged Marines were assigned to TF 38 late in 1944 to increase carrier complements. The first flattops to have Marine planes on their flight decks were the *Wasp* and the *Essex*.

General MacArthur's troops faced a gruelling task in their advance to Manila. This was not taken until mid-February—during rain and gales and over muddy and hostile terrain—after almost fanatical enemy resistance. It received strong and efficient support by the fast carrier groups, escort carriers, and Marine and Army aviation. The march on Manila is an enduring monument to good soldiering by splendid soldiers.

In mid-December, after reducing attacks by Kamikaze pilots to al- most zero by clever tactics, the Third Fleet ran into a typhoon. It caught the Third Fleet by surprise some 300 miles east of Luzon, causing the loss of three destroyers and inflicting great damage to numerous vessels. Planes on carriers ran amuck on flight and hangar decks; many aircraft crashed into each other and started fires; others were ripped from their lashings and blown overboard. Pilots and crews fought, and faced great dangers, to hold the damage down. Even so, 146 planes were either blown or deliberately tumbled into the sea. When the storm passed, the fleet was scattered over miles of ocean. Since many of them had lost aerials and other communications equipment, herding the vessels together proved an arduous task.

According to Fleet Admiral Nimitz' review of the typhoon, dated 13 February 1945, about 790 officers and men were lost or killed and 80 injured. In discussing causes and effects, the admiral noted that it is possible to place too much reliance on weather broadcasts and that some of the damage was caused by efforts to maintain fleet courses, speeds, and formations during the storm. He wrote:

> A hundred years ago a ship's survival depended almost solely on the competence of her master and on his constant alertness to any hint of change in the weather . . . . Seamen of the present day should be better at forecasting weather at sea, independently of the radio, than were their predecessors, because of better understanding of the general laws of storms and year-round weather expectancy. It is possible that too much reliance is being placed on outside sources for warnings of dangerous weather and on the ability of our splendid ships

to come through anything that wind and wave can do. If this be so, there is need for a revival of the age-old habits of self-reliance and caution in regard to the hazard from storm, and for officers of all echelons of command to take their personal responsibilities in this respect more seriously.

For Bill Halsey, 9 January was a big day. That was the day his job of making prelanding strikes and providing landing cover for troops going ashore in Lingayen Gulf ended. After much urging he had received permission from Admirals King and Nimitz to conduct a ten-day raid in the South China Sea that would carry him as far south as Saigon and as far north as Hong Kong. This was the first American surface offensive in those waters. Besides wrecking docks and other installations, the Allied force sank about fifty ships, including several large tankers; total tonnage: 150,000. Despite inclement weather, it was a most successful outing. Unfortunately, the raids ended on a low note due to intense air attacks from Luzon and Formosa on the return trip. Luzon planes inflicted neither damage nor death, and fifteen were splashed before the attackers were driven back. But Formosa launched heavy waves of both orthodox and Kamikaze fliers. All but four planes were knocked down or put to rout. Little harm was done by a bomb dropped on *Langley;* one Kamikaze plunged onto the DD *Maddox,* killing 4 men; two others hit the *Ticonderoga,* causing extensive damage to her flight deck and killing 140 men.

On 26 January the Third Fleet dropped anchor at Ulithi. On the following day Bill Halsey returned command to Admiral Spruance; and with that the Third Fleet became the Fifth Fleet once again. Similarly, TF 38 became TF 58, with Pete Mitscher back on the flag bridge of the *Lexington,* perched on his familiar long-legged chair, a lobsterman's cap on his head. During his five months of command, Bill Halsey, according to Admiral King's reckoning, had destroyed 4,370 enemy planes and sunk 82 combat ships and 372 enemy auxiliaries and merchant ships, against a loss of 449 planes and the CVL *Princeton.*

In a communication, which was issued in December and which displayed a great deal of foresight, Admiral Nimitz made the following comment:

> During the battles for the Philippines, carriers and planes engaged major forces for the first time in history. The Japanese network of airfields throughout the islands enabled them to throw large numbers of planes into the air over a given spot at one time.

This sets a precedent for action still to come as we approach closer to the heart of the Japanese Empire. The nearer we get, the more the Japanese can constrict his air defenses. Our choices of strategy will be reduced. He will not have to guess so much as to what we will do next. As Knute Rockne once said: "It is harder to score a touch-down from the 40-yard line because the defense is packed more tightly."

This was the situation as Admirals Spruance and Mitscher took the helms, respectively, of the Fifth Fleet and TF 58. There were stirring and strenuous days ahead as they prepared to go to sea; destinations: Iwo Jima and Okinawa.

While admirals changed commands and Nick Carter's miracle workers performed essential repairs on ships and equipment, officers and men of the fleet were given as much liberty ashore as possible. They needed the welcome change of feeling solid ground beneath their feet instead of the pitch and roll of steel decks; they needed the relaxation of mind and body seldom found during operations at sea; they needed respite from the endless chain of watches and constant vigilance against Kamikaze pilots. The latter had filled carrier personnel, if not with fear, at least with justified apprehension. There was welcome relaxation in games, swimming, or just shooting the breeze in groups over a couple of bottles of beer. Aside from that, there was little of anything else on Mogmog Island, the "recreation center" of Ulithi; not even enough coconut trees to offer pleasant shade against the broiling sun.

A lift from the monotony was provided by a communiqué that appeared on bulletin boards on 28 January. It was from CincPac, Fleet Admiral Chester Nimitz, and read:

> The Third Fleet, in the last four months, has hit the enemy hard in the Philippines, Ryukyus, Formosa, Indo-China and South China. It has demolished and damaged aircraft, ships and land objectives to a degree which has materially reduced Japan's ability to make war. It has paved the way for and covered the Philippine re-occupation. It has written proud pages in our nation's history.
>
> Submarines of the Pacific Fleet and the Army Air Forces in China and the Pacific Ocean Areas have provided extremely effective cooperation and support and have continued to destroy the enemy wherever found.
>
> Well done to the officers and men of these gallant fighting forces!

GLOSSARY

AA: antiaircraft weapons
AAF: (U.S.) Army Air Force
AKA: attack cargo ship
ammo: ammunition
amtrac: tracked landing craft, often armored
AO: fleet oiler
AP: armor piercing shell
APA: attack transport
APD: destroyer transport
AT: proximity fuze
ATF: fleet ocean tug
Avenger (TBF, TBM): USN torpedo-bomber
B-17 (Flying Fortress): AAF heavy bomber
B-24 (Liberator): AAF heavy bomber
B-25 (Mitchell): AAF medium bomber
B-29 (Superfortress): AAF heavy bomber
BB: battleship
Betty: IJN torpedo-bomber
Bogey: unidentified aircraft
CA: heavy cruiser
CAP: combat air patrol
Catalina (PBY): USN flying boat
CIC: combat information center
CL: light cruiser
CNO: Chief of Naval Operations
Corsair (F4U): USN fighter plane
CoS: Chief of Staff
CV: heavy aircraft carrier
CVE: jeep or escort aircraft carrier
CVL: light aircraft carrier

Dauntless (SBD): USN dive-bomber
DD: destroyer
DE: destroyer escort
Div.: division
Dumbo (PBY): USN air-to-sea rescue plane
F4F (Wildcat): USN fighter plane
F4U (Corsair): USN fighter plane
F6F (Hellcat): USN fighter plane
GP: general purpose bombs
Hamp: IJN fighter plane
HDQ or HG: headquarters
HE: high explosive shell
Hedge-hog: antisubmarine contact exploder
Hellcat (F6F): USN fighter plane
Helldiver (SB2C): USN dive-bomber
IJN: Imperial Japanese Navy
Jake: IJN reconnaissance plane
JCS: Joint Chiefs of Staff
Jill: IJN torpedo-bomber
Judy: IJN dive-bomber
Kate: IJN dive-bomber
Kingfisher (OS2U): USN observation-scout plane
LC, or Elsie: landing craft
LCT: landing craft, tank
Liberator (B-24): AAF heavy bomber
LSD: landing ship, dock
LST: landing ship, tank
LVT: landing vessel, tracked
Mavis: IJN transport plane
Mitchell (B-25): AAF medium bomber

OOD: officer of the deck

OS2U (Kingfisher): USN observation-scout plane

PBY (Catalina): USN flying boat

PT: motor torpedo boat

radar: surface ranging and detection device

RCT: regimental combat team

RN: Royal Navy (Brit.)

Ron: squadron

SBD (Dauntless): USN dive-bomber

SB2C (Helldiver): USN dive-bomber

Sea-Bee: naval construction battalion

sonar: underwater ranging and sound detector

SS: submarine

Superfortress (B-29): AAF heavy bomber

TBF (Avenger): USN torpedo-bomber

TBM (Avenger): USN torpedo-bomber

TBS: voice radio for talk between ships

TF: task force

TG: task group

tinfish: torpedo

TU: task unit

UDT: underwater demolition team

Val: IJN dive-bomber

Wildcat (F4F): USN fighter plane

Zeke: IJN fighter plane

BIBLIOGRAPHY

Arnold, Henry. *Global Mission.* New York: Harper & Brothers, 1949.
Arnold, Jackson D. Letter, August 4, 1965.
Bataan (CVL). Action report, June 1944. Washington, D.C.: U.S. Dept. of the Navy, Naval History Division.
Belleau Wood (CVL). Action report, June 1944. Washington, D.C.: U.S. Dept. of the Navy, Naval History Division.
Bunker Hill (CV). Action report, June 1944. Washington, D.C.: U.S. Dept. of the Navy, Naval History Division.
Cabot (CVL). Action report, June 1944. Washington, D.C.: U.S. Dept. of the Navy, Naval History Division.
Carter, Worrall R. *Beans, Bullets and Black Oil.* Washington, D.C.: U.S. Government Printing Office, 1952.
D'Alban, Andreiu. *Death of a Navy.* New York: The Devin-Adair Co., 1957.
England (DE). Ship's history. Washington, D.C.: U.S. Dept. of the Navy, Naval History Division.
Essex (CV). Action report, June 1944. Washington, D.C.: U.S. Dept. of the Navy, Naval History Division.
Field, James A. *The Japanese at Leyte Gulf.* Princeton, N.J.: Princeton University Press, 1948.
Fowler, Richard L. Action report, October 25, 1944, Washington, D.C.: U.S. Dept. of the Navy, Naval History Division.
Gambier Bay (CVE). Action report, October 25, 1944. Washington, D.C.: U.S. Dept. of the Navy, Naval History Division.
Halsey, William F., and Bryan, Joseph, III. *Admiral Halsey's Story.* New York: McGraw-Hill Book Company, 1947.
Hoel (DD). Action report, October 25, 1944. Washington, D.C.: U.S. Dept. of the Navy, Naval History Division.
Hornet (CV). Action report, June 1944. Washington, D.C.: U.S. Dept. of the Navy, Naval History Division.
Hurt, Samuel H. Letter, August 23, 1965.

Johnston (DD). Action report, October 25, 1944. Washington, D.C.: U.S. Dept. of the Navy, Naval History Division.

Johnston, R. R. *Follow Me.* New York: Random House, 1949.

Karig, Walter. *Battle Report—Victory in the Pacific,* vol. 5. New York: Rinehart, 1949.

King, Ernest J. *U.S. Navy at War.* Official reports, 1944, to Secretary of the Navy.

Kitkun Bay (CVE). Action report, October 25, 1944. Washington, D.C.: U.S. Dept. of the Navy, Naval History Division.

Lockwood, Charles A. *Sink 'em All!* New York: E. P. Dutton & Co., 1951.

MacArthur, Douglas. *Reminiscences.* New York: McGraw-Hill Book Company, 1965.

Masanori, Ito. *The End of the Imperial Japanese Navy.* New York: W. W. Norton & Company, 1956.

Monterey (CVL). Action report, June 1944. Washington, D.C.: U.S. Dept. of the Navy, Naval History Division.

Morison, Samuel E. *New Guinea and the Marianas.* History of U.S. Naval Operations in World War II, vol. VIII. Boston: Little, Brown and Company, 1953.

———. *Leyte.* History of U.S. Naval Operations in World War II, vol. XII. Boston: Little, Brown and Company, 1955.

Morton, Louis. *Japan.* Annapolis, Md.: *U.S. Naval Institute Proceedings,* February 1959.

Nimitz, Chester W. Pacific Fleet confidential letter, February 13, 1945.

Parsons, Charles. World War II letters, diaries, and personal files.

Potter, E. B., and Nimitz, Chester W. *The Great Sea War.* Englewood Cliffs, N.J.: Prentice-Hall, 1960.

Pratt, Fletcher. *Fleet Against Japan.* New York: Harper & Brothers, 1946.

Princeton (CVL). Action report, June 1944. Washington, D.C.: U.S. Dept. of the Navy, Naval History Division.

Ruddock, Theodore D. Letter, August 24, 1965.

St. Lo (CVE). Action report, October 25, 1944. Washington, D.C.: U.S. Dept. of the Navy, Naval History Division.

Samuel B. Roberts (DE). Action report, October 25, 1944. Washington, D.C.: U.S. Dept. of the Navy, Naval History Division.

San Jacinto (CVL). Action report, June 1944. Washington, D.C.: U.S. Dept. of the Navy, Naval History Division.

Sherman, Frederick C. *Combat Command.* New York: E. P. Dutton & Co., 1950.

Sherrod, Robert. *History of Marine Corps Aviation in World War II.* Washington, D.C.: Combat Forces Press, 1949.

Sprague, Clifton A. F. Action report, October 25, 1944. Washington, D.C.: U.S. Dept. of the Navy, Naval Historical Division.

Task Group One, TF 58, 5th Fleet. Action report, June 1944. Washington, D.C.: U.S. Dept. of the Navy, Naval History Division.

Taylor, T. *Magnificent Mitscher*. New York: W. W. Norton & Company, 1954.

U.S. Coast Guard. *Pacific War Report*. Washington, D.C.: U.S. Coast Guard, 1945.

U.S. Navy Department Communiqués, 301–600 (1943–45). Washington, D.C.: U.S. Dept. of the Navy.

U.S. Strategic Bombing Survey, Pacific. *Campaigns of the Pacific War*. Washington, D.C.: Department of Defense, Naval Analysis Division.

Wasp (CV). Action report, June 1944. Washington, D.C.: U.S. Dept. of the Navy, Naval History Division.

White Plains (CVE). Action Report, October 25, 1944. Washington, D.C.: U.S. Dept. of the Navy, Naval History Division.

Woodward, C. V. *Battle for Leyte Gulf*. New York: The Macmillan Company, 1947.

Yorktown (CV). Action report, June 1944. Washington, D.C.: U.S. Dept. of the Navy, Naval History Division.

Index